Armies in Homeland Security

Armies in Homeland Security: American and European Perspectives

Edited by
John L. Clarke

National Defense University Press
Washington, D.C.
2006

Opinions, conclusions, and recommendations expressed or implied within are solely those of the contributors and do not necessarily represent the views of the Defense Department or any other agency of the Federal Government. Cleared for public release; distribution unlimited.

Portions of this work may be quoted or reprinted without permission, provided that a standard source credit line is included. NDU Press would appreciate a courtesy copy of reprints or reviews.

Library of Congress Cataloging-in-Publication Data

Armies in homeland security : American and European perspectives / edited by John L. Clarke.
  p. cm.
Includes bibliographical references.
ISBN 1-57906-074-9 (hardcover : alk. paper)
  1. Civil defense—United States. 2. Civil defense—Europe. 3. Civil-military relations. 4. Armies—Organization. 5. United States—Armed Forces. 6. Europe—Armed Forces. 7. National security. I. Clarke, John L. (John Louie), 1952–
  UA926.A76 2007
  363.34'7094—dc22
                    2006026682

First printing, November 2006

NDU Press publications are sold by the U.S. Government Printing Office. For ordering information, call (202) 512–1800 or write to the Superintendent of Documents, U.S. Government Printing Office, Washington, D.C. 20402. For GPO publications on-line, access their Web site at: http://www.access.gpo.gov/su_docs/sale.html.

For current publications of the Institute for National Strategic Studies, consult the National Defense University Web site at: http://www.ndu.edu.

Contents

Introduction

Armies in Homeland Security: American and European Perspectives

John L. Clarke

Homeland security is a topic that has generated a great deal of attention in the past 5 years, on both sides of the Atlantic. With the increased focus on the homeland, or domestic, security of states in the aftermath of the terrorist attacks on New York, Washington, Madrid, and London, as well as the response to disasters such as Hurricane Katrina, senior officials have been challenged to provide adequate levels of domestic security consistent with the resources that advanced Western states have available for these purposes.

States have been hard-pressed to develop and equip security forces that will be able to perform the tasks required to maintain a high level of homeland security and support civil authorities in responding to catastrophes. In many instances, leaders have looked to the armed forces to carry out these key missions.

Military forces bring many advantages to these challenges; they are usually well organized, trained, mobile, well equipped—and available. In many countries, there is a tradition of using military forces in support of civil authorities, a tradition that has often included a broad range of homeland security and civil support tasks.

Military forces, however, are normally trained for missions that are quite different from those necessary for achieving effective homeland security. This is particularly true with regard to the use of force. While law enforcement officers are trained to use force as a last resort, soldiers are trained to use it in the first instance. As a consequence, while the temptation to employ existing military forces to carry out homeland security missions is great, it is also replete with dangers. Soldiers are not police officers, and the danger is always present that they will use force in a manner that is inappropriate in the domestic context.

This book is designed to look at how a number of states are meeting these challenges. The authors examine how Austria, Bulgaria, the European Union, France, Germany, Hungary, Italy, Romania, Ukraine, the United Kingdom, and the United States have approached the issue of the employment of military forces in domestic security. This collection of essays offers readers the opportunity to compare and contrast these experiences and the lessons they offer for future contingencies involving the employment of military force in support of civil authorities.

These countries have different traditions of using military forces domestically; they have different national security strategies; and they have different perceptions of the level of threat to their domestic security. Each nation approaches these issues in a different manner, reflecting their unique histories and status of the armed forces in the respective states. This volume examines how these states may choose to employ military force in support of a range of homeland security missions, with particular emphasis on defending against potential terrorist attacks.

These missions include the protection of critical infrastructure, border and transportation security, domestic counterterrorism, protection against catastrophic threats, and military civil support. Civil support includes how military forces may aid law enforcement authorities and provide assistance during periods of crisis or other key events.

A number of the essays examines the changes in missions and structure that many armies in central and eastern Europe went through in the post-Soviet period, when armies changed from instruments of political domination to agents of change in the national security structures of these countries. The essays on Bulgaria, Ukraine, Hungary, and Romania, for example, highlight this transition, as these armies have shed their Soviet orientation and become active partners in support of civil authorities.

Of particular interest, a number of these states have armed forces that are uniquely suited to the requirements of homeland security support. These include gendarme and other paramilitary police forces of France, Italy, and Romania that have long experience in the often-gray area between law enforcement and military operations. The capabilities and range of operations of these forces are well documented in the following chapters.

Military forces in Europe and the United States have made major contributions to homeland security. The benefits of these future contributions must be carefully balanced with the costs—in terms of both resources and opportunities—of engaging military forces whose primary mission remains the defense of the country. This book is designed to highlight these costs and benefits in comparative perspective, with a view toward providing examples of different approaches to the employment of armed forces in these key missions.

Chapter 1

Homeland Security and Homeland Defense: America's New Paradigm

Thomas L. LaCrosse

The United States Constitution divides authority over the military between the President, in his role as Commander in Chief,[1] and the Congress, which has the authority to "raise and support Armies…provide and maintain a navy…and make Rules for the Government and Regulation of the land and naval forces."[2] After the devastating terrorist attacks against the United States on September 11, 2001, President George W. Bush reaffirmed that "The United States government has no more important mission than protecting the homeland from future attacks."[3] *The National Strategy for Homeland Security* outlines the policy of the United States to achieve this goal.[4] It defines homeland security as "a concerted national effort to prevent terrorist attacks within the United States, reduce America's vulnerability to terrorism, and minimize the damage and recover from attacks that do occur."[5] Further evidence of the U.S. Government's commitment to this mission can be found in statements made by senior Department of Defense (DOD) leadership: "Protecting the United States homeland from attack is the highest priority of the Department of Defense."[6]

DOD has developed a homeland "defense-in-depth" strategy for covering all defense domains.[7] A key element of this strategy is addressing threats at the earliest possible opportunity and as far away from our domestic shores as possible. The strategy acknowledges there will be times and instances when military forces will be employed domestically. These instances can be broken down into three broad categories of employment.

- *Lead*: The Department of Defense conducts military missions to deter, prevent, and defeat attacks on the United States, its population, and its defense-critical infrastructure.[8] Flying combat air patrols to ensure airspace security as well as maintaining physical security around military installations and defense-critical infrastructure are examples where the department, always guided by civilian leadership, exercises leadership.

- *Support*: At the direction of the President or the Secretary of Defense, DOD provides defense support to civil authorities to prevent terrorist incidents or manage the consequence of an attack or a disaster. Support is often requested when DOD has unique capabilities to contribute, or when civilian responders are overwhelmed.[9]

- *Enable*: Efforts to share capabilities and expertise with domestic agencies and international partners reinforce DOD's leadership and support activities. At home, the department works to improve civilian capabilities for homeland security by lending expertise and sharing relevant technology. For example, DOD is sharing training and simulation technologies with the Department of Homeland Security (DHS), as well as unmanned aerial vehicle technologies with Federal law enforcement organizations responsible for surveillance along the Nation's borders.[10]

Legal Authority for Employment

Within civilian communities in the United States, the primary responsibility for protecting life and property and maintaining law and order is vested in state and local governments. Generally, Federal military forces are employed to enforce civil law and order only when circumstances arise that are beyond the control of state and local authorities. The basic policy reflects the Founding Fathers' hesitation to raise a standing army, and their desire to render the military subordinate to civilian authority. The policy is rooted in the Constitution and laws of the United States, and allows for exceptions only under extreme emergency conditions.[11]

Exceptions to the restrictions on the use of Federal armed forces to assist state and local civil authorities are also grounded in the Constitution, in the same article that provides the basis for Federal legislation allowing military assistance.[12] The President has a constitutional duty to see that the laws of the United States are faithfully executed.[13]

Just as there are legal authorities and exceptions allowing for the domestic use of the military, there are legal restrictions on its use as well. Principal among these is the Posse Comitatus Act.[14] The law was enacted in 1878, primarily as a result of the military presence in the South during Reconstruction following the U.S. Civil War.[15] Congress' intent in passing the act was to prevent direct military involvement in civilian law enforcement duties without congressional or constitutional authorization. For many years, the Posse Comitatus Act remained obscure and all but forgotten. In the early part of the 20th century, local officials used U.S. Army troops to break strikes, prevent labor meetings, stifle political dissent, and arrest or detain workers without the right of habeas corpus.[16]

In 1956, the act was incorporated into Title 18 of the United States Code, Section 1385, and amended to include the newly formed U.S. Air Force. An attempt was made to subject the Navy to the act in 1975, but the bill died in committee. It is a matter of DOD policy, however, that the act applies equally to naval forces. The Posse Comitatus Act does apply to members of the military reserves who are on active duty or active duty for training. Members of the National Guard are only subject to the act when they are in Federal service. Similarly, the act does not apply to the Coast Guard in peacetime, unless it is brought under the control of the Secretary of the Navy.

Historical Precedents

Postwar: 1945–1990

The Civil Defense Program. Soon after the end of World War II and the Soviet acquisition of nuclear weapons, the United States recognized a new vulnerability and acted accordingly. A comprehensive program of civil defense was designed to address the survival of individual Americans in the event of a massive Soviet nuclear attack. This single, monolithic state threat was dealt with through a combination of deterrence (via massive nuclear retaliation) and an active civil defense program at all levels of domestic government. The military's strategic nuclear forces had the mission to detect and retaliate in the event of a Soviet nuclear attack. In his 1963 budget request to Congress, President John F. Kennedy transferred the responsibility for the civil defense program to the Department of Defense, with the intent of more closely integrating offensive and defensive activities.[17] The program was driven and funded by the Federal Government, but was implemented at the state and local levels with voluntary individual participation. In addition to funding salaries of state civil defense officials and national scientific research, under most plans the military was used to provide equipment and training for shelter evacuation programs. Support for civil defense programs declined in succeeding administrations, due in part to the political climate of détente, and in part to improvements in satellite reconnaissance that resulted in earlier warning of impending attacks.

Civil Rights, Civil Disturbance, and Insurrection. Article II of the Constitution gives the President of the United States the inherent authority to protect the property and functionality of the Federal Government when state and local officials cannot or will not. In Title 10 of the United States Code, Section 332 (the Insurrection Act), Congress gave the President the authority to commit the military to enforce Federal laws.[18] In addition, the President may call into Federal service the National Guard units of any state and use the Armed Forces as he considers necessary to enforce those laws or to suppress a rebellion.[19] The provisions of this law were used to enforce public school desegregation in Arkansas in 1957 and in Alabama in 1963.[20] The same provisions were used to send in troops to help quell civil rights protests in Mississippi in 1962 and in Alabama in 1963.[21]

In addition to the civil rights movement that swept the Nation in the late 1950s and early 1960s, the protracted involvement in South East Asia during this period led to countless antiwar demonstrations. In several instances the military was used to help restore or maintain order in Washington, DC.

Post–Cold War: 1991–2001

Support for Operations against Drug Trafficking. In 1981, Congress passed Chapter 18 of Title 10, entitled "Military Cooperation with Civilian Law Enforcement Officials."[22] This act, with its subsequent amendments and a series of Congressional mandates, enabled DOD to assume an increasingly active role in supporting domestic civil law enforcement agencies to fight the flow of illegal narcotics into and through the United States. In addition to passing specific statutory authorities for providing countertrafficking support, Congress has annually appropriated specific funds to DOD for the effort.[23]

As part of the U.S. Defense Authorization Act of 1991,[24] Congress designated the Department of Defense as the single lead agency for the detection and monitoring of the aerial and maritime transit of illegal drugs into the United States.[25] Section 1206 of the same act stated that the "Secretary of Defense shall direct that the Armed Forces, to the maximum extent practicable, shall conduct military training exercises in drug interdiction areas." Many of the military activities provided under Section 1004 of this act fall into the category of logistics support operations: procuring and maintaining equipment, providing transportation to personnel and equipment, and providing communication support. National Guard forces have become a critical part of military support to civilian law enforcement agencies in the counterdrug effort.[26]

California Riots. In May 1992, after an unpopular ruling in the trial of police officers accused of beating an African-American motorist, civil unrest, arson, looting, and riots broke out in Los Angeles. Governor Pete Wilson requested Federal military support from President George H.W. Bush to assist with restoring law and order in the city.[27] Governor Wilson advised President Bush and the U.S. Attorney General that the violence in Los Angeles exceeded the capabilities of available law enforcement resources, including National Guard forces that had been called to duty by the Governor on May 1, 1992. President Bush ordered the federalization of the California National Guard and the deployment of soldiers of the Army's 7th Infantry Division from Fort Ord, as well as Marines from Camp Pendleton, to assist in restoring order in Los Angeles.[28]

Post-9/11

Airports. On September 27, 2001, President Bush asked state governors to deploy the National Guard at more than 420 civilian airports around the country. Governors and their adjutant generals responded, and deployed over 9,110 Army and Air National Guard personnel to supplement civilian law enforcement and security forces. Their deployment lasted for 6 months. During that time, the Transportation Security Administration was created and subsequently assumed the responsibility for passenger screening, and later the screening of checked baggage. The physical presence of uniformed military in U.S. airports reassured the traveling public that their Government would go to extraordinary lengths to ensure their security. It should be noted that the National Guard personnel remained under the command and control of their respective governors and adjutant generals, but that their deployment was paid for by the Federal Government.[29]

Anthrax. In fall 2001, while the Nation was in the grips of managing the consequences of the September 11 terrorist attacks, additional attacks occurred. Rather than using force to hijack a commercial airliner to kill innocent civilian noncombatants, these terrorists—who are as yet unknown—used the United States Postal Service to distribute a deadly anthrax virus to news media outlets around the country, and to two

United States senators in Washington, DC. Thirty-nine individuals developed anthrax infections, and five of those died from inhalation anthrax.[30] When anthrax-laden letters were discovered in the Hart Senate Office Building, next to the United States Capitol, the United States Marine Corps' Chemical/Biological Incident Response Force (CBIRF) was called in to conduct agent detection and identification as well as limited decontamination. During this event and a subsequent anthrax threat on Capitol Hill, CBIRF provided assistance to Federal and District of Columbia authorities, including the U.S. Capitol Police, the Federal Bureau of Investigation, the Environmental Protection Agency, the Federal Emergency Management Agency, the DC Metro Police, and the Emergency Management Office.

Borders. Prior to the creation of the Department of Homeland Security, the responsibility of securing the Nation's borders was shared by the Immigration and Naturalization Service and the U.S. Border Patrol—both of which were part of the Department of Justice—and the U.S. Customs Service, which was part of the Department of Treasury. In February 2002, through a cooperative arrangement between the Departments of Defense, Justice, and Treasury, DOD mobilized, trained, and deployed National Guard personnel to assist in border operations. Missions included cargo inspections, traffic management, terrain and trend analysis, and limited flights of fixed- and rotary-wing aircraft to provide basic observation flights over remote portions of the U.S. border with Canada. Unlike the deployment to provide airport security, where National Guard personnel remained under the command and control of their respective state governors and adjutants general, National Guard personnel were mobilized and brought into Federal service for this mission. The rationale behind that decision was debated at the senior levels of government, with the prevailing thought being that border security is the responsibility of the Federal Government and cannot be delegated to individual states. Once mobilized and trained, personnel were detailed to provide technical assistance and support to the Border Patrol, Customs, and the Immigration and Naturalization Service. Because they were performing a support function rather than enforcing laws, there was no violation of the Posse Comitatus Act.

Types and Capabilities of Forces

Active Military Forces

The primary mission of the military is to fight and win the Nation's wars.[31] The Department of Defense will sometimes be called upon to assist civilian authorities with active duty military forces. Domestic laws, Presidential directives, Executive orders, departmental directives, and Service regulations provide the framework for and set limits on the domestic use of military forces. Virtually any active duty unit or individual of any branch of the Armed Forces can be deployed domestically, under the proper authority. In testimony before Congress, the Secretary of Defense described four categories or circumstances in which DOD will use military forces domestically:

- *Extraordinary*: When the Nation is under attack, including by terrorist use of weapons of mass destruction, local and state officials may not be equipped to identify and repel the adversary

- *Emergency*: During disasters or emergencies, DOD will deploy troops domestically when directed to support local and state officials who are overwhelmed, or when there is an identified capability that is unique to the military

- *Temporary*: Forms of temporary support provided by the military to civil authorities include support during National Special Security Events (NSSEs) or other support to law enforcement. Recent well known NSSEs include the 2002 Winter Olympic Games in Salt Lake City, Utah; the 2004 G–8 Summit in Sea Island, Georgia; the 2004 political conventions in Boston, Massachusetts, and New York, New York; and the 2005 Presidential inauguration in Washington, DC

- *Routine*: Traditional military missions, including maritime interdiction and airspace security.

Each of these circumstances is discussed below. Whenever the deployment of active duty forces is contemplated for a domestic mission, critical consideration must be given to the impact on training and readiness for core DOD missions.

Reserve Component Forces

Army and Air National Guard. The National Guard has a unique dual mission that consists of both *Federal* and *state* roles. For state missions, the governor, through the state adjutant general, commands National Guard forces. The governor can call the National Guard into action during local or statewide emergencies, such as storms, fires, earthquakes, or civil disturbances.[32]

In addition, the President of the United States can activate the National Guard for participation in Federal missions. Examples of Federal activations include Guard units deployed to Bosnia and Kosovo for stabilization operations, and units deployed to the Middle East and other locations in the war on terrorism. When federalized, Guard units are commanded by the combatant commander of the theater in which they are operating.

Army, Marine, Navy, and Air Force Reserve. Each of the Services maintains a Federal reserve force whose mission is to provide trained and ready personnel and units with the critical capabilities necessary to support national strategy during peacetime, contingency situations, and war. The reserves are a key element in the multicomponent unit force, training with active duty and National Guard units to ensure that all three components work as a fully integrated team.[33] The reserve forces consist of the ready reserve, the standby reserve, the inactive reserve, and the retired reserve.

Other

United States Army Corps of Engineers. The Corps of Engineers is made up of approximately 34,600 civilians and 650 military men and women. These military and civilian engineers, scientists, and other specialists plan, design, build, and operate water resources and other public works projects for both the military and the interagency community. Much of their work involves inland waterway navigation, flood control, environmental protection, and disaster response.[34]

United States Coast Guard. The Coast Guard is one of the country's five armed services. In times of peace, they now operate as part of DHS, serving as the Nation's front-line agency for enforcing laws at sea, protecting the Nation's coastline and ports, and conducting life-saving operations. In times of war, or on direction of the President, the Coast Guard serves under the Navy Department.

The Coast Guard also maintains a reserve, similar to the reserves of the other services. In addition, the Coast Guard maintains an auxiliary as a nonmilitary organization, administered by the commandant under the direction of the Secretary of Homeland Security. In addition to the Coast Guard reserves, there are also private citizens who make up the Coast Guard Auxiliary, which assists the commandant in performing peacetime Coast Guard functions.[35]

Civil Air Patrol. The Civil Air Patrol is a civilian auxiliary of the United States Air Force with more than 64,000 members. The patrol is organized into 52 separate wings, with 1,700 units. The fleet consists of over 550 corporate-owned aircraft, and more than 4,000 privately owned aircraft. They conduct 95 percent of the Nation's inland search and rescue missions, as well as providing aerial reconnaissance for homeland security, disaster relief, and damage assessment. They are also called upon to transport time-sensitive medical materials.[36]

State Defense Forces. Twenty-five states have official militias. They are usually convened by the adjutants general, who head the state military services, with the governor as commander in chief. Their members train as volunteers, and also perform emergency and community support services. Unlike the National Guard, no Federal clearance is necessary for their formation, and they are obligated to serve on state active duty if so ordered by the governor.

National Response Plans and Programs

The National Response Plan (NRP) uses the foundation provided by the Homeland Security Act, Homeland Security Presidential Directive Number 5, and the Robert T. Stafford Disaster Relief and Emergency Assistance Act to provide a comprehensive, all-hazards approach to domestic incident management.[37] The NRP also establishes the coordinating structures, processes, and protocols required to integrate the specific statutory and policy authorities of various Federal departments and agencies in a collective framework for action to include prevention, preparedness, response, and recovery activities.

The NRP incorporates relevant portions of and supersedes the Federal Response Plan, the United States Government Interagency Domestic Terrorism Concept of Operations Plan, and the Federal Radiological Emergency Response Plan. The NRP also establishes national-level coordinating structures, processes, and protocols that will be incorporated into certain existing Federal interagency incident or hazard-specific plans, such as the National Oil and Hazardous Substances Pollution Contingency Plan. The NRP fully integrates emergency response and law enforcement elements into a single national strategy.

There are five key portions of the National Response Plan.

- The *Base Plan* describes the structure and processes that constitute a national approach to domestic incident management designed to integrate the efforts and resources of Federal, state, local, tribal, private sector, and nongovernmental organizations. The Base Plan includes planning assumptions, roles and responsibilities, the concept of operations, preparedness guidelines, and plan maintenance instructions.

- *Appendices* provide detailed supporting information, including acronyms, definitions, authorities, and a compendium of national interagency plans.

- *Emergency support functions annexes* detail the missions, policies, structures, and responsibilities of Federal agencies for coordinating resources and providing programmatic support to states and other Federal agencies or other jurisdictions and entities during what are referred to as "Incidents of National Significance."

- *Support annexes* provide guidance and describe the functional processes and administrative requirements necessary to ensure efficient and effective implementation of NRP incident-management objectives. Support annexes include financial management, international coordination, logistics management, private-sector coordination, public affairs, science and technology, tribal relations, volunteer and donations management, and worker safety and health.

- *Incident annexes* address contingency or hazard situations requiring specialized application of the NRP. The incident annexes describe the missions, policies, responsibilities, and coordination processes that govern the interaction of public and private entities engaged in incident management and emergency response operations. These annexes address the following types of incidents: biological, catastrophic, cyber, food and agriculture, nuclear/radiological, oil and hazardous materials, and terrorism law enforcement and investigation.

Protection of Critical Infrastructure

The majority of the Nation's critical infrastructure is under private, state, or local control. Likewise, most protection and preparedness efforts for critical infrastructure are being undertaken by state, local, and private-sector entities, without any Federal involvement. The Department of Defense relies heavily on the private-sector defense industry that provides the majority of the equipment, materials, services, and weapons for the U.S. Armed Forces. Ensuring that military forces are properly equipped is critical to maintaining DOD power projection and homeland defense capabilities. In that regard, the President recently designated the Department of Defense as the agency of primary responsibility for the defense industrial base sector. This is just one of 15 sectors of critical infrastructure that have been identified as needing protection in the "production industries" category in the Homeland Security Presidential Directive Number 7 (Critical Infrastructure Identification, Prioritization, and Protection), signed December 17, 2003.

In this role, DOD is responsible for national infrastructure protection activities for critical defense industries as set forth in Homeland Security Presidential Directive Number 7.[38] This includes:

- collaborating with all relevant Federal departments and agencies, state and local governments, and the private sector
- conducting or facilitating vulnerability assessments of the defense industrial base
- encouraging protective risk-management strategies to prevent and mitigate the effect of attacks on the defense industrial base
- preventing the loss of critical assets that are single points of failure.

Border and Transportation Security

In addition to the National Guard support provided in commercial airports in 2001, the Department of Defense supported the DHS Arizona Border Control Initiative in 2003 and 2004. This initiative was designed to strengthen control of the Arizona border in support of the detection, arrest, and prosecution of illegal cross-border traffic. DOD authorized both Hunter and Hermes unmanned aerial vehicles to perform aerial surveillance for DHS in accordance with the Economy Act.[39] Existing DOD contracts were used to operate and maintain the aircraft that had been placed under DHS control. No military personnel were employed in this operation, but missions were flown out of Fort Huachuca, Arizona, an active duty military installation.

Operation Winter Freeze. At the request of the Department of Homeland Security, DOD contributed to an interagency operation to deter, detect, and monitor transnational threats along the northern borders of Vermont, New York, and New Hampshire. A joint task force composed of both active duty and National Guard personnel provided technical support and analysis to the Customs Bureau in the Swanton Sector. The support provided included aerial reconnaissance and nonintrusive chemical, biological, radiological, and nuclear screening and detection.

Domestic Counterterrorism. Because of the United States' conventional military superiority, potential enemies, hostile nations, terrorist groups, or criminal organizations are increasingly likely to attack the Nation using unconventional means. The United States has established that terrorists who violate the law will be apprehended and tried, no matter where they hide and no matter how long it takes. The Department of Justice is the principal Federal agency responsible for domestic counterterrorism, but the Department of Defense can provide support in accordance with existing authorizations and appropriations.

Catastrophic Threats. In the event of a catastrophic threat, it is likely that local and state medical assets will become overwhelmed quickly. The National Disaster Medical System (NDMS) is designed to provide a national capability to deliver quality medical care to victims. DOD has a role in each of the three components of NDMS. When requested, DOD provides specialized deployable medical teams to disaster sites. When air evacuation is required from the affected area, DOD coordinates and tracks patient movement. Finally, DOD, along with the Department of Veterans' Affairs, monitors available hospital beds and staffs urgent care facilities.[40]

Civil Support

Disaster Relief. Throughout the history of the United States, the Department of Defense (and its predecessor, the Department of War) has assisted the victims of disasters.[41] The Robert T. Stafford Disaster Relief and Emergency Assistance Act is the primary legal authority for Federal participation in domestic disaster relief efforts. Under the Stafford Act, the

President may direct Federal agencies, including DOD, to provide personnel, equipment, supplies, facilities, and managerial, technical, and advisory services in support of disaster relief.[42] The DOD may be directed to provide disaster assistance in one of three different scenarios: a Presidential declaration of a major disaster; a Presidential order to perform emergency work essential for the preservation of life and property; or a Presidential declaration of an emergency. Although there is no specific statutory authority to do so, DOD established a commander's "immediate response" authority. This authority allows heads of military units to provide disaster relief when "imminently serious conditions resulting from any civil emergency or attack exist which requires immediate action to save lives, prevent human suffering, or mitigate great property damage."[43]

Support to Law Enforcement. The Secretary of Defense may, in accordance with other applicable law, provide military assistance to Federal, state, or local civil law enforcement officials. In addition to the Insurrection Act, specific statutory authority is granted for the protection of nuclear materials,[44] incidents of chemical and biological terrorism,[45] and in support to the United States Secret Service.[46]

Civil Disturbance. Title 10, Chapter 15 of the United States Code, entitled "Insurrection," allows the use of Federal forces to restore order during times of civil disturbance. Both the Department of Defense and the courts use one phrase, *civil disturbance*, to encompass the various situations allowing the use of military assistance under the Insurrection Act. Under this act, the President may commit Federal forces to support a request from a governor, enforce Federal authority, or protect constitutional rights.[47] As the use of Federal forces to quell civil disturbances is expressly authorized by statute, the proscriptions of the Posse Comitatus Act are inapplicable in these cases.[48] Historical examples of the use of Federal forces under this authority have been detailed previously in this essay.

National Special Security Events. Numerous special events regularly receive security support from the Department of Defense or another element of the Federal Government. Some of these, such as the Presidential nominating conventions, Presidential inaugurations, international summits, and large sporting events like the Olympics warrant special support. At the request of individual governors, or upon direction of the President, the Secretary of Homeland Security may designate these events of great magnitude and national or international importance as NSSEs.[49]

Once designated, the event receives the full protection and incident-management capabilities of the Federal Government. The Secret Service leads the development and implementation of the comprehensive security planning effort, which includes coordinating with local and state authorities, as well as identifying Federal capabilities to supplement but not supplant local resources. The Federal Bureau of Investigation serves as the lead agency for intelligence, Federal criminal investigation, hostage rescue, and counterterrorism efforts. The Federal Emergency Management Agency is the lead agency for the planning and coordination of response to and recovery from terrorist attacks and other emergencies. Other Federal departments and agencies, including the Department of Defense, provide a full range of resources to support the event based on their authorities and appropriations. For NSSEs, DOD usually provides specialized technical support like explosive ordnance disposal technicians, explosive detector dog teams, and chemical, biological, radiological, and nuclear detection and response capabilities. Depending on the scope and magnitude of the event, DOD may establish a joint task force to exercise command and control over its personnel providing support.

Conclusion

The domestic deployment of military resources is neither new nor limited to the United States. The military has long provided assistance in cases of disaster, and has routinely supported state and territorial governors, occasionally administering governmental affairs until local governance was reestablished. Military personnel and their associated equipment, although organized to conduct combat operations, can be rapidly deployed domestically with proper authorization.

Notes

[1] *The Constitution of the United States of America*, Article II, Section 2.

[2] Ibid., Article 1, Section 8.

[3] George W. Bush, "Letter from the President of the United States to the American People," transmitted as part of *The National Strategy for Homeland Security*, July 16, 2002; available at <www.whitehouse.gov/homeland/book/>.

[4] *The National Strategy for Homeland Security*.

[5] Ibid., 2.

[6] Donald H. Rumsfeld, "Message to U.S. Forces and Department of Defense Civilians," September 12, 2001.

[7] U.S. Department of Defense, "The Military Strategy for Homeland Defense and Civil Support," June 24, 2005.

[8] Ibid., 14.

[9] Ibid.

[10] Ibid.

[11] *Constitution*, Article II.

[12] Ibid.

[13] Ibid.

[14] Title 18, United States Code (U.S.C.), Section 1385 (hereafter Posse Comitatus Act).

[15] Matthew C. Hammond, "The Posse Comitatus Act: A Principle in Need of Renewal," *Washington University Law Quarterly* 75, no. 2 (1997), 953–954; *Domestic Operational Law (DOPLAW) Handbook for Judge Advocates* (Charlottesville, VA: Center for Law and Military Operations, 2001), 8.

[16] Gary Felicetti and John Luce, "The Posse Comitatus Act: Liberation from the Lawyers," *Parameters* 34, no. 3 (Autumn 2004), 100–101.

[17] Amanda J. Dory, "Civil Security, Americans, and the Challenge of Homeland Security," CSIS Report (September 2003), 12.

[18] Title 10, U.S.C., Section 331–335 (hereafter the Insurrection Act), July 29, 1861.

[19] Title 10, U.S.C., Section 332 (Use of Militia and Armed Forces to Enforce Federal Authority).

[20] Executive Order Number 10,730, 22 Federal Register 7,628 (September 24, 1957); Executive Order Number 11,118, 28 Federal Register 9,863 (September 10, 1963).

[21] Executive Order Number 11,053, 27 Federal Register 9,681 (September 30, 1962); Executive Order Number 11,111, 28 Federal Register 5,709 (June 11, 1963).

[22] Title 10, U.S.C., Subtitle A, Part I, Chapter 18 (Military Support for Civilian Law Enforcement Agencies).

[23] In 2001, Congress appropriated $869 million for DOD support for countertrafficking operations. This amount has continuously grown. See the National Defense Appropriations Act of 2001, Public Law 106–259.

[24] The National Defense Appropriations Act of 1991–1992, Public Law 101–189.

[25] Ibid., Section 1563.

[26] Title 32, U.S.C., Section 112(a).

[27] Proclamation Number 6,427, 57 Federal Register 19,359 (May 5, 1992).

[28] Executive Order Number 12,804, 57 Federal Register 19,361 (May 5, 1992).

[29] This duty status is authorized by Title 32, U.S.C., Section 525(f).

[30] Barbara Hatch Rosenberg, "Analysis of the Anthrax Attacks," *Federation of American Scientists* (September 22, 2002).

[31] Joint Chiefs of Staff, *Joint Vision 2020* (Washington, DC: U.S. Government Printing Office, 2000).

[32] National Guard Bureau Web Site, <www.ngb.army.mil/about>.

[33] U.S. Army Reserve Web Site, <www.armyreserve.army.mil/usar/mission/statement>.

[34] U.S. Army Corps of Engineers Web Site, <www.usace.army.mil/>.

[35] U.S. Coast Guard Web Site, <www.uscg.mil/USCG.shtm>.

[36] Civil Air Patrol (U.S. Air Force Auxiliary) Web Site, <www.cap.gov/>.

[37] Title 42, U.S.C., Section 5121, et seq. as amended (Robert T. Stafford Disaster Relief and Emergency Assistance Act).

[38] Homeland Security Presidential Directive No. 7, Critical Infrastructure Identification, Prioritization, and Protection (December 17, 2003).

[39] Title 31, U.S.C., Section 1535 (Economy Act) authorizes Federal agencies to provide supplies, equipment, and materials on a reimbursable basis to other Federal agencies.

[40] See National Disaster Medical System Web Site, <www.ndms.dhhs.gov>.

[41] U.S. Department of the Army Field Manual 100–19, *Domestic Support Operations* (July 1993), 1–2, addresses historic precedence of Army support to disaster assistance including the Chicago fire, the Johnstown flood, and the Charleston earthquake.

[42] The Stafford Act.

[43] U.S. Department of Defense Directive 3025.1, "Military Support to Civil Authorities," Para 4.5 (January 15, 1993).

[44] Title 18, U.S.C., Section 831, criminalizes certain acts involving nuclear material and authorizes the Attorney General to request DOD assistance to enforce the prohibition.

[45] Title 50, U.S.C., Section 2313 (Defense Against Weapons of Mass Destruction Act).

[46] Title 18, U.S.C., Section 3056 (Presidential Protection Assistance Act of 1978).

[47] Title 10, U.S.C., Section 332, et seq. (Insurrection Act).

[48] The Posse Comitatus Act makes it unlawful to use any part of the Army or Air Force in a civilian law enforcement capacity to execute local, state, or Federal laws. The language of the act itself specifies that activities expressly authorized by the Constitution or by statute are exempt from the act's restrictions.

[49] Presidential Decision Directive No. 62, "Protection Against Unconventional Threats to the Homeland and Americans Overseas" (May 22, 1998).

Chapter 2

The Role of the Armed Forces of the United Kingdom in Securing the State against Terrorism

Jonathan Stevenson

The horror of the terrorist attacks of September 11, 2001, led to worldwide condemnation. All parts of the world mourned the victims of the attacks with a sense of shared loss that was heightened by the fact that many of the victims were of nationalities other than American. Allies rushed to the support of the United States, and the North Atlantic Treaty Organization (NATO) promptly declared that the attack on the United States could be considered an attack on the entire 19-nation alliance. But while the United States chose to hike defense spending and intensify its efforts on homeland security, the effect on European countries was somewhat different. The terrorist attacks constituted a watershed in American threat perceptions, but to a large number of European countries, the threat seemed less novel.

Terrorist activities within national borders are not new to many states in Europe. Indeed, the continent's history is scarred by a relatively large number of terrorist activities and groups, including the Provisional Irish Republican Army (IRA), the Basque separatist organization *Euskadi ta Askatasuna* (ETA), the Greek far-left group November 17 Organization, the Red Army Faction in Germany, and the Red Brigades in Italy, to name but a few. Europeans did recognize that the "new terrorists"—that is, transnational Islamist terrorists—posed the threat of mass casualties, and were generally uninterested in bargaining or other modes of formal conflict resolution. But European governments also had more experience than did Washington with terrorism, and they tended to see the new terrorism more as a continuation of old forms of terrorism than did the United States. At least initially, for instance, European officials were less inclined to think that terrorists would use weapons of mass destruction (WMD).

Furthermore, the United States was perceived—justifiably—as the prime target of al Qaeda and the transnational Islamist terrorist movement over which it loosely presides. Therefore, threat perceptions did not change as dramatically in Europe, and the sense of an urgent need to boost homeland security was not as strong as that prevailing in the United States. For most European governments, existing counterterrorism measures were seen as basically adequate, although some adjustments were made to deal with the perceived threat of terrorism from WMD. Yet because the proportion of Muslims in European populations—especially in France, Germany, and the United Kingdom—is far higher than it is in the United States, and Muslim populations are generally less integrated, the challenges in terms of technical counterterrorism (intelligence collection through surveillance and penetration, pursuit by police and/or special operations forces) in Europe are in some ways greater than they are in the United States. However, falling military spending across Europe put a damper on any push to expand most homeland defense programs or jumpstart new initiatives.[1]

The United Kingdom, perhaps due to its singularly close strategic alignment with the United States, constitutes the starkest European exception to this trend. In the United Kingdom, there is no statutory constraint comparable to the U.S. Posse Comitatus Act, which substantially bars U.S. military operations on U.S. soil and against American citizens, though the pressures of the global war on terror may be marginally eroding some of the act's restrictions. Centuries of European political instability and warfare, two world wars centered in Europe in the 20th century, and a persistent low-intensity guerrilla insurgency waged by the IRA in Northern Ireland since 1969 have resulted in a substantial role for military forces in protecting national territory. The rising threat from al Qaeda and its affiliates and sympathizers indicated by the attacks of September 11 have prompted the government to extend the territorial mandate of British armed forces in areas related to homeland defense. Especially in light of the previous demand for military action in protecting both infrastructure and the general population against IRA attacks on the British "mainland" (that is, England, Scotland, and Wales) as well as Northern Ireland itself, the post-9/11 enhancement of the military's mandate on British soil should be considered evolutionary rather than revolutionary.

Historical Perspective

The Cold War Era

During the Cold War, the UK military was focused primarily on the defense of Europe (mainly through NATO) against a Soviet ground invasion across Europe's central front. The military defense of the homeland against an advancing Warsaw Pact was, in that context, a subsidiary concern. There was, however, a significant additional role for the military in homeland defense in countering the IRA's terrorist insurgency in both Northern Ireland, where it originated as a means of forcing the British government to permit the province to unite with the Republic of Ireland, and the British mainland. From 1969, when the Northern Irish "troubles" became a full-blown insurgency, until 1976, the British Army had the lead responsibility for quelling IRA violence and pacifying Northern Ireland. In 1976, however, the British government sought to "criminalize" Northern Irish terrorism and "normalize" law enforcement in the province to the greatest extent possible by according primary authority to the Northern Irish police force, then known as the Royal Ulster Constabulary (RUC). The army continued to play an important support role, however. British soldiers routinely patrolled the streets of Belfast, Londonderry, and other locales in the province in armored vehicles, and participated in joint armed foot patrols with the RUC. The Special Air Service also ran covert operations against the IRA, and the British Army maintained a garrisoned presence in Northern Ireland of between 20,000 and 30,000 troops between 1976 and 1994.

Beyond prosecuting counterinsurgency and securing airspace and surrounding waters, British policy did not contemplate a wholesale role for the military in homeland security, except at the request of debilitated civil authorities in the event of a strike by nuclear weapons or other WMD. As in the United States, however, the notion that civil defense could be effective against such devastation met with popular and, to a lesser extent, official skepticism.

After the Cold War

While the standoff between the Soviet Union and the West was ongoing, Northern Ireland remained a potentially important source of military-industrial capacity (missiles and shipbuilding) for the United Kingdom. Furthermore, London might find tactical use for Northern Irish port facilities and military bases in any North Atlantic strategic confrontation, and therefore had an interest in keeping Northern Irish territory from becoming part of the Irish Republic, which was politically neutral. But as the Cold War drew to a close in the early 1990s, the British government acknowledged that Northern Ireland was no longer of intrinsic economic or strategic value to the Crown, and quietly but clearly promoted dialogue on the question of the province's sovereign status between the pro-British and mainly Protestant "unionist" majority there and the largely Catholic "nationalist" minority that favored Irish unification, including the IRA and its legal political wing, Sinn Fein. The IRA declared a unilateral cease-fire in August 1994, and 6 weeks later, the pro-British "loyalist" paramilitaries followed suit. The political culmination of these developments was the Belfast Agreement of 1998 (also known as the Good Friday Accord). While there have been numerous violations of the cease-fires, and the implementation of the Belfast Agreement remains stalled, the cease-fires and political advances have resulted in a most likely permanent reduction in the level of terrorist violence. As a consequence, the military's role in domestic counterinsurgency has become residual and secondary; only about 10,000 troops are presently deployed in Northern Ireland.

More broadly, in the post–Cold War world, military planners saw the prospect of strategic attack on the British homeland as remote, perhaps even negligible. After the Soviet threat evaporated, no other power was regarded as having a ballistic missile force capable of threatening British soil. Contingencies in distant locations such as Bosnia and Sierra Leone suggested that expeditionary and force-protection capabilities—not homeland defense—should constitute the main military priorities. Foreign Minister Robin Cook commented in 1998 that "in the post–Cold War world, we must be prepared to go to the crisis, rather than have the crisis come to us."[2] While this sentiment accurately reflects some current Western strategic inclinations towards preemption and prevention, it also downplays the military's role in securing the homeland. By the millennium, the United Kingdom appeared poised to become a substantially demilitarized homeland.

After 9/11

The 9/11 attacks drove home to the British government the point that the military could be required to support the civil authorities in the event of a mass-casualty terrorist attack. Although the strongest

British precedent for heavy military involvement in homeland security was counterinsurgency in the Northern Irish conflict, the emergent need for such involvement was mainly in the areas of infrastructure protection, first response, and civil defense. In February 2003, the British Army was called upon to ring Heathrow Airport on the basis of current intelligence that Islamist terrorists could be planning a surface-to-air missile attack on a jetliner. In September 2003, British authorities simulated a chemical attack on a subway station in downtown London to test (and demonstrate) government response capacities. Although government policy does contemplate military assistance to civilian authorities if necessary in the event of a chemical, biological, radiological, or nuclear (CBRN) attack, the military was not involved in this exercise. Its nonparticipation could support the House of Commons Defense Committee's conclusion at the end of 2001 that the circumstances in which the Ministry of Defense expected to call out units of the reserve forces—particularly the Territorial Army (TA)—in conditions short of general war were too limited, and that a more proactive role resembling that of the U.S. National Guard should be explored.

Legal Authority

The United Kingdom has no hard-and-fast statutory bar to the application of military resources to domestic threats comparable to the U.S. Posse Comitatus Act.[3] Nevertheless, longstanding political and legal custom and common law circumscribe such application. The Ministry of Defense considers the principle that military support for domestic civilian authorities must be provided at their specific request in order to be effectively "constitutional."[4] This view was reinforced in discussions of the then-prospective new Strategic Defense Review chapter in the House of Commons in December 2001, when British Defense Doctrine was quoted as follows:

> [T]he use of the Armed Forces for domestic purposes is potentially controversial, and strict limitations are placed on their domestic employment. The relationship between the Armed Forces and civil authorities in the UK is the subject of aspects of constitutional and administrative law and there has developed, over three hundred years, a legal doctrine governing the domestic use of military personnel. At the core of that doctrine is the absolute primacy of civil authorities; when Armed Forces personnel are used on domestic tasks they are only employed in support of relevant and legally responsible civil authorities.[5]

Even in a state of emergency, then, the British military has no primary or independent authority on British soil absent a complete breakdown of civil authority and at least an implicit delegation of that authority to the military.

Types and Availability of Forces

On October 31, 2002, the Minister for the Armed Forces announced that an enhanced domestic military reserve capability would take the form of 14 Civil Contingency Reaction Forces (CCRFs)—one for each of the army brigade regions in the United Kingdom, each composed of 500 volunteers. Some 7,000 volunteers will make up the CCRFs. The Territorial Army is the United Kingdom's largest reserve body, with a strength of 40,350 troops. The army comprises 15 infantry, 4 light reconnaissance, and 2 special forces battalions, as well as 5 engineering, 4 air defense, and 3 artillery regiments, and 1 aviation regiment. Home service forces also include 3,390 troops (2,100 full-time) recruited in Northern Ireland. As of October 2004, some 10,700 regular armed forces personnel—overwhelmingly from the British Army—were deployed in Northern Ireland for residual counterinsurgency and counterterrorist operations.[6] British military doctrine, of course, also contemplates the use of regular armed forces in homeland emergencies.

Protection of Critical Infrastructure

Owing to the entrenched support role of the British military in homeland security, efforts in critical infrastructure protection—including information technology, nuclear facilities, power generation capacity, communications networks, civilian government installations, and industrial capacity—remain primarily the responsibility of civilian authorities and private owners. They are advised by the Security Service (also known as MI5), which is the United Kingdom's domestic intelligence agency, and wholly civilian in nature. Nevertheless, since 9/11, the role of the military in infrastructure protection, while still extraordinary, has become considerably more salient.

Indeed, that role became conspicuous in February 2003, when over 1,000 soldiers (initially 450) were deployed for over a week in West London to help police protect Heathrow International Airport on the strength of a civilian intelligence assessment that commercial passenger airliners could be the targets of terrorist surface-to-air missile attacks. The soldiers were armed with automatic weapons. Some patrolled the airport on foot, while others assisted local police in stopping vehicles on roads underneath Heathrow's flight path at checkpoints set up inside an 8-mile radius of the airport. Others monitored the airport perimeter in armored reconnaissance vehicles (mainly 8.7-ton Scimitars, equipped with 30 millimeter (mm) cannon and 7.62mm machineguns, with a top speed of 50 miles per hour). The soldiers were drawn from the 1st Battalion of the elite Grenadier Guards, as well as the Household Cavalry. While the army was enlisted through designated official channels, specifically at the request of the police, the Heathrow operation was the first time that the military had been involved in securing the airport since 1994, when the IRA launched mortar rounds at Heathrow.

Some skeptical observers apprehended the Heathrow operation as a kind of publicity stunt, designed to condition the public for more draconian security measures in other realms of life. One British Muslim, for instance, remarked: "I think probably the authorities feel that they should build up emotions—what I call the 'war spirit.'"[7] The overall danger of surface-to-air missiles, however, was credible. Two had been launched at an Israeli jetliner leaving Mombasa, Kenya, in November 2002, narrowly missing the plane, and tens of thousands of the hand-held missiles were in illicit—or at least unregulated—circulation. In any case, the operation demonstrated that, after 9/11, a lower threshold of intelligence warning would trigger military support for civilian authorities generally, since the consequences of the kind of mass-casualty attack preferred by the "new" transnational Islamist terrorists superseded its probability from the standpoint of prevention.

Andrew Marr, a thoughtful British Broadcasting Corporation journalist, noted the "appalling dilemma" faced by ministers who had to implement effective day-to-day domestic security operations when faced with a mountain of intelligence to analyze as well as "a political blame culture and an unquantifiable threat."[8] In the United Kingdom, such officials are now more likely to call on the military to support civilian authorities. Yet they have done so sparingly since February 2003—probably, at least in part, as a result of the criticisms that the Heathrow operation elicited. Indeed, in June 2002, Assistant Metropolitan Police Commissioner David Veness testified in Parliament to the Select Defense Committee that, while the military could be useful in certain limited domestic contexts, the United Kingdom had no "gendarmerie," no "third force," and no "national guard." Thus, he continued, if faced with "a threat that required [civil authorities] to protect a sector of British industry which is pretty geographically spread"—and therefore beyond regular police capacities—the first resort would be to the special constabulary, and the second to the private security industry. The fact that the military was not in his "batting order" is a telling indication of the reluctance of civilian officials in the United Kingdom to call on the military for support.[9]

Border and Transportation Security

Except for operating armed checkpoints on the border between Northern Ireland and the Irish Republic, the fact that mainland Britain is an island has resulted in little direct military involvement in territorial border security. The key agencies in border control—the police (including Special Branch and a National Coordinator for Ports Policing), the Security Service, and Immigration and Customs—are all civilian, and the approach is intelligence-driven. Should terrorists breach border security, however, there is a paramount role for the military—especially special operations forces—in search operations, a role that is duly acknowledged by law enforcement professionals to require skills "beyond that which can be provided by any UK police force."[10] The skills of the Special Air Service, for instance, has been famously (to some, infamously) employed against the IRA in Northern Ireland and on other British soil, notably Gibraltar.

Similarly, transportation security in the United Kingdom has been largely a matter for the civil police authorities. In general, the British government has a great deal of confidence in its civilian transportation security apparatus—mainly, the Transportation Security Directorate of the Department of Transport—which was reinforced following the destruction of Pan Am Flight 103 over Lockerbie, Scotland, by a terrorist bomb in 1989. In particular, British law enforcement officials place great stock in the extensive closed-circuit television camera surveillance systems now in place in transportation venues.[11] Nevertheless, the specific prospect of a sea-based attack on the United Kingdom has raised government awareness of a potential need for maritime military assistance in securing the homeland. For example, in December 2001, the British Royal Marines were dispatched to board a merchant vessel suspected of carrying terrorist materials—possibly materials required for producing WMD—or perhaps even being itself the vehicle for a coastal attack. This operation required close cooperation and coordination among intelligence services, customs officials, police, and the military, and has led to enhanced standing lines of communication and regular procedures among these four groups. And of course, the Heathrow operation was, from one perspective, a special instance of transportation security.

Domestic Counterterrorism

At the request (usually) of the relevant police chief—through the Home Office, and then by formal agreement with the Ministry of Defense—the UK military can provide specialized military aid to the civil power in the form of bomb disposal and other specialized equipment and expertise. In most cases, the police request would be very specific and circumscribed. In extraordinary circumstances, though, if the police demonstrate the need, the Home Office can agree to general military support. This occurred when the army was deployed around Heathrow Airport. Even then, however, the police operational commander determined jointly with the military commander what, where, and how the military equipment and personnel would be deployed.

As discussed above, except for the first 4 or 5 years of the Northern Irish conflict, during which the situation in the province sometimes verged on civil war, the armed forces have officially played a police support role in countering domestic terrorism, which the British government has approached as an essentially criminal problem since 1976. The reality is more nuanced, however, as Irish republican insurgents have killed more than twice as many soldiers as police. In addition to supporting the RUC, the army has played an important role in the area of intelligence in Northern Ireland. Nevertheless, MI5 has been the lead agency in a central body for collating and coordinating intelligence from all relevant sources, including the Royal Ulster Constabulary's Special Branch, its Scotland Yard counterpart, as well as army intelligence. From that position, MI5 has exercised control over intelligence-driven counterterrorist operations. This special arrangement, however, effectively accorded MI5 a key role in overseeing law enforcement—the execution of which remained the RUC's responsibility—by lowering the institutional barriers between intelligence collection and law enforcement. Perforce, army intelligence played a role in domestic counterterrorism. But it is unlikely that the level of input reached during the Northern Irish "troubles" has been sustained as they have wound down over the past decade.

First Response and Consequence Management

The general implication of the more particular doctrinal and legal limitations on the UK military's role in securing the British homeland is that the military is most likely to be summoned by civilian authorities in the case of a catastrophic terrorist attack for which civilian response and consequence management capabilities are inadequate. Relatively unspectacular tasks unrelated to terrorism for which the British armed forces were rallied to offset such incapacity include the control of traffic during a fuel strike in summer 2000, the disposal of livestock affected with foot-and-mouth disease in 2001, and the provision of firefighting services during a national firefighter strike in 2003. In the event of a mass-casualty terrorist attack, there would appear little doubt that the military would be called on for assistance in some capacity. The possible tasks specifically enumerated by the Ministry of Defense for the CCRFs, for example, include cordoning, evacuation, provision of temporary lodging and feeding facilities, and logistical support: all paramount needs in the event of most conceivable catastrophic attacks.

Current Formal National Policy

The British government's philosophy of civil contingency planning is based on the concept of resilience, which is defined as the ability "at every relevant level to detect, prevent, and, if necessary, to handle and recover from disruptive challenges."[12] It is fundamental to this concept that domestic emergencies are in the first instance to be handled at the local level. If local capacity is insufficient, the next resort is to neighboring jurisdictions. Only when such mutual local- and regional-level assistance is unavailing does the central government become involved through a lead government department; which department takes the lead varies depending on the nature of the emergency. That department is then required to alert the Civil Contingencies Secretariat (CCS) in the Cabinet Office.

The CCS in turn assesses the whole situation and determines which resources (potentially including military ones) need to be marshaled. The CCS, through the Civil Contingencies Committee (CCC), "is to provide the central focus for the cross-departmental and cross-agency commitment, coordination, and cooperation that will enable the UK to deal effectively with disruptive challenges and crises."[13] In particular, the CCC will determine whether overall strategic (as opposed to tactical or operational) responsibility for dealing with the contingency in question should be delegated to one of several devolved administrations or assumed by a central authority.

Combined response—with an emphasis on multi-agency command, control, and coordination—remains key to the British approach to homeland security. The CCS specifically contemplates the "armed forces" as well as emergency services, local authorities, central government, the health service, and the voluntary sector as potential elements of a combined effort.[14] In turn, British military doctrine establishes a relatively muscular (but still strictly secondary) role for the armed forces in securing the British homeland. Military doctrine considers maintaining the freedom and territorial integrity of the United Kingdom as chief among the goals of British security policy. This goal expressly includes "sustaining the rule of law and internal order within the United Kingdom."[15] British military doctrine also specifies, as one of three overlapping defense roles, ensuring the protection and security of the United Kingdom "even when there is no external threat."[16] Thus, the potential scope for the military's role in securing the British homeland is doctrinally broad. Indeed, the very first of the seven mission types for the military officially enumerated is "military aid to the civil power in the United Kingdom."[17] In turn, British doctrine enunciates three forms of military aid to civil authorities:

- military aid to the civil community, which is the provision of military personnel and equipment in both emergencies (e.g., natural disasters) and in routine situations to assist the community at large

- military aid to civil ministries, which is the use of military forces for nonmilitary government tasks, including ensuring the essential safety of members of the community and undertaking matters of national importance

- military aid to the civil power, which provides for the direct maintenance or restoration of law and order in situations beyond the capacity of the civil power to resolve using any other resources. The rule of thumb for the military is to respond to a civilian request for assistance, resolve the immediate problem, and return control to the civil power as expeditiously as possible.[18]

Indeed, military aid to the civil power has been provided continuously to combat the IRA's terrorist insurgency campaign since 1969. This long involvement in counter-insurgency and counterterrorism on UK soil gave the British military arguably unique, and certainly extraordinary, experience in thwarting asymmetric threats. The UK military has also recently assisted civil authorities in dealing with fuel strikes, floods, and the foot-and-mouth epidemic, as well as filling in for striking firefighters.

London, like other European capitals, had underestimated the threat posed by al Qaeda. The United Kingdom did begin to wake up before 9/11, outlawing 21 terrorist front organizations—16 of them Islamist in nature—early in 2001. But Britain has remained a key indoctrination, staging, and logistics center for al Qaeda members. In December 2001, the UK parliament responded decisively to the increased terrorist threats revealed by 9/11, passing laws comparable in effect to the USA PATRIOT Act. These included requirements that communications companies retain accessible records of calls made and emails sent (though not their contents), more rigorous recordkeeping requirements for transport companies, enhanced financial surveillance and restriction authorization, provisions for greater interagency exchanges of intelligence, and a controversial power of indefinite detention applicable to suspected international terrorists. In June 2002, a security and intelligence coordinator was appointed at permanent secretary rank. It is noteworthy, however, that none of these admittedly muscular provisions involved the British military.

Furthermore, in practice, the British military was unprepared for the extreme and novel demands that apocalyptic terrorism of the 9/11 variety—which differs plainly from the IRA's relatively restrained use of political violence—could place on the military in the domestic context. The UK Ministry of Defense's Strategic Defense Review (SDR), completed in 1998, emphasized primarily improvements in conventional warfighting capabilities—that is, in reconnaissance, surveillance, rapid deployment, target acquisition, precision-strike capability, and command and control. The SDR did not account for the increasing possibility that discontented nations and non-state groups would refuse to meet in the UK military's preferred and contemplated theater of action. In a 2002 Public Discussion Paper calling for a new chapter in the SDR to deal with the threat of apocalyptic terror, the Ministry of Defense itself noted:

> The SDR admitted the potential existence of asymmetric threats, but it is fair to say that it did not treat such threats as a strategic risk, but more as one of a range of tactics that an adversary might use. It was the emergence of asymmetric action as having the potential for strategic change that has prompted the work we are now undertaking.[19]

Included in the ministry's prospectus for the content of the new chapter of the SDR was "the contribution that the Armed Forces make to protecting the UK itself."[20]

While the UK Home Office has primary responsibility for counterterrorism on British soil, the military has always provided for the overarching physical defense of the realm in guarding airspace and territorial waters. After 9/11, Royal Air Force fighters were placed on heightened alert and have been scrambled to monitor suspect aircraft several times. The Ministry of Defense observed that the American experience on and after 9/11 demonstrated that transnational terrorism implicated these homeland defense functions, and that they required some rethinking, particularly as to the operational tempo and the speed of decisionmaking. Also inferred from the aftermath of the 9/11 attacks in the United States was the need for closer coordination between civilian and military authorities "in order to maximize the utility and suitability of responses to any future requests [by the civilian authorities for military assistance] at the national, regional, and local levels."[21]

In the Report of the House of Commons Defense Committee on the new chapter, published in May 2003, the committee concluded that, while the events of September 11 had raised the priority of homeland defense in the British military's thinking, the new chapter contemplated not a greater role for the armed forces in assisting civil authorities, but rather a greater role for the reserves.[22] As noted, the enhanced domestic military reserve capability would take the form of 14 CCRFs: one for each of the army brigade regions in the United Kingdom, each made up of 500 volunteers. Thus, the CCRFs' total strength would be about 7,000 troops. (By comparison, France's Directorate of Territorial Security has about 1,500 employees.) Along with the CCRFs, the Ministry of Defense has established an enhanced regionally based planning and command capability that is intended to facilitate rapid support from the armed forces (both regular and reserve) to civil authorities, as well as an integrated communications structure to be provided by a Territorial Army (TA) formation and two signal brigades. In total, the reserve forces were to receive 700 new posts and an additional 130,000 man-training days. The CCRFs do not encompass or overlap with the TA, the UK's main reserve force, though they would be mobilized through TA centers. Start-up costs for the CCRFs were estimated at £2 million (approximately $3.56 million USD), the annual cost of the CCRF scheme at £4.5 million (approximately $8 million USD), and costs over 4 years in the civil contingencies arena at £60 million (approximately $106.7 million USD).[23] The CCRFs were to have achieved full operating capability by December 31, 2003. The CCRFs would be used mainly for civil support in the aftermath of a major disaster, the consequences of which were beyond the capabilities of civil authorities. Likely tasks include cordon and evacuation, providing temporary accommodation and feeding facilities, and general logistical support.

It is worth noting, however, that the CCRFs' utility was contemplated only at the margins; the Defense Committee hastened to add that, in a serious terrorist contingency on British soil, regular army units would probably still be preferred for their superior training and experience, and that the CCRFs were intended merely to give British commanders an additional source of manpower. Accordingly, the Committee concluded:

> Overall, we have seen little evidence that the Ministry of Defense has taken seriously the need to rethink the capacity of the Armed Forces to provide predictable support to the task of home defense in the event of a mass-effect terrorist attack in the UK.[24]

Indeed, there appears to have been little articulation of British military or defense doctrine around a number of security challenges that have increased in salience since September 2001—for example, airline hijacking and hostage-taking, both of which could well occur on UK soil.

Conclusion

Since the September 11 attacks, the role of the UK military forces in securing the British homeland has increased only incrementally. The primary reason for the merely marginal enhancement of that role is the United Kingdom's well-established principle that civilian authorities should manage crises to the maximum practicable extent in a mature democracy. The consensus among UK officials is that this principle remains valid. At the same time, the extraordinary and largely uncharted character of the global jihadist threat has prompted some to question the government's conservatism in this area. To be sure, since 9/11 the British government has emphasized civil defense and national resilience, having simulated a chemical attack in central London to sharpen its preparedness. In light of transnational Islamist terrorists' preference for mass casualties, British law-enforcement agencies are more inclined than they were when the IRA was the main terrorist adversary to arrest suspects preventively.

The British are probably as ready to deal with such an attack as any jurisdiction in Europe. Yet local and regional officials, through the Emergency Planning Society, have criticized the United Kingdom's level of civil defense preparedness, noting that its first responders could handle a limited IRA-style operation but not a no-warning mass-casualty attack on the order of the Madrid bombings. Although the UK's civil-defense budget has increased by 35 percent over pre-2001 levels, it is still only £35 million (approximately $62.2 million USD) per year and the government faces a considerable challenge in rebuilding a system that was dismantled in 1991–1992 after the Cold War ended. Even when it was intact, with a network of regional headquarters, the system's response time was measured in days. It would be difficult, and perhaps impossible, to deploy comprehensive preventive means to compensate for any first-response deficiencies. For instance, the UK's 11,000-mile, 2,500-station rail network, which is used by 5 million people a day, is extremely vulnerable. Metal detectors and baggage scanners are used only on the Eurostar service running between London and Brussels and London and Paris. Universal airport-style security checks would be impractical and prohibitively expensive.

Thus, there are strong arguments for making the military's contemplated involvement in UK homeland security efforts more substantial. These may prompt greater activity in training and equipping regular army units as well as the CCRFs and the TA to assist civilian authorities, particularly in the event of a CBRN attack. Given the UK government's longstanding—and, indeed, supportable—philosophical bias in favor of civil domestic control, however, it is likely to respond to these arguments mainly by enhancing civilian capacity rather than doctrinally or operationally augmenting the military's role in homeland security.

Notes

[1] In general, see Jonathan Stevenson, "How Europe and America Defend Themselves," *Foreign Affairs* 82, no. 2 (March/April 2003), 75–90.

[2] Quoted in House of Commons Defense Committee, *A New Chapter to the Strategic Defense Review*, Second Report, December 2001, para. 116.

[3] The Posse Comitatus Act is found at 18 United States Code, Section 1385, which bars the use of the military in activities customarily reserved for law enforcement, such as arrest, seizure of evidence, searches of buildings, interrogating witnesses, pursuing escaped prisoners, and searching for suspects. However, "passive" assistance such as logistical support, technical advice, use of facilities, and training is not prohibited. Nor is technical support like explosive ordnance disposal or advice and assistance with respect to WMD. See, for example, Jeffrey D. Brake, "Terrorism and the Military's Role in

Domestic Crisis Management: Background and Issues for Congress," CRS Report for Congress (Washington, DC: Congressional Research Service, April 19, 2001), 12.

[4] UK Ministry of Defense, *The Strategic Defense Review: A New Chapter*, Public Discussion Paper (February 2002), 6.

[5] UK Ministry of Defence, *British Defence Doctrine* (2d edition, October 2001), 6–9.

[6] Figures are from International Institute for Strategic Studies, *The Military Balance 2004/2005* (Oxford: Oxford University Press, 2004), 73, 75.

[7] "Blair Authorised Terror Alert Troops," BBC News, February 17, 2003; available at <news.bbc.co.uk/1/hi/uk/2747677.stm>.

[8] "Ministers Highlight UK Terror Threat," BBC News, February 14, 2003; available at <news.bbc.co.uk/1/hi/uk/2751361.stm>.

[9] See, for example, United Kingdom Parliament, Select Committee on Defense, Examination of Assistant Commissioner David Veness, CBE, and Deputy Chief Constable Alan Goldsmith, May 7, 2002.

[10] Ibid.

[11] Ibid.

[12] Civil Contingencies Secretariat, *Dealing with Disaster* (revised 3d edition), chapter 1; available at <www.ukresilience.info/contingencies/dwd/c1introduction.htm>.

[13] Ibid., chapter 7, <www.ukresilience.info/contingencies/dwd/c7central.htm>.

[14] Ibid.

[15] *Design for Military Operations—The British Military Doctrine*, Prepared Under the Direction of the Chief of the General Staff, Army Code 71451 (1996), 1.

[16] Ibid., 2.

[17] Ibid., 3.

[18] Ibid., 5.

[19] *Strategic Defense Review: A New Chapter*, 3.

[20] Ibid., 4.

[21] Ibid., 6.

[22] House of Commons Defense Committee, *A New Chapter to the Strategic Defense Review*, Sixth Report of Session 2002–2003, 26.

[23] Ibid., 27.

[24] Ibid., 30.

Chapter 3

The Weight of History: Germany's Military and Domestic Security

Gerhard J. Klose

Introduction

To arrive at a correct understanding of the German attitude toward homeland security, homeland defense, or military involvement in domestic operations, it is important to know that Germans think of their *Bundeswehr* as an institution designed for nothing else but to guarantee homeland defense and security. The defense of the German homeland has always been the main task of the German armed forces. And, through most of Germany's history, providing homeland security and defense has taken place as a domestic operation. Situated at the center of Europe and being nearly completely surrounded by potential enemies, there were always only two options for Germany in conducting this defense of its soil: to make it happen either inside or outside of the homeland.

For centuries, Germany was prepared to use its terrain as the battle-field for homeland defense. This became especially true during the Cold War, when German territory was accepted as the theatre for the main ground conflict of a potential third world war. It was also accepted that Germany was very likely to be affected by nuclear weapons in the event that this war erupted. During the 45 years of the Cold War, Germany got used to the idea of limiting its defensive actions to its own territory. There were never official plans in place to cross borders and take steps for the defense of the homeland outside Germany's borders, as in former days.

This understanding of homeland defense is still valid for most Germans. However, the fact that traditional military forces no longer threaten German territory has not yet supplanted the old understanding of homeland defense—not even among soldiers. In addition, the majority of the German population does not identify the new threat from international terrorism as a potential military threat. So the mental and legal framework for military activities of the German armed forces on domestic soil is still founded on the two old basic notions: the presence or the absence of a conventional military threat, and an attack on German territory. Thus, there is a clear distinction between the two legal states of war or peace in Germany, states that are determined by the German parliament.

The legal framework that is in place to meet the requirements of these two basic situations still appears valid to most Germans. German society will probably stick to this simple black-and-white picture as long as there is not a huge failure resulting from this approach.

The U.S. approach to homeland security appears completely different. There has never been a serious threat to the territory of the United States, at least not by conventional land forces. Therefore, their response to the new global security environment is different. In Germany, the problem is to change a system that everyone has become used to over the years and that has apparently worked well so far.

There is a second peculiarity in the German situation. After World War II and the defeat of the Nazi regime, there was a complete revision of German society, the entire political system, and, as a part of that, the armed forces. This new start, which began during the Allied occupation of Germany after the war, included strict restrictions on the exercise of political power. Understandably, a first priority was to prevent Germany from becoming so powerful and dangerous again.

There was also a second effect. The German politicians who were assigned the task of creating the new legal-political framework had a strong desire to eliminate all possibilities of the abuse of central political and military power. Most of the authors of the constitution themselves had suffered severely under the Nazi system. Taking as their guiding maxim "it shall never happen again," it was inevitable that there would be compromises in the new political system.

The historical background to the constitution shaped the legal framework for both the foundation of the new German democracy and its military forces. To understand the limitations of the existing system and the scope for its future development, it is essential to recognize this fact.

The Historical Background of the German Constitution: The Basic Law

After World War II, Germany was completely under the authority of the four occupying Allied Powers. The road back to full sovereignty proved to be long and arduous. It was not until 1992, in the course of the reunification of East and West Germany, that Germany regained its full sovereignty.

The level of mistrust of Germany in 1945 was great, and easily understandable. So the first steps back toward self-administration were made from the bottom up, following the principle "divide and conquer." Beginning with regaining local and regional self-administration, the first major step toward future independence came with the reestablishment of the German states, the *Bundesländer*. These states, however, produced different and independent laws and regulations, very much depending on the individual Allied Power in charge of that region. The differences between the *Bundesländer* that were established in those early days still exist today. It can be compared with the independence of the different states of America; in fact, their example might have influenced the development of the diversity of law in the German states. There are two important differences in the German case, however. First, most of the *Bundesländer* are much smaller than the states in the United States. Second, Germany had already experienced the greater effectiveness of a more centralized political and administrative system, a historical situation that was never present in early America.

It was not until 1949 that the three Western Allies decided to put their administrative zones together and form a union out of these states. The constitution for this newly created union, the Federal Republic of Germany, had to be of a somewhat preliminary and provisional nature, of course, as the possibility of reunion with the eastern part of Germany could not be excluded. As much power as possible stayed with the individual states. This is still the case today, with all the well-known disadvantages that result when dealing with matters that would benefit from central coordination.

It was not the sole intention of the victors of World War II to prevent Germany from becoming dangerous again. The vast majority of German society, represented by the authors of the constitution, also had the same strong desire never to let fascism and militarism rise again in Germany. Strong governmental centralization had been an excellent defense for both phenomena in the prewar years. Therefore, precautions against the possible misuse of central power were sometimes favored over the effectiveness or efficiency of public administration.

These general principles are still in effect today and make actions difficult in situations where centralized governmental management would be essential (for example, in planning domestic defense against international terrorism).

There is a second effect that should also be taken into account before trying to understand the German military system. When the new constitution came into effect in 1949, there was no intention ever to have German military forces again at all. Germany was still strongly committed to demilitarization and denationalization. This led into a broader current of pacifism. To have no military at all was thought to be the safest way to ensure that the excesses and abuses of the fascist era never took place again. So when it was finally decided to once again have a military, the constitution had to be substantially rewritten, which faced intense resistance.

Because of this strong opposition from the German population and an important part of the political elites, the legal framework for the German armed forces was carefully crafted to prevent the forces from being used against the civil population by the central government. The German constitution is therefore very clear and strict about how the armed forces can be used. This is especially evident when it comes to actions other than fighting against unambiguously identified combatants. Once again, optimum effectiveness was not the first priority, but rather the prevention of potential abuse.

Even though the legal framework governing the formation and use of the German armed forces has been amended from time to time, particularly when it proved to be impracticable in essential areas, the restriction on the use of military power has remained a dominant attitude to this day. So the constitution clearly restricts the armed forces to engagement only for purposes of defense. In Article 87a, it states in paragraph 1, "The Federation establishes forces for defense." The following paragraph states, "Apart from defense, the forces may only be employed in ways explicitly allowed by this Basic Law."

In addition—and in this way it differs from other nations—Germany's constitution has the quality of law, a superior law. It might therefore be called a *Grundgesetz* (Basic Law[1]), and not a *Verfassung* (Constitution). The Basic Law does not solely bind the processes of legislation and jurisdiction, but is also applicable to every individual citizen. Laws that are found to be in conflict with the Basic Law will automatically be overruled. A special Court of Constitution (*Bundesverfassungsgericht*) exists, where affairs with a constitutional dimension will get a final interpretation. The sentences of the Court of Constitution bind the government and the parliament. There are many cases where laws that had passed both chambers of parliament had to be repealed and reworked under clear restrictions established by the Court of Constitution.

Moreover, the legal framework for and the structure of the new German armed forces, the *Bundeswehr*, were intentionally designed to make them as different from those of the former *Wehrmacht* as possible. Once again, operational effectiveness was not the first priority.

With the German armed forces being limited to the defense of their home territory, all these limitations on a more effective engagement model seemed to be acceptable. And the resulting system proved to work quite well under the unique circumstances of the Cold War. However, 40 years of experience for the *Bundeswehr* in this mode have created attitudes that may have to some extent become entrenched.

After the terrorist attacks of recent years, Germany, like all other nations, is confronted with a completely new threat, in a completely different security environment. It is questionable whether the new types of threat might successfully be met with the existing capabilities and attitudes of both German society and its military.

Options for the German Armed Forces to Act in Cases of Defense or Tension

The German constitution clearly relates the engagement of the armed forces to two different states, with two different substates: one is the state of defense or tension; the other is the absence of a state of defense or tension. Under this there are two substates: operations against combatants and operations against noncombatants.

Article 87a of the Basic Law states in paragraph 3 the options for military engagement against noncombatants:

> In the case of defense and tension, the armed forces are allowed to protect civilian property[2] and to control traffic as far as it is necessary for the completion of their defense mission. Moreover, in times of tension and defense, the armed forces might additionally be tasked to support the police in protecting civilian property. In this case, the forces act in cooperation with the related civilian administration.

Of course, it is hardly necessary to mention that the armed forces are permitted to act militarily with every means allowed by the Geneva Conventions against hostile combatants. But the Basic Law clearly limits the options for actions against noncombatants, even in defense situations. For example, the protection of civilian property is normally a task of the police forces. Protection by the military is only authorized if a site or structure is of military importance to German forces. Other civilian property, being of no direct military interest to German forces, may only be protected by the military if it is likely to be attacked and is of importance to the enemy (critical infrastructure). Nuclear power plants might fall into this category of property, but military protection would always be limited to attacking combatants. Acting against noncombatants in this case would always have to follow the regional police guidelines, which differ from state to state. That makes the situation more complicated.

The same applies to the control of public movement and traffic. As stated in the Basic Law, traffic may only be controlled as far as the requirements of the defense operation demand. These strict legal limitations, even in cases of homeland defense, very clearly show the attitude and intention of the new German democracy concerning the use of military power against noncombatants in general.

As is laid down in the Basic Law, the same regulations apply in states of defense, as well as in states of tension. Both terms are defined in the Basic Law. Article 115 says everything about the state of defense and how it is declared. Parliament has to approve this step with a two-thirds majority. The Basic Law also states what is to be done when there is not enough time to reach a decision in this way. In essence, it is vital that the state of defense will come into effect as soon as an attack has been launched across the German border.

Contrary to the rather broad definition of the state of defense, the preconditions for declaring a state of tension are not defined at all in the Basic Law, even though it offers the same amount of additional rights to the armed forces as the state of defense. But the commentaries on the Basic Law are unanimously of the opinion that the state of tension describes a phase when it is evident that an attack by combatants is soon to be launched.[3]

In opposition to the unclear definition of the state of tension, Article 80a clearly describes how it is reached. Again, a decision of the parliament is needed, with a majority of two-thirds. However, there is also a second option as to how this status may be achieved—that is, if an international executive body of a defense alliance (such as the North Atlantic Treaty Organization [NATO]) officially states this to be the case. (This exemption was specifically inserted on behalf of NATO obligations.) Such an external decision becomes effective subject to its approval by the federal government.

In this case, parliamentary approval is not necessary. But how sensitive the authors of the Basic Law were regarding the legitimization of extra rights for the armed forces becomes evident in a further description in Article 80a, which declares that a state of tension can be terminated at any time by a decision of parliament with a simple majority.

All the provisions in the Basic Law concerning the armed forces make very clear that they were made exclusively to enable the German armed forces to conduct the defense of German territory, together with the Allies, and for no purposes beyond these. Security against abuse was always the first priority.

It should be noted that nothing from either earlier military traditions or constitutions was included in the Basic Law that would have allowed more latitude regarding the use of military power. It is now evident that the German Basic Law originally was not equipped to handle and regulate threats of the kind that Germany is now facing.

Options for the German Armed Forces to Act in the Absence of a State of Defense or Tension

Apart from acting under the conditions of the states of defense or tension, there are more options set forth in the Basic Law for the use of military abilities and capabilities to support the security of the country.

Military Assistance in Civil Disturbances and Insurrections

In Article 87a, paragraph 4 of the Basic Law (in conjunction with Article 91), a very sensitive issue is touched on: the situation of internal disturbances and tensions, such as riots. It states:

> In order to avert an imminent danger to the existence or to the free democratic basic order of the federation or a state, the federal government may, should the conditions of Article 91 apply, and the police forces and the Federal Border Guard be inadequate, use the armed forces to support the police and the Federal Border Guard in the protection of civilian property and in combating organized and military armed insurgents. Any such use of armed forces must be stopped at parliament's request.

Article 91 reads as follows:

> 1. In order to avert an imminent danger to the existence or to the free democratic basic order of the federation or a state, a state may request

the services of the police forces of other states, or of the forces and facilities of other administrative authorities and of the Federal Border Guard.

2. Should the endangered state not be willing or able to combat the danger, the federal government may place the police forces of other states under its own control and commit units of the Federal Border Guard.

The order for this shall be rescinded after the removal of the danger or else at any time on request of the senate.[4]

This regulation is clearly intended to address circumstances of great internal unrest, caused by Germany's own citizens. But the rights granted to the central government for intervention are limited to cases of unrest so large that they might endanger the existence of the whole federation, a single state, or substantially endanger the basic democratic order of society. Following the commentaries, the authors of the Basic Law were mainly thinking of a form of communist revolution, beginning in one state and then spreading out through the republic. In this case, they wanted special rights for the central government to enable them to reestablish the democratic order. The possibility of military support was granted, but again under very strong limitations:

- The scale of the unrest had to be capable of endangering the existence of at least one of the states.

- The armed forces were only to support the police forces. That meant that, once again, they would have to act not in a military, tactical way, but under the legal conditions applicable to the police force of the relevant state.

- The options of engagement for the armed forces in this case are limited to "protection of civilian property" and "fighting against organized and military armed insurgents." By this provision, the engagement of the armed forces against unarmed people is clearly prohibited.

- Finally, the engagement of the armed forces, when requested by the federal government, can be immediately stopped by the vote of the senate, the parliamentary chamber of the states.

Fortunately, no situation has ever arisen in the Federal Republic of Germany to call this regulation into effect. However, this is not to say that it could not happen in the future. Chemical, biological, radiological, and nuclear (CBRN) scenarios could quickly assume such scope that an entire state might be affected and would no longer be able to manage the situation.

This very special type of engagement for the German armed forces has to be recognized as a core task of the *Bundeswehr*. Therefore, the costs of such an intervention would have to be covered by the defense budget.

This is quite different from all the other following options. They fall under the legal principle of subsidiarity. That means that interventions of these types—if requested—would be mandatory but would have to be executed only using the existing means and capabilities of the armed forces. In addition, the types of engagements discussed below will have to be paid for by the relevant state or the entities receiving support.

Emergency Aid and Rescue Support

The provision of support in the form of emergency aid and rescue equipment is mentioned here only to provide a complete picture of the legal possibilities for the German military's contribution to homeland security.

The provision of emergency aid is an obligation, although it is not directly derived from the Basic Law; rather, it stems from general legal principles.[5] It is not so much an obligation placed on the armed forces, but rather on each individual citizen. If emergency aid is required to support individuals or private organizations, then any immediately required measures may be engaged for rapid assistance. But this general permission, which has to be ordered by any present military authority, is very much limited by clear conditions[6]—the aid may involve only a few personnel, single cars, and a minimum of equipment, and may be committed only for a short period of time. No law enforcement functions can be undertaken, and as soon as there is enough civilian support present, the military support has to be withdrawn. In addition, the cost for this support must be reimbursed.

The same restrictions apply to the provision of support in the form of rescue equipment. In this case, the armed forces may assist civilian rescue services in accordance with a corresponding regulation, which states that the armed forces may use their rescue equipment to support the civil sector in emergency situations and may also provide practical training of medical personnel.[7] Again, no law enforcement operations can be carried out along with this option, and reimbursement is required to the same extent as with civilian rescue services.

If emergency aid is required by the public administration, the case is different. This is an issue of great importance for the engagement of the

German military in homeland security affairs. Such aid is called—literally translated—administration assistance (*Amtshilfe*). For the following discussion, it will be called Military Assistance to Civil Authorities (MACA) to keep it close to the language of similar U.S. regulations.

Military Assistance to Civil Authorities

MACA in Germany is part of the general scope of administration assistance that all parts of the government have to provide for each other, if their own capabilities are exceeded. This obligation is basically described in Article 35 of the Basic Law and is detailed in a special federal law about the principles of public administration.[8]

Article 35, paragraph 1, of the Basic Law reads: "All administrations of the federation and the states provide mutual assistance in legal and administrative affairs." The special executive law mentioned above gives explanations and elaborates more details. The most important are:

- Support is only granted at the request of a public administration whose own capabilities are exceeded. Permanent mission transfer for regular or recurring obligations is not allowed.

- Support consists only of the means that the supporting administration has available for its core tasks. So, for the *Bundeswehr*, it would not be legal to stock special equipment only for cases of administration assistance. That is the first condition of the principle of subsidiarity.

- Support is to be given only to the extent that it does not affect the core task of the supporting administration. That means that necessary military activities would always remain the first priority.[9] That is the second condition of the principle of subsidiarity.

- The costs of the deployment would have to be reimbursed by the supported administration. This applies only to material costs; no costs for personnel are reimbursed.

Commentaries about the first paragraph of Article 35 are unanimous of the opinion that this paragraph addresses technical and logistic support only.[10] Thus, unlimited manpower and/or equipment might be provided by the armed forces, but their participation in law enforcement functions would remain strictly prohibited. On the basis of this paragraph, the German armed forces have until now mainly provided their support only in cases where they came into action in broader homeland security operations, such as disaster relief engagements. In such situations, they would not bring any weapons or armaments with them beyond hand-held weapons for guarding and self-defense.

During such a MACA-type mission, the military structure of command and control would remain in action. However, the supporting forces would be put under the direction of the civil authorities as far as the disaster management effort would be concerned. They would receive their tasks from the civil authority, but to transform these directives into militarily relevant orders, a military superior is required.

Paragraphs 2 and 3 of Article 35 of the Basic Law go significantly beyond technical and logistic support. They allow the police forces of an affected state to receive support from the police forces of other states, from the federal police (*Bundespolizei*),[11] or from the armed forces. This type of support could include law enforcement activities being carried out by the armed forces, such as the protection of critical infrastructure or the protection of disaster areas against looting. But the military support would always be under the direction of the regional police force, and the rules of such an engagement would be the laws of the relevant state. Moreover, this law enforcement support is clearly limited to the cases of natural disasters and catastrophic accidents.

As this regulation gives the federal government an opening to exert powerful influence against the sovereignty of the states, this kind of MACA has to be stopped immediately once the situation is stabilized again, or it is requested by the senate. And there is another strict limitation on the use of the armed forces for law enforcement purposes. Legal scholars are quite unanimous (so far) that the engagement of the armed forces in these cases is only legitimate when the disaster or catastrophic accident has already happened or is about to. Any engagement to prevent an anticipated or generic threat from happening is prohibited. Allowing participation in preventative actions, however, is the key to permitting military support of homeland security against any terrorist threat.

In summary, the legal framework of MACA allows the *Bundeswehr* to provide technical and logistic support to the greatest extent possible, even for purposes of prevention. However, it is primarily intended for exceptional cases, rather than predictable events. Military assistance in law enforcement affairs is intentionally kept very restrictive and does not allow the German armed forces to participate in preventive measures.

This very restrictive attitude became evident in the recent discussions about the new Air Policing Act. After the September 11 disaster in New York and Washington, DC, and an incident involving an uncontrolled sports plane in Frankfurt, the German government prepared a bill to close an important loophole in the legal system. It had become evident that the extant German law would have made it impossible to stop a civilian airplane from being used as a weapon. Fortunately, the airspace over Germany is a federal responsibility and does not fall under the states' sovereignty.[12] Although this was one less administrative hurdle to clear, the bill was still difficult to prepare, and the issues are not all yet resolved.

The reasons for the legal difficulties are that, first, the relevant aircraft is not a military aircraft, and neither the (potential) terrorists nor the passengers are combatants. Thus, dealing with such an aircraft should be the responsibility of the police forces. The police, however, have no means of dealing with such an aircraft, and nobody intends to provide the federal police with fighter jets or antiaircraft weapons for such an unlikely scenario. Therefore, military support was requested under MACA. But, as it is a permanent threat and needs permanent readiness to react, it would require a permanent transfer of a mission from the police to the armed forces. That is in conflict with the law that details the modalities of administration assistance. Second, another law forbids the military to use firearms against unarmed groups of civilians if it cannot be ruled out that children might be hit.[13]

Even though the Air Policing Act became effective in January 2005 when it was signed by the president, no one knows whether it will remain in effect. The president had serious concerns and therefore applied for a revision by the Court of Constitution.

Another area of concern is the area of special security events. Germany is preparing to host the soccer World Cup in 2006. Currently, there is no possibility of involving the German armed forces in protective and preventative activities. General patrolling, as we saw during the Olympic Games 2004 in Athens, and see every day in France, is not possible in Germany under present legal conditions.

Command and Control of the German Armed Forces in Homeland Security Engagements

Everything concerning security in Germany is still based on the tradition of defending German territory that is left over from centuries past.

This general basis was even reinforced by the unique security situation that was in place during the Cold War years. According to this vision of the military's responsibility, the protection of civilians and civil property has always been the responsibility of the police forces and is under the control of the Ministry of the Interior and the Ministries of the Interior of the *Bundesländer*. This distribution of responsibility was widely accepted, as it was evident to everybody that the armed forces could not be spared for that simple purpose. All of the military's resources had to be reserved to fight (potentially) against enemy combatants. Even in the combat zone in the event of war, it would have been the responsibility of the police to protect civilians against attacks by noncombatants.

In the combat zone, the main defense operation against hostile combatants would have been managed by the field army, in combination with NATO. Outside the combat zone, it would have been up to the Territorial Army to organize support for the field army and to conduct operations against airborne combatants or hostile troops that had broken through the front lines. For that purpose, each civil district had a military district command headquarters,[14] and each county had a county command headquarters.[15] Above that level, there were six regional commands headquarters[16] and two territorial commands headquarters.[17]

To carry out territorial defense in the rear of the combat zone against combatants, many homeland protection forces were put in place. These constituted the Territorial Army and consisted almost entirely of reservists. After the end of the Cold War, these forces were significantly reduced, but even today there are approximately 75,000 reservists still employed in such home defense companies, battalions, and brigades.

The territorial command structure was mainly designed to organize support for the field forces from civil sources and to control defensive operations against the threat from combatants in the rear of the main deployed force. Beyond that, this command structure was also used in peacetime to manage civil-military coordination and MACA efforts in cases of disaster relief.

After the end of the Cold War, the territorial command structure was cut down somewhat, but the organization still remained primarily built around the requirements of territorial homeland defense. It also retained responsibility for managing MACA and disaster relief operations. This concept remained in effect until March 2003.

At that time, the Minister of Defense released a new security doctrine, which stated in essence:[18]

■ In the future, territorial defense would be extremely unlikely to be necessary in Germany, and there would be no longer a justification to commit resources to that purpose.

■ The most likely missions for the armed forces would be operations outside of Germany, and all resources should be concentrated on this type of operation.

The new doctrine stated explicitly that permanent organizations designed for territorial defense alone would no longer be justified. In consequence, the existing territorial defense organization, the territorial command structure, and the homeland defense forces came in for a stringent review to find out what roles would remain for them aside from territorial defense.

The review confirmed that there is still a need for a body to manage civil-military coordination and cooperation with the civil authorities of districts, counties, and states, and that there is still a substantial requirement for the armed forces to provide MACA, especially for disaster relief. The latter role was given even more importance because of the challenges posed by the international terrorism.

To meet these residual requirements, a new structure was developed to reduce manpower requirements but to continue providing at least the same amount of assistance to civil authorities as before. The cornerstones of this new structure, which has been operating on a pilot basis since October 2004 in three states, are outlined below.

For each district (*Kreis*)—being the lowest level of disaster relief authority—there will be one staff officer of the reserve as a permanent representative of the armed forces for civil-military cooperation and coordination.[19] He/she will also support the public administration in contingency planning for disaster relief plans. The staff officer is supported by a section of approximately 10 reservists (3 officers, 3 senior noncommissioned officers, and 4 junior noncommissioned officers), all volunteers for the posts and available for shift duty. Together they form the military section of the district's crisis management headquarters, which forms in cases of real disasters and for exercises. All of the reservists should be residents of that particular district. They should also have experience in many exercises in reserve positions with the active military. They might also be retired professional soldiers. This military headquarters element will be called the KVK (*Kreis Verbindungs Kommando*), or District Liaison Command. Their job will be to provide general advice on military matters to the local civil authority responsible for disaster management. They have to consider options for military support and prepare, coordinate, and support the deployment of the armed forces within their district. The KVK will not be equipped or authorized to exercise tactical control over a military engagement in their district. Instead, they will be part of the civil authority responsible for the management of disaster relief efforts and will advise, coordinate, plan, and provide direction.

On the next higher administrative level, the county (*Regierungs-bezirk*), a colonel of the reserve will be appointed, again along with approximately 10 reservists to form a BVK (*Bezirks Verbindungs Kommando*), or County Liaison Command, to perform the same role at the county level. In total, there will be around 470 KVKs and BVKs throughout the country, with approximately 4,700 voluntary reservists.

On the level of each state, there will be a permanent headquarters, formed with roughly 50 active-duty soldiers, called *Landeskommando* (LKdo, or State Command). The commander of an LKdo unit will be the official delegate of the armed forces to the state and will coordinate civil-military cooperation at that level. In cases of disaster, the state command forms a military branch in the state's crisis management headquarters, and the commander of the LKdo unit for that state becomes the military advisor of the president of the state. In principle, the system operates on the state level in the same way as described above for the lower levels, but in a permanent way and with active-duty soldiers instead of reservists. In addition, the commander of a State Command is authorized to form an initial ad-hoc disaster battlegroup from troops stationed in his state and make it available for that mission. He will also appoint the first tactical commander and establish the field headquarters for this battlegroup. However, as with the KVK and the BVK, neither he nor his branch is equipped for military command, control, and communication (C^3) purposes, so the military field headquarters will have to establish communications in the civil headquarters.

The necessary military type of command and control for the soldiers engaged in disaster relief missions will be established by the four regional command headquarters, called *Wehrbereichskommandos* (WBK). They form the next level of the territorial command structure. Today, these regional commands, which during the Cold War were at the division level of military homeland defense, have become the primary divisional level for the recently formed new arm, the Joint Support Service (*Streitkräftebasis*), or SKB.[20] It will remain the job of the regional commands to establish regular military C^3 capabilities and provide military logistics and sustainability for the forces deployed on missions related to homeland security. The commands will do this mainly by drawing on resources from their area of responsibility, which could comprise up to five *Bundesländer*.

If military support from other areas of Germany were required, it would be the responsibility of the Armed Forces Support Command (*Streitkräfte Unterstützungs Kommando*, or SKUKdo) to manage that. They are the highest command level of the Joint Support Service, and wholly responsible for management of the armed forces' involvement in MACA and disaster relief activities. They would report directly to the Ministry of Defense.

The old (but still valid) C^3 structure for the engagement of German forces in MACA, the new structure, and the future command and control (C^2) relationships are all discussed below. The main differences are that the new command structure is more closely adapted to the civil administration. Civil-military cooperation is now their main task, having replaced homeland defense operations. And the liaison job on the county and district levels is no longer done by active-duty soldiers, but by reservists. These reservists will find themselves occupying a new status. They will no longer be legitimized only by the state of defense. Instead, they will cover a part-time but permanent military task in peacetime. For Germany, that is a revolutionary change that will take some time to be accepted. The greatest progress for the civil administration is that they will now have a dedicated permanent military element in their crisis management headquarters.

The first results from the trial phase of the new structure, as well as two major disaster relief exercises staged in 2004, have already proved that the new approach is very much welcomed by the civil administration. It seems that it is even preferable to the existing system. The intention is to complete the change to the new system and structure by 2006.

International Terrorism: A Military Threat?

Immediately after the terrorist attacks of September 11, Germany started reviewing the new threat and discussing how to protect the country against it. After the end of the Cold War, Germany had significantly reduced all preparatory measures for the protection of the civilian population against war-related threats. Germany no longer faced the risk of becoming the battlefield for World War III. In particular, the Ministry of the Interior, with its responsibility for the management of the protection of the civil population from war-related damages, had completely marginalized its management capacity and the related resources. Exercises, both for the military and other branches of the government, had been stopped. Capacities had been reduced to meet just the requirements of natural or industrial disasters. And the management of these cases was now completely under the responsibility of the *Bundesländer*.

With the new type of threat posed by international terrorism and the potential for mass casualties, it became evident that there might not be sufficient capacities remaining to address adequately the new security situation. In opposition to this need, the military capacities related to territorial defense were still kept substantially unchanged but were under strict review because of the change in defense policy. So the actual discussion was very much driven by the questions, "Who should have to pay for the necessary restoration of capabilities?" and "Why not give more responsibility to the Armed Forces? They still have enough capabilities." The discussion is ongoing. The answer will depend very much on the political decision that is made about how to categorize this new threat.

Germany has had some experience with terrorism in the 1970s, but this was internal German terrorism (led by such groups as the Red Army Faction), directed mainly against the German political system by attacks on civilians of major political and economic importance. All these terrorists were Germans. Besides killing individuals, the damage was rather limited and local, so there was no doubt that the states and their police forces were responsible for dealing with these incidents.

The threat itself was not a regional problem, but a national one. Therefore, prevention measures and prosecution needed to be coordinated at the national level by the federal Ministry of the Interior. And even though the terrorists themselves wanted to be seen as warriors and treated as combatants, nobody was seriously of the opinion that these situations might reach the scale of "defense" in its legal meaning. Thus it was never thought to support the fight against this terrorism with military means or to place it under the responsibility of the Ministry of Defense (MoD).

Today, the threat of international terrorism is different and so are the resources needed to fight it. The damage can reach dimensions that, in the past, were only possible to achieve through full-fledged warfare. The threat in general is organized from outside Germany, but the people executing it might live in Germany. The threat appears to be against our society in total and against the lifestyle and culture of Western civilization in general. The terrorists do not fight against other combatants, but against the citizenry as a whole. Thus it remains—using our traditional legal tools—a matter for the police, with the states and the federal Ministry of the Interior sharing responsibility. Even the responsibility for disaster relief management would stay with the states and the local authorities. Again, the armed forces could not be employed in preventative measures and can only act in a supporting role.

But more and more political and legal experts are beginning to change their minds. There is a growing body of opinion in Germany that the fight against international terrorism has to be seen as a new kind of war because the intentions of the terrorists and the extent of the damage they can bring about equate to war.

The perception of the fight against terrorism as a kind of war would have far-reaching consequences, and the responsibility for addressing it could be completely inverted. If this view were to prevail, the Minister of Defense would be in charge of the entire effort, and it would be the military budget that paid for preparatory and preventive activities. But even with such a change of perception, the responsibility for the protection of civil society would remain with the Minister of the Interior, like it was in the time of the Cold War. The armed forces would only be authorized to fight against this new type of combatant, the terrorist. Being no better prepared for such a war than the police are at this point, the armed forces do not find the idea terribly appealing. They see the danger that they might be given that responsibility without warning. On the occasion of a major terrorist attack, a state of tension could easily be declared by the parliament with a two-thirds majority. Having shown the complicated and sensitive relationship between the government and the states in Germany, and the strict separation of roles for the police and the military, the declaration of the state of defense would at least make the task of the management of prevention and damage much clearer.

This solution is not as unlikely as it sounds. A much greater interpretive leap regarding how the armed forces might be used was made when the Court of Constitution—which is responsible for the interpretation of the Basic Law—in connection with the first German military missions abroad accepted the premise that the "defense of Germany" could also take place outside NATO territory. Keeping this in mind, it seems much less difficult to allow the threat from international terrorism to trigger the declaration of a state of defense.

However, under the given legal framework for the state of defense to be declared, the German armed forces would only be authorized to manage the situation and to fight against combatants—in this case, the terrorists. The management of the protection of civilians and their vital networks would remain the responsibility of the Ministries of the Interior of the republic and the states.

The Attitude of the German Armed Forces toward Homeland Security Engagements

The *Bundeswehr* has not been used to having any serious obligations in homeland security affairs. As mentioned before, the defense of German territory against traditional combatants was always its first priority during the period of the Cold War. For that purpose, everyone and everything had to be maintained at a constant state of preparedness. Under these conditions, no one expected the armed forces to be officially engaged in relief efforts following natural disasters or catastrophic accidents. Of course, whenever such an event did occur, the military proved to be the only organization capable of providing the necessary management skills and capabilities to solve the problem. The generally accepted practice was that the armed forces would never guarantee the ability to provide any capabilities for disaster relief, but in cases when disasters happened they would help with all their available means and capabilities. That is what they proved to be capable of on many occasions.

After the end of the Cold War, the state's capabilities for civil protection in wartime were drastically reduced. Now, under the specter of international terrorism, many of them are required again. Therefore, the states, being responsible for disaster relief management, want more of a guarantee that the *Bundeswehr* will become engaged. That would help the states to save resources. Why should they set aside capabilities for a rather unlikely eventuality if these capabilities were permanently available within the armed forces?

The armed forces, on the other hand, have lost their main role of the territorial defense of Germany, under which 100 percent of their capabilities would have been engaged. And, following the official doctrine, no more than 40 percent of the armed forces would ever be engaged on missions abroad in the future. However, the *Bundeswehr* continues to stick with their traditional doctrine of not participating in disaster relief efforts on a more calculable basis. They refuse to declare officially any of their abilities and capabilities to be consistently available for the support of civil disaster relief.

The following reasons could account for this position: The doctrines from the Cold War era are still ingrained, even though the situation has changed completely. Nobody is interested in examining the validity of the doctrine that is an artifact from those days. This can be seen in many cases. To some extent, it applies to many areas of the Basic Law, which was created under the influence of World War II and the beginning of the Cold War.

The armed forces do not want to be slowly drawn into having responsibility for disaster relief, which legally is entirely the responsibility of the *Bundesländer*. They are concerned that they would no longer be free to make deployment decisions. The states are thought to be interested only to save money and to be unwilling ever to give something in exchange.

Even after the end of the Cold War, territorial defense remained the main task of the German military.[21] As a result, it was not possible to convert all resources to the preparation for the much more likely cases of operations outside Germany, for which a completely different structure and equipment are needed. The new defense doctrine from 2002 finally opened the way to getting rid of all the ballast remaining from the territorial defense obligation. Now the planners are concerned that, via the threat of international terrorism, the armed forces would again be drawn back into territorial-defense-type obligations, with no increased budget for this additional task. All in all, the armed forces are still reluctant to provide a higher level of engagement in antiterrorism activities.

Options for the Way Ahead

Immediately after September 11, 2001, discussions began regarding what options Germany would have if anything similar to the attacks on New York and Washington should occur in Germany. Scenarios were examined to consider what further options could be chosen by international terrorists to shock the sensitive, technology-dependent civilization of German and European society. The United States took it as a military challenge, reacted accordingly, and persuaded NATO to treat it as a military affair as well. However, Germany still views this threat from the traditional, criminal perspective. The states are responsible for the prevention of criminal activity (including—under this view—terrorism), and damage control and management is within the portfolios of the Ministries of Interior of the affected states and the federal Ministry of the Interior. The German armed forces play only a supportive role for damage management efforts, if they are not committed to defense missions. They are not allowed to participate in prevention measures apart from providing technical support.

Following the events of September 11, it was quite clear that Germany's existing "toolbox" would provide no tool to prevent a terrorist attack under the given legal conditions. It was also clear that only the *Bundeswehr* had the capabilities to respond to the threat of a civilian passenger airplane used as a weapon. The complete helplessness of the German administration in such a case became evident again in January 2003, when a small leisure aircraft flew around the skyscrapers of Frankfurt's banking area unabated. Even though the small plane could have done no serious harm to the multistory buildings, it did happen, and gave the final motivation to close an evident loophole in the German legal system. Immediately a bill was prepared that would give the German secretary of defense the authority to order such an airplane shot down by fighter aircraft of the air force as a "last resort." The law, called the Air Security Act (*Luftsicherheitsgesetz*), was to be based on the established interpretation of the Basic Law, Article 35, sentences 2 and 3, which deal with administrative assistance by the armed forces in a law-enforcement situation, as described above. But from the beginning, many constitutional scholars did not feel comfortable with this solution. Most of the experts were of the same opinion as Christof Gramm, who argued that the Basic Law in its present version would not allow the permanent delegation of authority to the armed forces to counter a foreseeable and permanent threat.[22] Instead, the amendment of the Basic Law would be required. Others, like the member of parliament Dieter Wiefelspütz, are of the opinion that everything would fit easily within the existing framework of the Basic Law and that at present no amendments would be needed.[23]

The Air Security Act was finally signed by the German president in January 2005, effective as of January 26. The president released the bill with the caveat that it should be revised by the Court of Constitution, since he was concerned about the legality of the act, especially because of the need to consider the certain death of innocent civilian victims in the airplane against the possible death of victims on the ground. This eventuality, being a completely new and unique situation, was not covered by the extant legal framework.

In addition, the political opposition has announced that they would bring this act to the federal Court of Constitution to have it reviewed. Whether the act will remain valid under these conditions is uncertain. A similar act is in preparation, dealing with the response to terrorist actions on sea and land, especially in the vicinity of harbors.

More and more scholars and politicians have come to the conclusion that this type of terrorism is a new general type of external threat and that the armed forces should be responsible for providing more calculable protection and leading prevention efforts, just as they did in the past for traditional homeland defense.[24] The chances that this perspective will meet with wider acceptance seem relatively good. Some states would reap a benefit if this were the case because the resources used to fight terrorism would have to be taken from federal sources, instead of from the individual states. That, of course, is not in the interest of the federal government; the states as well as the Ministry of Interior, being the entities traditionally responsible for the protection of the civilian population in peacetime and wartime, would have dramatically reduced their level of expenditure for this increasingly important activity. To close the gaps that were identified in the meantime will require a great deal of money.

Above all else, the legal framework for declaring a state of defense only allows the military to use their abilities to defeat these new types of combatants and to be responsible for the protection of the homeland against this threat. The protection of civilians, however—the so-called Civil Defense, established during the Cold War—would remain the responsibility of the Ministry of the Interior.[25] To fall back into such a traditional mode seems attractive to many people because then many patterns and methods from that period could still be used.

In case of a disaster, such as the train bombings in Madrid in March 2003, the German parliament would decide to declare a state of defense. That would be the easiest way to come to a clear distribution of roles and responsibilities. It was much more difficult for the German parliament to change the interpretation of defense from the traditional territorial focus to a global view than it will be to declare international terrorists to be combatants, and their method of asymmetric attacks on German territory as a new form of war.

But such a quick solution would only go half way. Most of the capabilities needed to fight terrorism in Germany have more of a nonmilitary character. This fight begins with an investigation of how to identify the enemy and his intentions; this approach is quite different from the military method of reconnaissance, be it inside or outside of the home territory. It ends with the analysis of the targets. For terrorists, the main target is not the combatant, but unprotected civilians and the insecure civilian infrastructure.

So a separate approach has to be developed to meet the challenges of this new situation. No doubt such an approach would lead to even more obligations for the German armed forces than they envision at present. The *Bundeswehr* is in a kind of euphoric phase of transformation to an expeditionary army. But German society still wants them to feel more responsible for direct homeland security, defending the nation inside Germany rather than in Afghanistan. So a clear way ahead cannot be predicted.

Conclusion

The existing German options to involve the military in homeland security affairs can be put quite simply. In case of an attack by traditional combatants, all necessary actions to meet this challenge can be taken by— and are the responsibility of—the armed forces. This includes all actions to prevent such an attack from happening.

However, when the possible attackers are not of the traditional combatant type covered by the Geneva Convention, the situation becomes more complicated. The legal framework for the scope of the activities of the *Bundeswehr* is clearly and strictly laid down in the German constitution, the Basic Law. There is little leeway given for interpretation in the Basic Law, and this document, unlike many other constitutions, is effective for jurisdiction. The German Basic Law was developed with the clear intention to minimize the possibilities of the misuse of central political and military power to the greatest extent possible. The disadvantages in effectiveness that this approach implies were taken into account and were in fact seen as helping to optimize that intention. Changes to the Basic Law have been made only in response to imperative challenges, never to improve the administrative management of the republic. The reestablishment of the German armed forces in 1955 is one example of such an imperative challenge. And the threat by the international terrorism might be another. The authors of the Basic Law did not foresee this kind of threat; therefore, there is no suitable article in the constitution that outlines how the German state is to respond to this new threat to its security. In spite of that, the existing legal framework allows a wide variety of possibilities that may be helpful in the new security environment. The armed forces might provide technical support and even tools to support prevention efforts. But so far there is a common understanding that the participation of soldiers in actions of law enforcement to prevent terrorism-related disasters from happening is prohibited.

As soon as an attack has happened or is about to happen, the military might be engaged, even in a law enforcement role. However, even in this case, they may not act in a military manner, but only under the legal conditions of the regional police forces.

At this point it remains unclear who should feel responsible for taking preventive measures against an attack by international terrorists in the future. There is still no legal permission for the German armed forces to participate in preventive management or to support prevention management efforts by engaging their special capabilities, even if they are the only entity with the appropriate means to counter the threat. The controversial discussion about the Air Security Act in January 2005, which would allow a German military aircraft ultimately to destroy a civil aircraft that has been captured by terrorists, highlighted this situation clearly.

But following German tradition, this gap will be closed. The timing of this will depend on the perception of how urgent the threat is felt to be. Hopefully, it will not be the day after the first massive terrorist attack has happened in Germany. The first initiatives have been taken not only by legal experts but also by some states and political parties. They all want the military to bear a greater level of responsibility for meeting these new challenges.

But the *Bundeswehr* is not pressing in that direction. On the one hand, they are very positive about promising any support that is legally permitted in case such a catastrophe occurs. On the other hand, they do not want to be held accountable for all such cases in the future. Now that they finally have started the difficult process of transformation to gain expeditionary capabilities, they especially do not want to divide their very limited budget to address this issue. But all ongoing discussions go into the same direction: this form of homeland security should no longer be only an obligation in subsidiarity but should become a core function of the German armed forces. Terrorism is a new form of external threat, waged by a new form of combatant. And the German armed forces are well advised not to remain too reluctant. The German people will fail to understand—on both an emotional and intellectual level—why German soldiers should prevent Serbs from being attacked by Albanians in Kosovo but should not defend Germans from being attacked by international terrorists.

Notes

[1] To make clear the special quality of the German constitution, the name *Basic Law* is used for the rest of this chapter.

[2] The term *civilian property* stands for critical infrastructure. The commentaries are quite clear about the interpretation in this case. As all critical infrastructure is of military interest to an attacking force, it can become a military target. Effective protection requires combatants.

[3] See Bruno Schmidt-Bleibtreu, *Kommentar zum Grundgesetz*, 10th ed. (Verlag Luchterhand); see also Dieter C. Umbach, *Grundgesetz, Mitarbeiterkommentar und Handbuch* (Berlin: Deutsche Bibliothek, 2001).

[4] The German parliament has two chambers. The *Bundestag*, similar to the U.S. House of Representatives, represents the people. It is here referred to as the *parliament*. The *Bundesrat*, similar to the U.S. Senate, represents the states (*Bundesländer*). It is here referred to as the *senate*.

[5] See, for example, *Strafgesetzbuch der Bundesrepublik Deutschland* § 34 (Penal Law of Germany § 34).

[6] *Bundesministerium der Verteidigung, Ministerialblatt* (VMBl), *Hilfeleistungen der Bundeswehr bei Naturkatastrophen bzw besonders schweren Unglücksfällen und dringender Nothilfe* (1978), 86.

[7] *Bundesministerium der Verteidigung, Ministerialblatt 1988, Richtlinie über den Einsatz von Rettungsmitteln der Bundeswehr im Rahmen des zivilen Rettungswesens* (1988), 270.

[8] Hans Günther Henneke et al., *Verwaltungsverfahrensgesetz*, 8th ed. Kommentar, § 4–8.

[9] This fact is supposed to be the reason why the German armed forces never accepted any regular responsibility for disaster relief efforts. During the Cold War, they always had to be prepared to become 100 percent engaged in defense of the German territory. This is an argument that is no longer valid under the new strategic conditions.

[10] See, for example, Schmidt-Bleibtreu, *Kommentar zum Grundgesetz*; Phillip Kunig, *Grundgesetz-Kommentar*, 5th ed., vol. 2, section on Article 35; or Klaus Müller, *Grundgesetz-Taschenkommentar für Studium und Praxis*, 11th ed. (Cologne: Heymanns Taschenkommentare, Carl Heymanns Verlag, 2002).

[11] The former Border Guard Police (*Bundesgrenzschutz*).

[12] The airspace above Germany only recently came under federal responsibility because until 1992 it was under international (NATO) control.

[13] *Gesetz über die Anwendung von unmittelbarem Zwang durch Angehörige der Bundeswehr* (UZwGBw) § 15 and 16 (Federal Law about the Exercising of Violence by Members of the *Bundeswehr*).

[14] *Verteidigungskreis Kommando* (VKK).

[15] *Verteidigungsbezirks Kommando* (VBK).

[16] *Wehrbereichskommando* (WBK).

[17] *Territorial Kommando* (TerrKdo).

[18] *Bundesministerium der Verteidigung, Verteidigungspolitische Richtlinien für den Geschäftsbereich des Bundesministerium der Verteidigung* (Berlin, March 21, 2003).

[19] He will be called the *Beauftragter der Bundeswehr für die Zivil-Militärische Zusammenarbeit* (BeaBwZMZ), which means "representative of the *Bundeswehr* for civil-military cooperation."

[20] All joint support functions were put together and now form the Joint Support Service (*Streitkräftebasis*).

[21] While other European nations quickly changed their national security policies, Germany left it substantially unchanged for a while. Germany was very much diverted by the problems of German reunification, among which the integration/dissolution of the armed forces of the former East Germany was one of the most complicated.

[22] Christoph Gramm, *"Bundeswehr als Luftpolizei: Aufgabenzuwachs ohne Verfassungsänderung?" Neue Zeitschrift für Wehrrecht* (2003), 89–101.

[23] Dieter Wiefelspütz, *"Sicherheit vor den Gefahren des Terrorismus durch den Einsatz der Streitkräfte," Neue Zeitschrift für Wehrrecht* (2003), 45–65.

[24] Christian Lutze, *"Abwehr terroristischer Angriffe als Verteidigungsaufgabe," Neue Zeitschrift für Wehrrecht* (2003), 101–115; and Martin Hochhut, *"Militärische Bundesintervention bei inländischem Terrorakt," Neue Zeitschrift für Wehrrecht* (2003), 154–167.

[25] See the German Society for Military Law and Humanitarian Law, "Civilians and the Military," Report submitted to the 12th Congress of the International Society for Military Law and Law of War (Brussels: May 1991); Alexander Poretschkin, *"Zivilverteidigung als Verfassungsauftrag,"* Ph.D. Diss. *im Fachbereich Sozialwissenschaften der Universität der Bundeswehr* (1990); and Bundesminister des Innern, Bundesminister der Verteidigung, *"Rahmenrichtlinien für die Gesamtverteidigung"* (Bonn: January 10, 1989), BMI-KN7-731800-51; BMVg-VR II 6/FüS VI 5-31-02-04, GMBl 1989, 107. In addition, see *Deutscher Bundestag, Zivilschutzgesetzt (ZSG)*, (March 25, 1997); *Bundesgesetzblatt I*, 726 (status April 27, 2004).

Chapter 4

A New NATO Member's Perspective: Hungary's Army and Homeland Security

Imre Takács

> . . . it is said that one who knows the enemy and knows himself will not be endangered in a hundred engagements.
>
> —Sun-Tzu, *The Art of War*[1]

Foreword

The last decade has brought substantial changes in the security environment of Europe and the Euro-Atlantic region in general. Hungary has not been immune to these trends. Some aspects of these changes appear to be positive, since the possibility of a purely European war was lessened, and the regional-ethnic conflicts of the 1990s have settled down, at least in a military sense. Nevertheless, new security challenges have emerged—most notably terrorism—that may require military intervention. The Republic of Hungary is currently in the process of developing a National Military Strategy, which—in accordance with the Basic Principle of the Security and Defense Policy,[2] the National Security Strategy,[3] and the Defense Reform[4]—meets the challenges of this new era.

The ultimate goal of maintaining the Hungarian Defense Forces (HDF) is to support the enforcement of Hungary's national security interests. It is imperative, therefore, to clarify the role of the HDF, the principles of engagement, and the primary courses of technical development and funding that will best support that mission.

Basics of the Defense Policy

Hungary understands its security in a comprehensive manner. Apart from political and military aspects, this includes economic, financial, national security, human rights, information technology, and environmental and legal dimensions as well. Hungary does not consider any state an enemy, and is willing to settle any dispute through the channels of international law and the peaceful tools of diplomacy. The Republic of Hungary's approach to military defense rests on two foundations: national self-defense and North Atlantic Treaty Organization (NATO) cooperation. In shaping its defense policy and developing its defense capabilities, Hungary contributes to collective defense, crisis management, and crisis response. Besides these efforts, the Hungarian Defense Forces, in cooperation with other national ministries and organizations, work in the field of homeland defense.

Security challenges currently confront Hungary at multiple levels: global, transnational, regional, in proximate areas, and local. A threat posed by conventional military aggression is not foreseen, even in the long run. Nonetheless, new challenges may arise that will require partial or total military action in response. In the period ahead, there are three main areas of concern:

- international terrorism and its implications for Hungary

- regional instability and the attendant possible increase in migration and illegal border crossing

- proliferation of weapons of mass destruction (WMD) and the means of their delivery.[5]

Apart from these three primary concerns, there are the national military responsibilities of protecting the civilian infrastructure, supporting civilian authorities in crisis management and response, and providing military support to law enforcement agencies as required by law.

General Objectives and Tasks of the Hungarian Defense Forces

The Defense Forces form an integral part of the state institutional structure in Hungary, and as such are indispensable elements of the nation's security and the enforcement of its national interest. The Hungarian Defense Forces are entrusted with the responsibility to defend the territorial integrity and airspace of Hungary, secure the borders of the state, and project real deterrent force. Furthermore, the armed forces of Hungary collect, process, and secure intelligence, and provide support to civilian authorities in such areas as crisis response, natural disaster consequence management, unexploded ordnance disposal, search and rescue, air-policing, and frequency management.

In the event of a threat to the territorial integrity of Hungary, or in a case where such an attack would need to be repelled, the full scale of the armed forces would be mobilized.[6] There also is the possibility that an internal conflict within a neighboring state might break out, or an extreme conflict situation between states might arise, the purpose of which is not to threaten the territorial integrity of Hungary. In such situations, armed formations or air force units from a neighboring state might cross the Hungarian border, in which case the Hungarian Defense Forces would be called upon to perform a border-guard function.[7]

In cases of natural or industrial disaster, the Hungarian Defense Forces use their existing capabilities to support civilian authorities in prevention and consequence management. Managing humanitarian crisis situations and providing help for displaced persons are also tasks in which the armed forces might be called upon to participate.[8]

Historical Precedents

Between the end of World War II and the present, the Hungarian military has been engaged on several occasions to deploy its capabilities in domestic matters, but mainly in a peaceful manner. It took part chiefly in disaster relief and consequence management operations; the only exception to this is its role in the 1956 revolution, which will be discussed below.

The Cold War Era (1945–1990)

After World War II, it is hardly possible to speak about an independent Hungarian military because of the presence of the occupying Soviet armed forces. Therefore, any military involvement in domestic contingencies could only have been carried out with the consent of the Soviet forces.

Nevertheless, events in the Soviet Union indicated potential major changes in Soviet policy in 1955 and early 1956. These included the Soviet leader Nikita Khrushchev's pilgrimage to visit Josip Broz Tito in May 1955; the signing of the Austria State Treaty in May 1955, which led to Soviet military withdrawal from and neutralization of Austria; and the acceptance of Finland's neutrality in September 1955. As one historian has written of the potential implications of these events:

> It appeared logical to believe in Hungary that, since policies of Austria and Finland were acceptable to the Soviet Union, Hungary could adapt their examples into a political concept that would be tolerated by the Soviet Union and at the same time would elicit Western support.[9]

The political situation in the Soviet Union had a profound impact on Hungarian domestic politics. Political changes in the Soviet Union in 1953 and the split in the Hungarian Communist Party resulted in changes in Hungarian politics as well. Imre Nagy, then Prime Minister, announced several economic reforms, namely abolishing the forced joining of collective farms and increasing consumer goods production, along with abolishing political terror. But the prevailing conditions of the era did not allow Nagy to fulfill his goals. The political wind changed in the Soviet Union in 1955, but Nagy's economic reforms failed mainly due to a lack of resources, which neither Western countries nor the Soviet Union were ready to provide. The first symptom of overt rebellion against Soviet rule in Hungary appeared in the fall of 1955. Moreover, "people now demanded tangible improvements [in economics], and the Poznan [Poland] riot in June 1956 showed that violent outbreak was no longer unthinkable."[10]

On October 23, 1956, a peaceful students' demonstration took place in Budapest, at the Bem Statue[11] and at the Polish embassy. Police tried to disperse the demonstration when students tried to break in to the radio station to broadcast their demands. Army troops, which were already on alert, were supposed to suppress the demonstration, but they refused to open fire on their compatriots, and joined them instead.[12] On October 26, Imre Nagy began to negotiate the withdrawal of the Soviet forces from Budapest (and eventually from all of Hungary), and ordered the military not to clash with Soviet troops. One of the miracles of the revolution at this point was that the Hungarian People's Army units had not actively taken any side. Nevertheless, in Mosómagyaróvár the military lost its "virginity." Insurgents, in an attempt to acquire weapons, attacked an army barrack. The commander of the barrack ordered his troops to fire in self-defense, leaving 23 insurgents dead. In the meantime, at the request of the Ministry of Defense, the 37th Motorized Infantry Regiment from Kiskunhalas approached the suburbs of Budapest, where it met resistance from insurgents. The 6-hour battle resulted in 100 dead and many injured.

Although Soviet troops were supposed to leave Budapest, on October 30 they still remained in the city. The Soviet leadership, under cover of further negotiations, sent more reinforcements to Hungary. The Soviets took no chances, using 11 divisions and 2,000 tanks. At 5:30 AM on November 4, Prime Minister Nagy went on the air to announce a full-scale

Soviet attack on Budapest: "At dawn this morning Soviet forces attacked our capital city. . . . Our forces are in action."[13]

The outcome is well known. "The clashes between revolutionaries and Soviet troops resulted in heavy casualties: 2,500 Hungarian lost their lives (1,950 in Budapest) and about 20,000 were injured. The Soviet Army lost about 2,000 men, including those who fraternized with Hungarians."[14] However, when the revolt first broke out, the government made the right decisions: first of all not giving the order for military units to crush the demonstrators, and second, not to fight the overwhelming Soviet military force. Quite surprisingly, these decisions resulted in a high respect for the military, since "the Hungarian Army either joined the revolutionists or remained intact."[15]

After the 1956 revolt, the Hungarian armed forces were mainly used in domestic affairs as augmentation forces in disaster relief. Cases of this sort of work are numerous. The most notable example was the flood of the Tisza River in 1970. The military provided thousands of troops as manpower, as well as heavy equipment.[16]

In 1979, military units around Szeged were used to put out a fire caused by an oil well explosion in Algyő. In winter 1986, only the Hungarian military, using its heavy armored vehicles, could sustain a normal flow of vital goods into the rural area in the vicinity of Székesfehérvár and Várpalota due to extremely heavy snowfall.

Although it was not the originally intended use for military resources, until the 1990s the Hungarian military's conscript corps was used in the "domestic economic area," meaning substituting and augmenting the agricultural work force during the harvest season. Military units were put to work harvesting grapes, potatoes, corn, and apples.

More tangible uses of military capabilities were for minesweeping and unexploded ordnance disposal. Since Hungary was a theater of substantial military engagements during World War II, its territory remained heavily littered with unexploded grenades, bombs, and mines after the war. The areas around Székesfehérvár, Lake Balaton, Debrecen, and Budapest, where the heaviest fighting took place, provided work for bomb-disposal experts for many years.[17]

Post–Cold War Examples (1990–2001)

The period from 1990–2001, with the end of the Cold War and the attendant changes in the regional security environment, did not alter the main function of the Hungarian Defense Forces. Even in this new era, the new Hungarian Constitution stated, "The main responsibility of the armed forces is the military defense of the homeland and the fulfillment of collective defense tasks deriving from international obligations."[18] The constitution elaborated further on the military's role:

> In domestic contingencies the armed forces could be deployed only in declared state of emergency according to constitutional regulation in the following situations: attempts to overthrow constitutional order or seize power with arms, or in events that endanger life and property of citizens, providing police forces are not in position to cope with.[19]

October 1990 saw the development of a relatively dangerous situation. After the decision of the government to drastically increase fuel prices, private entrepreneur taxi drivers blockaded the main roads entering Budapest. This groundswell of civil disobedience gained additional force within hours, when taxi drivers from the capital were joined by drivers in other cities, as well as private car drivers. Almost half of the country was paralyzed. The police were reluctant to disperse the demonstrators, mainly because the public sided with the drivers. Negotiations between representatives of the government and the demonstrators resulted in minor success for the government: only emergency vehicles were allowed to pass the impromptu roadblocks. Since the blockades threatened the normal flow of products vital to the public, the government—and most especially the Minister of Interior—wanted to invoke Section 1, Article 40/B§ of the constitution without any prior declaration of the constitutionally mandated period. General Kálmán Lőrinc, then commander of the Hungarian Defense Forces, announced he would resign from his post once the unconstitutional order for the deployment of military units to disperse the roadblocks was given. The tension was eased through further negotiations, which resulted in the withdrawal of the government's decision on increased fuel prices.

In 1990, Iraq occupied Kuwait, an event that has had a deep impact on world politics. The 1991 Gulf War and its implications in terms of international terrorism imposed a new task for the armed forces. Due to terrorist threats, the defense of important installations had to be heightened, a task for which the police did not have sufficient manpower. So border guard squads, which at that time were part of the armed forces, were sent as reinforcements to protect critical infrastructure.[20]

Another noteworthy example of the activity of the Hungarian armed forces' domestic deployment was the Balkan Wars. The broadening crisis in the former Yugoslavia, which was the result of the dissolution of the state of Yugoslavia,[21] culminated in the first Balkan War in July 1991. Military engagements in close proximity to the Hungarian border affected the interests of the Republic of Hungary. Therefore, a governmental decree stipulated the establishment of rapid-reaction military formations that would be able to immediately close Hungary's borders. Because of this new task, the Border Guard Directorates of Nagykanizsa, Pécs, and Kiskunhalas each deployed two companies to the most endangered part of the border in November 1991. The Hungarian Defense Forces provided trained personnel and specialized military hardware to the border guard. Companies were given armored personnel carriers and antitank equipment. In the event of defensive operations, the companies' standard operating procedures (SOP) would have been identical to the Army SOP for mechanized infantry formations.[22]

During the second wave of the Balkan War, in 1995, border guard units were organized into battalion formation and equipped with military armament and technology. These units were tasked with military defense operations; only with the de-escalation of the security situation in the former Yugoslavia did they take up border police functions. Thus a special conflict-management organization was established that combined border policing and military tactical defense function and was able to rapidly secure the nation's borders, react to border violations, and manage, limit, and repel military action.[23] After consolidating the situation and signing the Dayton Agreement, further rearmament of the border guard units took place, with several new armored personnel carriers put into service.[24]

Border guard units were not the only Hungarian units given assignments during the Balkan Wars. Due to the terrorist threat, a mobile radar company was deployed near the Yugoslavian border, and the Szentgyörgyi Dezső Tactical Fighting Regiment was given an order to enforce a no-fly zone over and near the nuclear plant at Paks. The Air Missile Defense unit in Kalocsa was also put on heightened alert status to provide air defense to Paks and the southern border of Hungary.

The years 1998 and 1999 were marked by severe flooding in Hungary. During fall 1998, the upper Tisza River and its various branches saw the heaviest level of flooding of the 20th century. The government declared a state of emergency, and military helicopters and amphibious vehicles provided help to those in need. In March 1999, in the middle section of the Tisza River, near Szolnok, a third-degree flood warning was issued. The police, military personnel, and members of the State Catastrophe Management Directorate worked together to prevent the flood waters from breaching the dike. The military provided 200 men and 3 amphibious vehicles to carry sandbags to the most remote and dangerous places.[25]

Post-9/11 (2001–present)

After the events of September 2001, public interest (not surprisingly) turned to the question of the defense of nuclear plants, as well as of Hungary's national borders. The physical defense of such plants was increased everywhere in the world. Balázs Kováts, the head of the visitors' center at the nuclear plant in Paks, said:

> In Paks, objective, subjective, and technological means are in place and functioning to defend the nuclear plant. Understandably, the organization of the security and defense system of the plant is restricted, yet it conforms to strict security regulations. There is a no-fly zone in and around the airspace of Paks, and air defense is provided.[26]

In 2002, heavy flooding occurred throughout the entire catchment basin of the Danube River, which affected Hungary along with much of the rest of Central Europe. Minister of Defense Ferenc Juhász said in his appreciation address to the personnel involved in the flood abatement effort:

> In August an incredible heavy flood took place on the Danube River. . . . . At the beginning, work was concentrated on the Mosoni-Danube branch of the river. The 12th Air-Defense Missile Regiment provided 400 personnel. . . . Close to Budapest, 250 personnel of the György Klapka Mechanized Infantry Brigade helped in flood prevention. . . . In the most endangered area of Esztergom, Nagymaros, Vác, [and] Szentendre 830 personnel from the Central Training Command, 1st Mixed Regiment and Central NCO Training School provided help in protecting civilian goods. In the Budapest area, 620 personnel from the 87th Tactical Helicopter Regiment, 89th Mixed Transport Air Mobile Regiment and Budapest Garrison carried out flood-prevention activities. Besides personnel, 22 helicopters from the 89th Mixed Transport Air Mobile Regiment and the 87th Tactical Helicopter Regiment respectively and ten amphibious and one engineering vehicle from the 37th Ferenc Rákóczi Engineering Brigade provided help.[27]

National Policies and Legal Authority for the Employment of Forces in Domestic Contingencies

The main guidelines for Hungary's security and defense policy and crisis management are determined by the constitution, and on a more detailed level by the following documents and acts approved by the parliament:

- Basic Principle of the Security and Defense Policy of the Republic of Hungary
- National Security Strategy of the Republic of Hungary
- Defense Act.[28]

The November 8, 2004, amendment to the constitution established a new qualified period, which it defined as a preventive defense situation. This is important because a new stipulation within the constitution abolished military conscription. The main significance of the amendment is that, in peacetime, compulsory military service is abandoned; in a preventive defense situation, it is left up to the National Assembly to reintroduce the draft, while in a state of attack on the state all male citizens have to serve. At the same time, the Defense Act defines the armed forces as the Hungarian Defense Forces only, and puts the Border Guard into the category of public order defense organizations.

It is important to note that, in peacetime—that is, without the declaration of any kind of qualified period—generally no person or authority has the right to employ military forces in domestic contingencies. However, the Constitution of the Republic of Hungary defines certain qualified periods that are exceptions to this rule. They are as follows (see table 1 as well):[29]

- preventive defense situation[30]
- state of emergency[31]
- surprise attack[32]
- state of danger[33]
- state of alert.

The Defense Act articulates the complexity of homeland defense in the most obvious way when it says: "Homeland defense is an issue of national concern."[34] In order to sustain its homeland defense capabilities, the Republic of Hungary relies on its own power—the resources of the national economy, the preparedness of its armed forces and public order defense organizations, and its citizens' patriotic commitment.

Table 1. Outline of Qualified Periods

Tendency of Danger	External Danger	Internal Social Conflict/Disaster	Disaster	External Danger
Constitutional state of affairs	State of war; danger of war	Attempt to overthrow constitutional order, seizure of power using force; terrorist-like activities; natural or industrial disaster	Natural disaster	Surprise attack by an external armed group
Constitutional qualification	Preventive defense situation or state of alert	State of emergency	State of danger	Constitution §19/E
Authority	National Defense Council or National Assembly	President	Government	Government

Table 2. Elements of Homeland Defense

National	Defense
Civil elements (preparation for defense and national mobilization)	Military element (armed security system)
Defense management	Hungarian Defense Forces
Civil protection (safeguarding health and property of inhabitants)	Public order defense organizations (Border Guard, police, fire brigades, catastrophe prevention directorate)
National economy	

When establishing the system of homeland defense, the possibility of war has to be taken into consideration for planning purposes. The organizational system and measures must be designed accordingly. It is easy to understand that the preparation and planning for a situation of war includes preparation for the prevention of smaller and simpler dangers, and consequence management as well. The rationale behind the establishment and operation of the national defense system is as follows:

- enforcement of the constitutional state

- establishment of an integrated system that is able to deal with the qualified periods

- implementation of a modular structured system of defensive elements (see table 2).[35]

The complex system of homeland defense can be divided into military and civilian elements. Military elements include the armed forces (the Hungarian Defense Forces) and those organizations responsible for defending public order (police, fire brigades, border guards, etc.).[36] The basic task of the Hungarian Defense Forces is the defense of the country's independence, territory, inhabitants, and material goods against external attack, along with the defense and protection of Hungary's airspace.[37]

Apart from the fulfillment of their basic duties, they cooperate in:

- the protection and defense of institutions that require heightened defense from the point of view of homeland security[38]

- the fight against international terrorism (with prepared and designated forces)[39]

- averting armed actions or violence committed with arms (as defined in §40/B, Section (2) of the constitution)[40]

- the disposal of unexploded ordnance[41]

- assistance in disaster prevention and relief activities[42]

- the provision of special military hardware and knowledge to other state institutions (on a reimbursable basis).[43]

The main guarantee of the constitutional use of the armed forces is governed by strict preconditions:

- military force can be used under stipulated conditions
- military force must be used in accordance with the provisions of the Constitution
- command of the armed forces is confined to the parliament, the president, the government, and the National Defense Council.

In an event of averting armed actions or violence committed with arms (as defined in §40/B, Section (2) of the constitution), it is imperative to define the objectives, timeframe, and location of the operation, along with the task, strength, and equipment (weapons) of the units that will be engaged. Deployed forces operate under their own officers' command.[44]

For disaster prevention and relief operations, and the lending of military hardware and knowledge, the chief of defense staff can give the order to deploy up to 100 personnel for up to 21 days. The minister of defense authorizes engagements for longer periods, or those involving more troops. If the situation requires more than 3,000 troops, the minister of defense authorizes the engagement, but he is required to notify the National Assembly.[45]

The amendment to the constitution notably stipulates that "the basic function of the police is to maintain public law and order," while "the basic function of the Border Guards is to secure the border and carry out border police duties."[46] Public order defense organizations, besides their basic duties, fulfill defensive tasks similar to those of the armed forces. These include:

- armed protection of facilities and persons
- support of the armed forces in certain activities
- participation in civil protection activities
- cooperation in fulfilling tasks in qualified periods.[47]

As is stated in the constitution, only the National Assembly, the president, the government, the Defense Council, and the responsible minister as organs of the management of national defense are authorized to direct military activities for purposes of homeland security. Administratively, Hungary is divided into 19 counties; the 20th administrative entity is the capital city, Budapest. Altogether, however, Hungary has about 3,150 settlements. To centrally govern all 3,150 settlements, 19 counties, 23 districts, and 1 metropolitan center would be unfeasible in the event of a security-related event.

Therefore, since all settlements have their own stakes in homeland defense, they each have their own local defense committee. The committee chief is the mayor of each settlement, who, under the guidance of the governor of the county, prepares a local defense plan and is responsible for fulfilling local homeland defense tasks.

These defense plans of the settlements are incorporated into the defense plans of the counties. The main responsible person for the realization of the county defense plan is the county governor, who is directly guided by the national government or the respective minister.

The counties' defense plans are submitted to the Defense Office of the Ministry of Defense, and together they constitute the country defense plan. Submitted plans are prepared for different contingencies—natural disaster prevention and relief, chemical and hazardous material incidents, nuclear incidents, and events of armed assault. Altogether, each county has 22 prepared plans for foreseeable contingencies. Due to the sensitive nature of the plans, they are classified.

Brigadier General Sandor Patyi uses a simplified model of the national defense command to show all the actors that play a role in homeland defense, and the chain of command as it exists either in peacetime or in qualified periods.[48] The command of homeland defense efforts, except in situations such as those described in §19/E of the constitution—that is, "an armed attack"—rests with the president, the National Assembly, and the government. In the events described in §19/E of the constitution, the National Assembly declares either a preventive defense situation or a state of alert, and establishes the Defense Council. The Defense Council in turn commands the homeland defense efforts of the Republic of Hungary.[49] The Defense Council consists of the president, the speaker of the parliament, party faction leaders, the prime minister, the ministers, and the chief of the defense staff.

Types of Available Armed Forces and Public Order Defense Organizations

Active Military Forces

The active military forces of the Republic of Hungary consist of the army, air force and air defense, central logistics and support units, and other organizations, such as the Joint Forces Operational Center, the Budapest Garrison Command, and units directly subordinate to the chief of defense staff and personnel of the Ministry of Defense and its subordinate organizations (see table 3).[50]

Table 3. Personnel Strength of the Active Military Forces (as of January 1, 2005)

Organization	Officers	NCOs	Contracted	Total
Army	1,357	3,366	4,895	9,618
Air Force, Air Defense	1,387	2,369	1,836	5,592
Central logistic and support units	917	1,143	507	2,567
Other organizations	1,716	1,857	939	4,512
Ministry of Defense and subordinate organizations	2,252	824	0	3,076
Total	**7,629**	**9,559**	**8,177**	**25,365**

Public Order Defense Organizations

Organizations responsible for defending the public order consist of the police, the Border Guard, fire brigades, and the catastrophe prevention directorate (see table 4).[51]

Table 4. Personnel Strength of the Public Order Defense Organizations (as of February 1, 2005)

Organization	Civil Servants	Active Duty	Total
Police	8,612	31,245	39,857
Border Guard	1,719	11,573	13,292
Catastrophe Prevention Directorate	725	1,043	1,768
Local governments' fire brigades	405	7,562	7,967
Total	**11,461**	**51,423**	**62,884**

Reserve Forces

According to the government's stated intentions regarding the introduction of an all-volunteer military, peacetime service in the armed forces is on a voluntary basis. Perhaps further diminishing the size of the Hungarian military, the reserve forces are also entirely composed of volunteers. The legal basis for these changes is set forth in the constitution and the Defense Act. By the virtue of the Defense Act, the Ministry of Defense's Military Administration and Data Processing Center and reserve commands keep records of eligible male citizens between 18 and 40 years of age for reserve service. These citizens are called "potential reservists" and are grouped into trained and untrained categories, depending on whether they have received any military training or not. Recently, in peacetime the Hungarian Defense Forces have had 165 voluntary reserve vacancies, out of which 50 to 60 have been filled. It is the ministry's intention to raise the level of peacetime reservists to 3,000 men in the next 2 to 3 years.[52]

However, in a preventive defense situation, after the National Assembly has decided to reintroduce compulsory military service, all male adult citizens are obliged to fulfill their military service duties.[53] This is automatically the case in a state of emergency; no decision by the National Assembly is necessary.

Protection of Critical Infrastructure

As a general rule, military forces do not engage in the protection of critical infrastructure in peacetime, except in defense of segments of the military infrastructure deemed important from the point of view of homeland security. But the public order defense organizations are responsible for fulfilling their tasks determined by law during peacetime (listed in the previous section).

In the meantime, the armed forces, under the direction of the minister of defense, contribute to the installation and maintenance of critical infrastructure such as medical, transport, and telecommunication networks, and to the operation of air warning, meteorological, and nuclear, biological, chemical, and radiological (NBCR) detection and warning systems.[54] The most visible element of this infrastructure is the military-operated Air-Sovereignty Operation Center (ASOC), which is part of the NATO Integrated Air Defense system and gives a real-time picture of activity in the skies over Europe. ASOC also cooperates with the civilian air traffic control system as a back-up system for it. In addition to managing ASOC, the Hungarian Air Force conducts routine air patrolling, provides an air defense capability to the nuclear plant at Paks, and maintains the no-fly zone over that plant.

After 9/11, the National Assembly authorized measures to cope with the terrorist threat with its 62/2001 (IX.25) Decree. With this measure, the government of Hungary attempted to implement the so-called *renegade concept* into the Defense Act as well. It says in particular:

> Forces participating in the air defense of the Republic of Hungary can open warning or destructive fire on an aircraft flying in the airspace of Hungary if:
>
> a) it uses its weapons system
>
> b) it, by any other means, commits life- or property-threatening activity or causes catastrophe
>
> c) by any means it is clear that it intends to commit activity mentioned in a), b), and deliberately does not answer to the air defense patrol call. In such cases air defense patrol or air defense units can open warning or destructive fire only at the command of the Air Force General on duty.[55]

In addition, the military operates the NBCR Detection and Warning System, which is designed to take samples continuously from the air and water. In the event of any contamination, the system makes recommendations on the course of action to be taken.[56]

In the case of an armed attack, or as a worst-case scenario for war, a defense plan has been worked out by the chief of defense staff. The plan covers all aspects of the command and control of the armed forces, combat support, and preparation of the country for a defensive operation. The minister of defense, via the prime minister, submits the defense plan to the president for approval. Due to their sensitive nature, details of the defense plan are classified.

Other Military Support Activities

Domestic Counterterrorism

As a rule, the Hungarian military does not participate in domestic counterterrorism activities. Nevertheless, the military performs some kind of counterterrorist function, although it is intended mainly to enhance its own protection.

In Hungary, there are five agencies that deal with gathering, processing, and disseminating intelligence. Two among them are under the direct control of the minister of defense: the Military Intelligence Service and the Military Security Service. The Military Intelligence Service collects covert and overt intelligence, mainly abroad. It focuses on the military aspects of national security. Furthermore, it collects information on terrorist organizations capable of posing a threat to military forces.[57] The main task of the Military Security Service, on the other hand, is force protection, including counterterrorist and counterintelligence activities.

The remaining three agencies are civilian national security agencies: the National Security Support Service, the National Security Office, and the Information Agency. The National Security Support Service provides all the necessary technical means to other national security services for performing their duties. It is the responsibility of the National Security Office to perform national security tasks in Hungary, while the Information Agency is responsible for operations abroad.[58]

As a result of the terrorist attacks on 9/11 in the United States, in November 2003 in Istanbul, and in March 2004 in Madrid, the government's National Security Cabinet decided to establish the Counterterrorism Coordination Committee (CCC), which includes the Military Intelligence Service, the Military Security Service, the National Security Office, the National Security Support Service, the Information Agency, the police, and the Border Guard. The aim of the CCC is to:

> elevate the cooperation of the National Security Services, enhance protection of persons, installations most threatened from the point of view of terrorism, [and] put under strict surveillance persons and organizations believed to be possible accomplices of terrorist attacks.[59]

Civil Disturbances

In general, the military is not designed to cope with civil disturbances, mainly because, as an American saying stipulates, "If you only have a hammer, you tend to see everything as a nail." Since the military is specifically prepared for fighting wars, civil riot control is the task of the public order defending organizations, such as the police. Nonetheless, according to §40/B, Section (2) of the constitution, the military can be deployed to suppress insurgents or disperse demonstrators, but only after the declaration of a qualified period and only if the police cannot cope with the task. In the course of military training, however, some riot control techniques are covered, but only military members who are in the preparation phase for peace support operations abroad get comprehensive riot control training.

Civil Support

The most visible and viable civil support function of the Hungarian military is that seen in the Tisza Multinational Engineering Battalion that was established on January 18, 2002. The battalion is an 800-strong military formation assembled by troops from Hungary, the Czech Republic, Romania, and Ukraine. Each country contributes no more than 200 men respectively, with no fewer than 100 engineer personnel in each contingent.

The purpose of this on-call battalion is to perform disaster relief operations within the catchment basin of the Tisza River in cooperation with other agencies and institutions performing relief operations. The battalion operates without arms or ammunition. Instead of fighting, the battalion performs reconnaissance (identification of the extent of a threat, investigating conditions for performing relief operations), flood relief (fortification of river banks, direct rescue of persons and property, evacuation of persons and property from endangered areas, clearing roads, removal of fallen tree trunks, basic diving operations, and building of temporary bridges), or other duties made necessary by unforeseen ecological events.[60] The units designated by Hungary to serve in this formation, from the 5th István Bocskai Light Infantry Brigade, take part in relief operations on request.

Peculiarities of Military Support Activities Without Declaration of Qualified Periods

Although there generally is no legal basis for the employment of military forces in domestic contingencies, the amendment to the constitution and the new Defense Act define special occasions when the government of Hungary may employ military forces in domestic contingencies without a formal declaration of qualified periods. The Amendment to the Constitution stipulates that:

> Preventing legislative delay in the Parliament, in case of imminence the government may decide on introduction of preventive defense situation. The government until the decision of the National Assembly, but no more than for 60 days, may take measures to prevent danger.[61]

The above passage means that the government has in its arsenal the ability to take the necessary steps for introducing preventive measures. It is worth noting that measures introduced within the 60-day period can only affect the state administration, the public order defense organizations, and the Hungarian Armed Forces, with no direct influence on civilians.

The government, in order to fulfill the tasks derived from §35, Section 1, Clause (m) of the constitution, may introduce measures that usually require the deployment of the military:

- using military air traffic control in civilian air transport

- implementing restricted measures in frequency management and broadcasting

- assigning designated personnel of the military forces and public order defense organizations and equipment to the defense of critical infrastructure

- operationally preparing Hungary's terrain for defense

- performing special counterterrorism operations with designated military forces

- tightening entrance procedures of persons and vehicles into installations of the government, the military, and other institutions involved in maintaining homeland security, including restrictions, bans, and evacuation

- searching the clothing and vehicles of persons entering into installations of the government, the military, and other institutions involved in maintaining homeland security; searching and destroying objects of unknown origin

- tightening border security and control

- tightening control of the postal service.[62]

Conclusion

The ultimate goal of the Hungarian Defense Forces is, according to the constitution and the Defense Act, to defend the country's independence, territory, inhabitants, and material goods against external attack, and to defend and protect the national airspace. In addition to these tasks, the armed forces protect and defend the institutions that require heightened defense from the point of view of homeland security, fight international terrorism with prepared and designated forces, avert armed actions or violence committed with arms (as defined in §40/B, Section (2) of the constitution), conduct unexploded ordnance disposal, contribute to disaster prevention and relief activities, and provide special military hardware and knowledge to other state institutions.

As a basic rule, the military cannot be deployed constitutionally in peacetime in Hungary. However, the constitution defines five qualified periods: preventive defense situations, states of emergency, surprise assault, states of danger, and states of alert. In doing so, it stipulates situations in which the military can play a role in domestic contingencies.

Deployment of the military in peacetime and in qualified periods (except armed attack, as it is defined in §19/E of the constitution) is controlled and conducted by the National Assembly, the president, the government, and the responsible minister. For these contingencies, plans drafted by the local Defense Committees are to be implemented. These plans contain measures (both civilian and military) for all foreseeable contingencies, beginning from fire to disaster prevention and consequence management, including NBCR disaster.

Hungary's armed forces thus have a highly varied and rich experience in assisting the civil authority in a broad range of homeland security missions. As a new NATO member, Hungary's civil and military authorities are working very hard to ensure that the country is ready and able to carry out all of its assigned missions, including domestic ones.

Notes

[1] Sun-Tzu, *The Art of War* (New York: Barnes and Noble Books, 1994), 79.

[2] "Basic Principle of the Security and Defense Policy of the Republic of Hungary," Resolution of the National Assembly 94/1998 (XII.29).

[3] "National Security Strategy of the Republic of Hungary," Governmental Decree 2073/2004.

[4] "Transformation and Establishment of a New Organization Structure of the Hungarian Defense Forces for the Period 2004–2013," Governmental Decree 2236/2003 (X.1).

[5] "Draft of the National Military Strategy of the Republic of Hungary," Sec. 1, para 20.

[6] Ibid., Sec 2, para 37.

[7] Ibid., Sec 2, para 40.

[8] Ibid., Sec 2, para 47.

[9] B.K. Király and Paul Jónás, *The Hungarian Revolution of 1956 in Retrospect* (New York: Columbia University Press, 1978), 41.

[10] Imre Kovács, *Facts About Hungary* (New York: Waldon Press, 1958), 78.

[11] Jozef Bem was a Polish-born revolutionary hero who commanded the Hungarian Defense Forces during the Hungarian revolution in 1848–1849.

[12] Imre Takács, *The Hungarian Revolution of 1956* (Monterey, CA: Naval Postgraduate School, 2001), 5.

[13] Király and Jónás, 55.

[14] Zoltán D. Bárány, *Soldiers and Politics in Eastern Europe, 1945–90* (New York: St. Martin's Press, 1993), 64.

[15] Király Béla, *Facts on Hungary* (New York: Waldon Press, 1957), 54.

[16] The Hungarian Defense Forces provided transport helicopters and amphibious vehicles for disaster relief.

[17] On average, bomb-disposal units have been called upon over 3,000 times per year. In 2004, their activities included disposing of more than 5,500 artillery shells, 1,366 mortar grenades, and 1,326 hand grenades.

[18] Constitution of the Republic of Hungary (XX. Law of 1949), 40/A§, Section 1. The amendment to the Constitution of November 8, 2004, stipulates that the "armed forces" constitutes only the Hungarian Defense Forces. The Border Guard became part of the law enforcement agencies.

[19] Constitution of the Republic of Hungary (XX. Law of 1949), 40/B§, Section 1.

[20] Border guard squads were deployed together with police regiments and Republican Guard regiments.

[21] 3065/1991 Governmental Decree. This order states that, besides securing borders, the functions of such formations are border policing and law enforcement. In Sándor Hopácsi, *Border Guard Formation at EU Accession*, available at <www.zmka.hu/kulso/mhtt/ hadtudomany/2003/1/horpacsiferenc/chapter1.htm>.

[22] Some chapters of the Standard Operational Procedures for the border guards are the same as in the Army's Field Manual, except law enforcement procedures.

[23] Hopácsi.

[24] Sixty-eight Russian BTR–80 armored personnel carriers were distributed among the border guard units. To date, they have never been used in operations.

[25] Maj. László Komjáthy, *Flooding on the Tisza River 1830–2001* (Budapest: BM Katasztrófavédelmi Oktatási Központ, 2002), 3.

[26] Announcement of visitors center at the Paks nuclear plant regarding the attacks of September 11, 2001.

[27] Excerpt from Juhász's appreciation address to personnel taking part in flood-prevention activities in August 2002, available at <www.honvedelem.hu/Archivum_index.php>.

[28] "On Defense and Hungarian Defense Forces," Law of the National Assembly, CV/2004 (November 8, 2004).

[29] Brig. Gen. Sándor Patyi and Lt. Col. László Tóth, "Cooperation of Civilian and Military Structures in Crisis Management," in *Conference on Civil-Military Relations in the Context of an Evolving NATO*, ed. Lt. Col. Ferenc Sipos (Budapest: MSZH Printing Office, 1997), 78.

[30] "On the Amendment to the XX/1949 Law (Constitution)," Law of the National Assembly, CIV/2004 (November 8, 2004). This law stipulates that §19, Sec. 3, is amended with clause (n), which says that "[The National Assembly] in event of imminent external armed attack, or in order to fulfill international obligations, declares [or sustains] preventive defense situation and authorizes the Government to employ necessary measures."

[31] "Constitution of the Republic of Hungary," §19, Sec. 3(i), states: "[The National Assembly] declares a state of emergency in the event of attempting to overthrow constitutional order or seizing power with arms, furthermore in events of natural or industrial disaster."

[32] Ibid., §19/E, Sec. 1, states: "In an event of surprise external attack, or for defending the territorial integrity of Hungary by standby national or Alliances air-defense and air force units or to protect the Constitutional order, citizens, life and property and to sustain public order the Government, guided by the defense plan approved by the President, until the declaration of state of alert, have to act immediately."

[33] Ibid., §35, Sec. 1(i), states: "[The Government], in the event of a natural disaster endangering life and property of citizens or for averting consequences of such disaster makes all necessary steps." See also "On Disaster Prevention," Law LXXIV/1999, §2, Sec. 1, 2 (June 22, 1999).

[34] "On Defense and Hungarian Defense Forces," §1, Law of the National Assembly, CV/2004 (November 8, 2004).

[35] Source: Presentation of the Budapest Defense Committee Secretariat.

[36] Amendment to the Constitution, §4, Sec. 1, Law of the National Assembly, CIV/2004 (November 8, 2004).

[37] "On Defense and Hungarian Defense Forces," §70, Sec. 1(a), Law of the National Assembly, CV/2004 (November 8, 2004).

[38] Ibid., §70, Sec. 1(d).

[39] Ibid., §70, Sec. 1(c).

[40] Ibid., §70, Sec. 1(f).

[41] Ibid., §70, Sec. 1(g).

[42] Ibid., §70, Sec. 1(h).

[43] Ibid., §70, Sec. 1(i).

[44] Ibid., §71.

[45] Ibid., §72, Sec. 1.

[46] Amendment to the Constitution, §4, Sec. 2, Subsections (2) and (3), Law of the National Assembly, CIV/2004 (November 8, 2004).

[47] "On Defense and Hungarian Defense Forces," §6, Section 1, and §42, Sec. 2(b)–(e), Law of the National Assembly, CV/2004 (November 8, 2004).

[48] Patyi and Tóth, 92.

[49] "On Defense and Hungarian Defense Forces," §61, Sec. 1, Law of the National Assembly, CV/2004 Law (November 8, 2004).

[50] Defense Forces' Military Administration and Data Processing Center.

[51] Human Policy Main Department, Ministry of Interior, Hungary.

[52] Phone interview with Col. Dr. János Kriszbai, Deputy Head of MOD Human Policy Department, and Col. Ferenc Takács, Deputy J1, Hungarian Defense Forces, on March 17, 2005.

[53] See Amendment to the Constitution, §6, Sec. 1, Law of the National Assembly, CIV/2004 (November 8, 2004); and "On Defense and Hungarian Defense Forces," §6, Sec. 1, and §83, Sec. 1, Law of the National Assembly, CV/2004 (November 8, 2004).

[54] "On Defense and Hungarian Defense Forces," §52, Sec. 1(d), Subclause (dc), Law of the National Assembly, CV/2004 (November 8, 2004).

[55] Ibid., §132, Sec. 1(a)–(c) and Sec. 4.

[56] Interestingly enough, the Hungarian military owns a unique mobile nuclear, biological, and chemical laboratory, which is part of the capability it offers to NATO. Until now, this laboratory has not taken part in action in Hungary. However, as Hungary's contribution to securing the 2004 Olympics in Athens, it was deployed to Greece. The uniqueness of the laboratory is that its deployability conforms with the NATO Response Force deployability criteria; it is able to detect any form of known agents within 1 to 6 hours.

[57] See <www.kfh.hu/hu/frame/rend.htm>.

[58] See <www.nemzetbiztonsag.hu/szolgalatok.php>.

[59] See <www.nbh.hu/terror.htm>.

[60] Technical Agreement between the Ministry of Defense of the Republic of Hungary, the Ministry of National Defense of Romania, the Ministry of Defense of the Slovak Republic, and the Ministry

of Defense of Ukraine concerning the implementation of the agreement between the Government of the Republic of Hungary, the Government of Romania, the Government of the Slovak Republic, and the Cabinet of Ministers of Ukraine on the establishment of a Multinational Engineer Battalion, signed on January 18, 2002, in Budapest, Article VI, Sec. 1–2.

[61] Amendment to the Constitution, §3, Section 2, Law of the National Assembly, CIV/2004 (November 8, 2004). See also: Constitution of the Republic of Hungary, §35, Sec. 1(m).

[62] "On Defense and Hungarian Defense Forces," §201, Clause (a-r), Law of the National Assembly, CV/2004 (November 8, 2004).

Chapter 5

The Role of Italy's Military in Supporting the Civil Authorities

Carlo Cabigiosu

Policy on Deployment of Military Forces

Italy has a long tradition of deploying military forces in domestic contingencies. Hence, we can look to a substantial and conspicuous body of legislation regarding this subject, as there has long existed a well-developed attitude among the various constituent bodies responsible for national defense to cooperate in all circumstances. Although the categories used in Italy are not the same as in America, for the sake of this chapter reference will be made to the general terms of classification as they are used in the United States.

Extraordinary Circumstances

National defense in Italy comprises all political, military, economic, industrial, and financial activities that are carried out by the state to ensure its own security and national integrity in all given circumstances. National security is based upon two main branches—military defense and civil defense—which are strictly interconnected through a permanent structure called the Agency for Civil-Military Cooperation (COCIM). COCIM has the responsibility to face any kind of extraordinary circumstance. This structure is based on the Military-Political Nucleus (*Nucleo Politico Militare*), which is part of the prime minister's cabinet and is headed by the prime minister himself (or his delegate). All relevant institutions are represented, among them the Ministry of Defense, the Ministry of the Interior, and the Department for Civil Protection. At its headquarters, the National Decision Center, there are a number of operations rooms (one for each ministry or agency) activated at the beginning of an emergency situation, which manage the flow of information to and from the area of operation. Coordination is the main purpose and is exercised by the Nucleus in permanent session.

Under the rubric of "military defense" are grouped all those activities
typically carried out by military forces in cases of threats to national territory by an external aggressor. The principles for the deployment of the Italian armed forces are laid out in the Constitution of Italy, where two main
points are stated: the defense of the homeland is a sacred duty of all citizens,
and war is a means of last resort to settle international disputes, unless the
Italian territory is under attack.

The president of the republic is the supreme commander of the armed
forces, but he does not have the authority to decide upon their deployment.
This decision is made by the government with the approval of the parliament, and the execution of the following actions falls under the responsibility of the Ministry of Defense and is coordinated within the COCIM (in
fact, within the Political Military Nucleus) in coordination with the other
ministries concerned.

The chief of staff for military defense, a four-star general or admiral,
is responsible for keeping the armed forces ready for deployment and for
updating the operational plans for extraordinary circumstances, such as
armed attacks on the nation. He operates through an operational staff,
namely the *Comando Operativo di Vertice Interforze* (COI), or the joint
operational headquarters, based in Rome. Forces are made available by
the chiefs of staff of the army, navy, and air force, and by the *Carabinieri
Comando Generale.*

Civil defense comprises a vast number of activities, which are linked
to all sectors of the socioeconomic life of the country. Its most relevant aim
is to ensure:

- continuity of government
- survival of the telecommunication system
- operation of the national warning and alert system
- protection of the civilian population
- safeguarding of public health
- continuation of public information activities
- preservation of the nation's cultural and artistic patrimony.

The various elements of civil defense fall under the primary responsibility of the minister of the interior, who coordinates (according to the
directives of the Military-Political Nucleus) all other institutions through

the Inter-Ministerial Technical Committee for Civil Defense. Responsible for civil defense throughout the national territory are the prefects, who represent the government at the provincial level. Each of them has an operations room that replicates the central organization. Hence, those responsible for civil defense have the difficult task of coordinating the activities that are to be carried out by the various state departments and other nongovernmental organizations, developing prevention capabilities, and ensuring that everything is accomplished in good order and subject to the financial constraints established by the government. In other words, the framework of civil defense is the organizational pillar of the country in cases of extraordinary circumstances for all activities except combat.

Chemical, biological, radiological, or nuclear (CBRN) attacks are actions that have to be dealt with as an emergency and must be faced by the organization established to manage disaster consequences. The armed forces contribute within the limits of the priorities established by their primary mission: the defense of the nation.

Emergency

The declaration of a state of emergency is a governmental responsibility that has been exercised rather frequently in Italian history, mainly on the occasion of natural disasters. In fact, due to the geological structure of the nation, the intervention and effort of military forces as part of the civil protection organization have often been required to face the consequences of heavy earthquakes and floods, as well as hurricanes and other natural calamities.

Military participation in these relief efforts is established by law whenever the armed forces operate within the structure of the National Service of Civil Protection (PROCIV), but only when the dimension of the disaster is of such a magnitude that it cannot be dealt with by the nation's firemen (organized in fire brigades and in fire mobile units), who are the first institutional asset to be used in emergency situations.

The National Service of Civil Protection is an independent department of the ministries' council that is under the direct authority of the prime minister and head of the government. Once a state of emergency is declared, the Operational Committee of Civil Protection coordinates the intervention. This committee is led by the chief of the Department of Civil Protection; the Ministry of Defense is represented by the commander of the

COI (joint operational headquarters). A senior prefect is also present on behalf of the Ministry of the Interior.

At the local level, the provincial prefect represents the central government, but the operational instrument is the Civil Protection Operational Center, headed by an official of the regional, provincial, or city Civil Protection Department. Other members are the appointed military commander and representatives of the firemen's organization, police forces, health department, and others.

To manage an emergency, PROCIV has the authority to issue *ordinances*, acts that have the force of law, enabling PROCIV to carry out requisition and expropriation, establish limits to the freedom of movement of the population of a certain area, and possibly to mobilize doctors, drivers, and so on.

PROCIV has in its headquarters an operations room (the *Sala Crisi Italia*), which is open around the clock and receives all alerts, requests for intervention, and available information about any event. The director of the operations room has the power to initiate all immediate measures that are foreseen by the emergency plan that is in place.

As for the role of the armed forces, there are two general cases. When there is immediate danger to human life, local commanders are authorized to intervene on their own initiative, without waiting for formal approval from their superior headquarters (which, of course, they keep informed at all times). Nevertheless, these units must be replaced as soon as the situation allows PROCIV to operate with its own assets. In all other cases, the deployment of military units must follow the normal procedures that foresee a formal request to the cabinet of the Ministry of Defense. The approval is conditioned by the necessity to maintain the capability to carry out their primary task and is granted only when civilian resources are not sufficient. In this case, the cost of the military contribution requires a special governmental financial act or must be reimbursed by the requesting authority. The military intervention, under the guidance of the Department of Civil Protection's chief, is carried out by one of the two operational headquarters commanders (one for the North and one for the South), who share responsibility over the whole of the Italian Peninsula.

Special mention should be made of cases of the intervention of military units in emergency situations resulting from natural disasters abroad. These interventions are possible on the basis of specific requests or bilateral agreements with other countries or by a request coming from one of the numerous international organizations established to coordinate international assistance (the United Nations [UN] Office for Coordination of Human Affairs, the Euro-Atlantic Disaster Response Coordination Center, or the European Union Monitoring Information Center).

As far as terror attacks are concerned, this is a case that has been intensively studied and implemented by the armed forces since after World War II. However, during the period of the Cold War, it was dealt with mainly as a national (or internal) threat. In the last 15 years, however, increasing stress has been put on the threat deriving from international terrorism. It is considered that the highest risk in this respect is linked to the possibilities of CBRN attacks and to attacks carried out from the air using civilian aircraft, similar to the terrorist attacks of 9/11 in New York City and Washington, DC.

The initial response to terror attacks is the responsibility of the Ministry of the Interior, as far as the security measures to be immediately taken in the area are concerned. In terms of rescue of and assistance to the victims of such an attack, there are a vast number of organizations that will respond according to existing local plans—local hospitals, the Red Cross, voluntary assistance organizations, elements of the state civil protection apparatus—but their coordination is the responsibility of the local prefect and/or the local mayor. In the immediate aftermath of an attack, units of the armed forces will intervene to assist in the rescue operation only if they are in the area. In the longer term, their participation will occur within the framework of the overall measures decided by the governmental authorities.

The response to terror attacks relies almost entirely upon the military only in case of air-terror attacks. For these emergencies, the National Governmental Authority is the Ministry for Defense, and the assets of the Italian Air Force are always ready to scramble to face the threat posed by detoured civilian aircraft.

Temporary

The provision of temporary support to civil authorities by the military is a relatively common practice within the Italian security system, both as a means of providing direct support to law enforcement, and as a contribution to the security measures for special events.

The armed forces—and particularly the army—have provided temporary support for civil law enforcement agencies since the beginning of the history of the Italian nation-state in 1860, when a large part of the army was deployed to fight rebel formations in the south of Italy that opposed the newly united Italian Kingdom. Nowadays, these interventions are always carried out under the authority of the Ministry of the Interior in support of the state police. The juridical status of the military units deployed in these situations can be different, ranging from the status quo, to active military status, to the awarding of soldiers the full status of public security agents. In the first case, all units, down to the lowest level, must be accompanied by police officers in the accomplishment of the assigned missions; in the latter case, soldiers are entitled to carry out directly the usual functions of the police. The duration of these deployments can vary from a few weeks to several years and must always be supported by a governmental decision, followed by a specific decree, where the purpose, duration, status of soldiers, and the financial limits of the mission are described and approved.

The military contribution to providing security for special events has become common due to the prevalence of terrorist threats. All the services of the military can be involved in different areas, and often particular military capabilities are required. The air force has to maintain air surveillance over the area of the event and be ready to counter possible aircraft trying to strike the area where the special event is taking place. Fast- and slow-moving targets require different responses, including antiaircraft batteries, armed helicopters, fighter aircraft, and surface-to-air portable missiles. If the event takes place near the coast—which in Italy, due to its geographical profile, is rather common—navy and coast guard units will also play a role. The army deploys infantry units to form security cordons around the area of the event and provides rapid response forces and special forces to ensure the evacuation and special protection of very important people and distinguished visitors. Military capabilities are also required for the establishment of a command and control network, to man operational or situation rooms, or to grant an immediate response to biological or chemical attacks. Engineer units and ordnance disposal teams are always present to deal with explosive devices. In addition, these contributions need to be exercised within the framework of a decree or some other governmental act that legalizes the deployment of the military in such events.

Routine

The most traditional mission carried out by one component of the armed forces in support of the Ministry of the Interior is the routine and practically permanent assignment of the *Carabinieri* for the execution of police tasks. The *Carabinieri* are the fourth service of the armed forces and are a gendarmerie corps. They are established under the authority of the Ministry of Defense and perform security and military police tasks for the other three services, but in the aggregate these are limited in number. The majority of their units are dedicated to the security of the nation's territory through about 5,000 *Carabinieri* stations spread across the country. Moreover, they have a number of battalions (called territorial battalions) that are a sort of general reserve that can be deployed to secure law and order in antiriot situations to sweep areas where searches have to be carried out or as reinforcements to other security forces when required. Another component of the *Carabinieri* is the mobile brigade, which is usually engaged in providing the Italian contribution to the various multinational specialized units deployed on peacekeeping missions overseas. It should be noted that the *Carabinieri* are the only force that is always present in all kind of contingencies, performing a military and a police role simultaneously.

The navy and its coast guard component are in charge of providing security in Italian territorial waters. They operate in international waters or at their limits, in the so-called blue waters. In territorial waters (brown waters), maritime security is mainly provided by the *Guardia di Finanza*—a force with military status, but technically part of the Ministry of Finance, that has been established as a maritime border and customs police unit. Along the long Italian coast, the *Carabinieri* have also developed some control and security missions, although they usually confine themselves to waters very near the shore. Their task has become particularly relevant during the last decade, due to the problem of illegal immigration, which is virtually always accompanied by illicit traffic of a different nature: drugs, tobacco, and weapons. Due to the proximity of the Balkan and North African coasts, Italy is particularly engaged in combating this trend, and it has become a routine activity that constantly involves all the forces that have been mentioned.

Other duties, which are routinely carried out by the navy, either directly or by the coast guard, are:

- search and rescue at sea, including the entire logistical support structure that this activity requires (coordination, control, and communications, around the clock)

- navigation security, carrying out regular inspections on all national merchant shipping and acting as the state port control authority over foreign ships in transit through Italy's ports
- water supply in support of a number of islands
- assistance and control of the Italian fishing fleet
- maritime policing in territorial waters (performed by the coast guard) and international waters (the navy).

The air force also provides permanent control over Italian national airspace. This is an assignment that is carried out by a special unit, the Airspace Brigade, which is responsible for the management of all radar stations, allowing the air force to monitor the airspace along with the civilian air traffic control organization and elements of the air defense units (which include aviation units and missile units). The Italian air defense, as such, is normally carried out within the framework of the North Atlantic Treaty Organization (NATO), through the Combined Air Operations Center (CAOC) 5, whose commander is dual-hatted, always being an Italian general. Within the CAOC 5 structure, there is also a national cell; in the case of a threat that has to be dealt with at the national level, a transfer of authority immediately takes place, and the Italian air force's operational headquarters assumes responsibility for the conduct of defense operations.

Historical Precedents

Post–World War II

During the period from 1945 to 1990, the Italian military went through an initial period of reconstruction and reorganization due to the events of World War II. Resources were limited and the financial constraints that existed imposed the necessity to build an instrument capable of facing a possible conflict more through quantity rather than quality. Quantity in fact was available through the institution of the national service, which provided a large number of young men at a very low cost.

The Italian forces slowly started their renovation when, in 1949, Italy joined NATO, and the Alliance gave a great boost to their effort to improve the level of their preparation. One good example of this international consideration was the decision of the United Nations, in 1950, to give to the Italian Republic the responsibility for the temporary administration of Somalia. The Italian military played a significant role in this enterprise, which had a positive influence upon the morale of the rank and file, who were still frustrated by the events of the recent war. The NATO exercises also played an important role in bringing the Italian armed forces into a cycle of continuous verification of their capabilities, compelling a large number of officers and other ranks to learn English as a vehicle of more modern ways of thinking, modifying the curricula of most of the military schools, and procuring the essential equipment to update the navy and the air force and then the army. Beginning in 1963, Italian troops regularly took part in the Allied Command, Europe, Allied Mobile Force training, with both land and air components. The experiences of these activities were spread out to a large number of other units, bringing up the standard of many of the Italian formations, especially the Mountain Brigades.

During the 1960s Italy had to face an insurgency in the northern region of Alto Adige carried out by local clandestine organizations belonging to the German-speaking minority, who were demanding a higher level of autonomy from Rome. The army was called in to support the police forces, and a number of units were deployed along the border with Austria to prevent the illegal movement of armed groups across the Alps. Units were deployed in the rest of the region to secure railways, electric power stations, to guard national institutions, and to carry out—in direct support of the police—cordons and searches, checkpoints, and other similar activities. The deployment required an average of 10,000 men, under the command of the Fourth Army Corps of Bolzano. After about 7 years, the problem reached a political resolution, and the army units in the region went back to their normal duties. During that time, in 1963, a terrible disaster occurred in the province of Belluno, where an enormous landslide collapsed into an artificial lake, the Vajont. A mass of water was pushed over the dam and swept away a number of villages and their inhabitants, causing more than 3,000 deaths. For weeks, hundreds of soldiers from the surrounding units worked day and night to try to rescue people and to recover the bodies of those drowned in the flood.

At the end of the 1960s, the so-called Red Brigades, as in other European nations, started to attack national institutions in Italy with terrorist actions, assassinations, and kidnappings of politicians, journalists, judges, and police officers, and with bomb attacks against innocent civilians. Again, in a number of circumstances the army was brought in to support the police, to protect installations, railways, airports, ports, telecommunications sites, and, in particular cases, to organize checkpoints and to implement other measures to allow a strict control of the territory. Some units were also assigned to provide personal security to important people. This situation lasted about 10 years, until the end of the 1970s. Beyond the challenges posed by these deployments, this was also a difficult period for the military because the Red Brigades tried to influence the internal discipline of the armed forces, infiltrating among the draftees their own elements who carried out propaganda actions and stimulated a subversive attitude among the troops. Fortunately, they did not meet with much of a response, and major problems were avoided by the strenuous engagement of all the officers who stood against these attempts with great moral courage.

It was in this period (1975–1976) that the army went through a major reorganization. Doctrine, structure, training, and equipment were carefully reviewed and renovated.

Another major commitment for the army came about in 1976, when a tragic earthquake hit the Friuli region in the northeastern part of Italy, claiming more than 1,000 victims and the destruction of a huge number of houses. Troops were deployed in support of the local population, providing every kind of assistance. One of the local divisional commanders was appointed Governmental Extraordinary Representative, responsible for the coordination of all civilian and military rescue and assistance organizations. A few years later, in 1980, an earthquake of even greater magnitude occurred in southern Italy, in the Irpinian region. The difficult terrain, the damage caused to the communication network, and the lack of a capable civil protection organization in the region put the military on the front lines of the relief effort, and much of the weight of the rescue operation fell on their shoulders.

Aside from these major events, military forces were assigned to intervene in a number of other situations related to local natural disasters, thus giving continuity to the excellent relationship between the armed forces and the rest of the country and enabling the military to acquire more and more respect from the Italian populace, who appreciated the military's capability to provide an immediate response to their needs with generosity and efficiency.

As far as the institutional task of the armed forces is concerned, their integration within the structure of NATO increased over time, progressively closing the gap that existed earlier between Italy and some other members of the Alliance. By the 1980s, the general standard of efficiency of the Italian military reached acceptable levels. Most of the military effort in this period was aimed at countering the possible threat of the Warsaw Pact against Italy's northeastern border with Yugoslavia and Austria and, by the navy, in the Mediterranean Sea.

In 1981 and 1982, Italian forces took part in an international mission in Lebanon, together with troops from the United States, United Kingdom, and France. Italy's troops performed well on this mission and gained general recognition, which was another step in the right direction.

In summary, in the postwar period the Italian military stood ready to intervene in extraordinary circumstances, in particular to face possible aggression on the part of the forces of the Warsaw Pact, an event that never took place. On the other hand, they had to face a series of emergency situations at home caused by natural disasters and a number of temporary missions in support of civil authorities in a law enforcement role.

The variety of the missions accomplished in those 40 years, and the progress made in a number of areas, allowed the Italian armed forces to increase credibility and to contribute to the enhancement of Italy's relevance on the global stage. What is even more important, the armed services were ready to face the challenges of the post–Cold War strategic situation and ready to play a major role under any and all circumstances.

Post–Cold War Period (1991–2001)

In Italy, as in many other Western nations, the fall of the Berlin Wall opened a debate over the possibility of reducing the size of the defense budget in view of the fact that the threat posed by the Soviet Union was gone. But soon everyone realized that, having broken the existing balance established by the confrontation of the two superpowers, the Pandora's Box of global instability had been opened, and a number of minor conflicts started to take place. Just to mention a few in which Italian troops played a role:

- In 1991, Italy took part in Operation *Provide Comfort* in Iraqi Kurdistan.

- In 1992, one Italian brigade was sent to Mozambique for 2 years to support the peace process started after a long period of guerrilla warfare.

- Again in 1992, an additional brigade took part in Operation *Ibis* in Somalia, initially within a "coalition of the willing" and subsequently with the UN mission.

- Soon after this intervention, the Balkans were in flames, and the conflict quickly spiraled out of the control of the UN mission, the United Nations Protection Force. When NATO was asked to take over the mission, Italy deployed troops in Sarajevo from the Garibaldi Brigade, the first brigade to complete the transformation from being made up of draftees to an all-professional unit.

- In 1997, Italy led a multinational coalition in Albania.

- In 1999, a contingent was sent to East Timor and another one to Kosovo.

This was the nonmarginal commitment of Italian forces in overseas missions. However, in this same period, major changes were decided about the structure of the three services and in particular that of the army. The total strength of the forces was planned to be around 230,000, with 130,000 in the army and 50,000 each in the navy and the air force. In the process, the army lost about 60 percent of its previous manpower, decreasing from about 300,000 men to 130,000.

The second major change was the transformation of the Italian armed forces into a fully professional organization. Another relevant change was the recruiting of women without restriction in number or role. In the same period, the chief of staff for defense, through a legal decision, was given full authority over the armed services and acquired full responsibility for the functioning of whatever units were deployed in operations.

Besides these decisions, more changes occurred with reference to the structure of the three services. For instance, the army gave more mobility to its units, improved their equipment, provided a better command and control capability, introduced wheeled armored vehicles, dramatically cut the number of tanks and artillery, enhanced its helicopters' capabilities, and reviewed its procedures for logistic support. For the navy, an air/helicopter carrier was built, and an air component was acquired; special care was taken for the amphibious component; and the renovation of the fleet was started, modernizing the long-range support ships. The air force made a major effort in modernizing the air transport brigade, replacing the old C130–H "Hercules" transport aircraft with the "J." Other changes concerned the acquisition of tankers for in-flight refueling and assets for battlefield surveillance. At the same time, Italy was also heavily involved in the Eurofighter project.

Apart from what has just been described, which falls in the area of the traditional processes and missions of the military, the 1990s have seen the Italian armed forces deployed on a wide range of temporary missions in support of the police in a law enforcement role, and on a good number of emergency missions to help the National Civil Protection Service manage disasters caused by natural calamities. It must be emphasized that in this decade the National Civil Protection Service has become much better organized; hence, the army has in part been disengaged from the leading role that, in previous decades, it was compelled to assume due to the fact that no other state organization was capable of managing these events.

The most relevant missions accomplished in support of the police forces in a law enforcement role in this period began in 1991, when Albanian citizens started to cross illegally the gulf that separates the Italian coast from the Albanian one (a distance of about 150 kilometers). This was a mass exodus that involved up to 20,000 people at one time, causing both a humanitarian and a law-and-order problem of vast scale. A full brigade was put in charge of bringing the situation under control.

In the following years, between 1992 and 1997, the political authorities decided on a number of occasions to use the army to support the police due to the intensification of criminal activities carried out by gangs belonging to organized criminal groups and to enhance the control of Italy's borders to stop the wave of illegal immigration. To accomplish these missions better and to give the military a more proactive role, the government decided to grant the soldiers, through a parliamentary act, the status of public security agents, which enabled soldiers to stop people and identify them, to search persons and vehicles, and, in particular circumstances, even to arrest people.

The first deployment took place in Sardinia in the summer of 1992 to enforce the presence of the state in areas where the police did not have the capability to properly operate due to rough terrain. At the same time, a similar operation was started in Sicily to limit the freedom of action of elements of the local mafia. In 1995, Italian troops carried out border control operations on the Italian-Slovenian border and performed coast control functions along the Adriatic Sea near the city of Ancona and more to the south near the city of Brindisi. Subsequently, other anticrime operations took place in the Neapolitan area and in the region of Calabria, each lasting up to 2 years. In the first case, the main task was to protect local magistrates and judicial facilities (tribunals, the external perimeter of prisons, judges' residences) from attacks by criminal organizations that were being investigated. In the second case, the main task was to patrol areas where hostages were detained by criminal organizations.

Most of these activities have been carried out by infantry units, altering military techniques as needed due to the fact that all their activities were carried out among civilians and in streets and areas where often there were no particular restrictions on the movement of individuals. The employment of the military in a police support role sent a strong message to the local population, which sometimes was intimidated by members of the local gangs or, on the contrary, was part of the criminal network itself. But the locals—who had in the past in some cases complained about the lack of any state presence and about being left alone to face the impunity of the criminal organizations—in general appreciated the increased sense of security.

Post-9/11

After the terrorist attacks of September 2001, and the new awareness of the dangers posed by terrorist organizations to Western countries, the entire national security system in Italy has been reviewed. There is now a general understanding that a terrorist attack could come without warning, at any time, and be of an extremely violent nature. Therefore, two areas of security have been particularly enhanced: the gathering of intelligence and the prevention of attacks. The armed forces have been involved in the latter area in a variety of ways.

First of all, the concept that terrorist organizations have to be fought not only at a national level but also, when necessary, at an international level is a cornerstone of the antiterrorist security strategy. Italy's participation in Operation *Enduring Freedom*, and later in Operation *Iraqi Freedom*, is a clear signal of the Italian commitment to this concept.

As far as the military contribution to homeland security in Italy, all the services have new tasks to perform. The army has deployed a contingent of 4,000 soldiers to protect more then 150 possible targets from terrorist actions (Operation *Domino*). Such targets are distributed in different regions and include areas surrounding airports, ports, railway stations, telecommunications sites, and other specific installations, such as major electric power stations, water distribution systems, and similar facilities.

The navy is engaged with its own forces in Operation *Active Endeavor*, under the umbrella of NATO in the eastern Mediterranean Sea in an effort to control the maritime traffic in the region and to prevent any illegal use of ships to carry out activities linked to a terror organization. The navy is also ready to exercise a more stringent level of control over movements in international waters once these are detected by the intelligence network. The coast guard is also specifically tasked to maintain constant focus on possible clandestine immigration vessels trying to approach the Italian coasts, not only as a matter of respecting the Schengen immigration rules in Europe but also to enable the early identification of members of terrorist groups.

The air force has received a particularly difficult assignment: interventions against renegade aircraft. New rules have been established to define better the responsibilities of pilots and the responses to be made in case civilian aircraft should be used to carry out attacks. The existing procedures foresee that, in peacetime, the NATO air defense system is responsible for conducting the identification, interdiction, and eventually engaging the air asset that is violating the navigation rules and is suspected to be an aggressor. Up to this point, it was always assumed that it would have been a military plane that represented a threat, but this is no longer the case. To act against a civilian aircraft with possibly hundreds of innocent passengers on board is a different matter, one involving moral and political aspects. Due to the fact that NATO has decided that such cases are no longer an Alliance responsibility but that they fall under national sovereignty, the Italian government's decision was to delegate this authority to the Ministry of Defense, and special procedures have been activated to enable the minister to face whatever circumstances might arise. This applies mainly to fast-moving aircraft. The case of slow-moving targets has also been considered, but this requires a more articulated response. To achieve such an end, no-fly zones have been established around sensitive areas that can be defended using armed helicopters, and this system is always applied in case of special events (Group of Eight meetings, international summits, state visits, international sporting events), and on a case-by-case basis in other situations.

As far as the *Guardia di Finanza* is concerned, they contribute to the general security of the borders, both on land and at sea, with a much higher degree of attention since 9/11. In particular, their troops have been given specific responsibilities to implement the security measures foreseen by two projects that have been supported by the United States: the Container Security Initiative and the Proliferation Security Initiative.

In summary, all branches of the Italian armed forces have received new tasks to increase the efficiency of the national counterterror security

system, through the deployment of units, the introduction of new procedures, and an awareness campaign that is constantly carried out at all levels.

Deployment of Military Forces

National Legal Framework

To arrive at a clear definition of how military forces are employed
for purposes of homeland security in Italy, it is important to note that the
first bills promulgated to this end were issued as Royal Decrees as early as
1907 and 1909. They state that the armed forces can be called in to ensure
public security if/when the police forces are not available or insufficient.
Military units continue to be under command of their respective commanders, but the mission to be carried out remains under the responsibility of the police officers concerned. A request for the deployment of
military units to support the police should be forwarded by the provincial
prefect according to the established procedures. These laws still form the
basis of the present-day participation of military units in operations in
support of the police. Through subsequent legislation, the employment
of the military was extended to support the magistrates carrying out particular investigations (1941), to provide security during elections at the
polling stations (1957), and to the prison police in cases of disorder in
penal institutions (1976). In 1978, the parliament approved a complex act
concerning the armed forces, covering a number of important aspects,
above all their tasks. The first of these tasks, *homeland defense*, is described
as "to contribute to safeguard the national free institutions," which is a
wide definition that also includes what is meant by the term *homeland
security*. In 1981, another law was issued to define the new procedures to
be followed to ensure public security. Among other points, it includes the
confirmation of the possible requirement to support the police forces with
military augmentation, and the setting up of the National Committee for
Public Order and Security at the ministerial (of the Interior) and provincial
(prefect) level, with the presence of one representative of the armed forces
as a member of the committee.

Finally, in 2001, another law relevant to internal security was issued.
Three articles of this law (n. 128–26 March 2001) specifically concern
the armed forces. These articles confirm that, in specific and exceptional
situations, soldiers can be deployed to free police officers from their

surveillance and security tasks so as to allow them to dedicate all their efforts to fighting crime. These troops are made available to the provincial prefects involved, according to specific plans, for 6 months at a time. These plans are initially approved by the National Committee for Public Order and Security, which includes the chief of staff for defense (usually represented by the commander of the Joint Operational Headquarters [JHQ]). The JHQ commander makes sure that the level of forces required is compatible with the other priority tasks of the armed forces, in consultation with the chief of staff of the concerned service. The plans are then forwarded for final approval to the relevant parliamentary commissions.

Scope of Permissible Activities

The general principles established by these laws are supported by more specific regulations issued by the Ministry of Defense specifying, in more detail, the procedures and modalities to be applied in such cases. Military commanders, taking into account the general directives decided at the governmental level, will define the execution plan for the assigned tasks and will elaborate the subsequent orders. Plans and orders will have to be agreed upon by the prefect in charge, and shared with the police commander responsible for the area.

There are two main options for how the military is to be employed. The first one is in a relieving role; the second one is effective integration. The first one, in fact, allows a consistent number of police officers to disengage themselves from static duties and routine patrolling to be put to use in more qualified police duties. The second model allows the conduct of combined operations for dynamic actions, where army units provide territorial control over a large area while, inside that area, the police conduct more specific actions and investigation. The army commanders usually try to accomplish their mission while limiting the static activities (target surveillance, guarding) to the bare minimum, opting, whenever possible, for dynamic actions such as patrolling and conducting mobile checkpoints. This concept brings higher morale, good results, and keeps sections and platoons together without breaking formation ties. After years of intense cooperation with the police forces, an agreement has been reached in substance with the Ministry of the Interior to assign to the army units the following tasks:

- surveilling and protecting sensitive targets (tribunals, justice facilities, prisons, magistrates' residencies, persons at particular risk, peculiar installations and so on)

- establishing checkpoints and road blocks

- maintaining a cordon around urban areas where the police will carry out searches

- sweeping of rural areas

- patrolling along the rail and highway networks, verifying the integrity of bridges, tunnels, and flyovers. Mobile activities are carried out according to military standards adopted in area interdiction operations and in large-area surveillance. The static activities are also implemented as closely as possible in line with basic military criteria.

Authorizing Authority and Command and Control of Forces

As was described in the previous section, once the request for military reinforcement presented by one or more provincial prefects to the Ministry of the Interior has been processed and approved at the governmental level, the bodies that will exercise command and control functions over the deployed troops are:

- the National Committee for Public Order and Security (NCPOS), under the direction of the minister of the interior (to whom all provincial prefects report). The committee includes the chief of police (who is at the top of the nationwide police structure) and the commander of the JHQ (who reports to the chief of staff for defense). The NCPOS also includes the commander of the *Carabinieri* (part of the Ministry of Defense), who is subordinate to the chief of police and whose troops on the ground always respond to the local head police officer (namely, the *Questore*).

- the Provincial Committee for Public Order and Security, headed by the provincial prefect, which includes the local senior *Questore* as police chief, flanked by the provincial commander of the *Carabinieri*, and by the appointed military commander.

Before reaching any definitive decision about the scope of operations, discussions and negotiations about potential options take place within these bodies. Once their respective positions are clarified and all constituents agree, final orders are issued.

As far as the military chain of command is concerned, the chief of staff for defense is at the top. He can delegate his authority to the commander of the Joint Operational Headquarters or, in case only one branch of the armed forces is involved, to the chief of staff of that particular service. The next level down in the military chain of command is the army operational commander, followed by the other commanders according to the normal hierarchical sequence (Divisional HQ, Brigade HQ, Regimental HQ, and Battalion HQ). Bottom-up reports go straight from the commander on the ground to the provincial operation room and in parallel to the military chain of command.

A special chain of command is envisioned to face airborne terrorist attacks best. In this case, a direct link would be established between the commander of the air force and the minister of defense, who is the national governmental authority responsible for issuing the order of engagement.

Rules of Engagement

All units deployed in support of police forces for purposes of homeland security are given specific rules of engagement to be followed in case the use of force is required. Weapons can generally be used only for self-defense, and proportionality must be observed in relation to the severity and nature of the offense. The use of weapons is allowed:

- by individual initiative, to face an attack that endangers a soldier's own life or the lives of others

- on order, given by the commander of the unit, when it is necessary to counter threats against the unit or to safeguard the lives of others.

Rules of engagement are also issued to define the procedures to stop unauthorized people from approaching protected targets, and they are to be followed in cases of resistance to inspections or searches. Rules of engagement are usually issued in catalogues and are graduated according to the situation. The closer the situation is to normal, the stricter the rules of engagement.

Navy units are given specific rules of engagement to be followed in order to stop suspected vessels, board them, and deal with possible clandestine materials or illegal immigrants on board. To face the case of a civilian aircraft suspected to have been diverted to execute a terror attack, specific rules are also set by the commander of the air force and approved by the minister of defense.

While NATO rules of engagement are usually followed during peacekeeping operations, they are adopted without relevant changes and are substantially the same for all missions. In case of interventions that are being made for homeland security purposes, the rules of engagement must be agreed upon by the Ministry of the Interior, and must reflect those being used by the police.

Types and Capabilities of Available Forces

Active Military Forces

The Italian military is made up of four services: the army, the navy, the air force, and the *Carabinieri*. All forces are built on a base of professional soldiers, since national conscription came to a halt at the end of 2004.

The armed forces are under the authority of the chief of staff for defense, who exercises his authority through the Joint Operational Headquarters. This headquarters, as was mentioned above, is also responsible for exercising the necessary command and control capability over all forces deployed nationally for missions related to homeland security, and overseas for all peacekeeping and other stabilization missions.

The army, navy, and air force are all organized along the traditional lines of all other Western military forces. The *Carabinieri* reflect in their structure the basic model of the army, but with the necessary adjustments to carry out their gendarmerie duties nationwide.

The army is 120,000 soldiers strong. Its operational structure is based upon one operational command, located in Verona, which is responsible for the preparation of subordinate commands and units. The subordinate commands are:

- Command, Control, Information Command
- Air Defense Artillery Command
- Army Aviation Command
- Artillery Brigade
- Engineers Brigade
- Logistic Brigade.

There are three headquarters at the divisional level:

- First Defense Force Command, with three brigades (one armored, one mechanized, one paratrooper)
- Second Defense Force Command, with five brigades (one armored, four mechanized)
- Alpine Troop command, with two mountain brigades.

From these forces the army draws the necessary units in case it is required to contribute to any of the possible scenarios foreseen for matters of homeland security or to the National Civil Protection Service in cases of natural disasters. All regiments are trained to accomplish infantry-type missions, even the artillery and the armored units. This allows the army to count on having a sufficient number of units to carry out most of the activities that can be foreseen in support of the police units. From the other units—besides ensuring direct support to the army's own infantry units—the army can offer communications, logistic, air transportation, ground surveillance, engineering support, and medical assistance. Special capabilities, such as explosive ordnance disposal and CBRN abatement, can also be made available.

The navy is about 40,000 sailors strong, including the coast guard. Its operational structure is based upon the Naval Fleet Command, located near Rome, which is responsible for operational preparation and support and, in some cases, has direct command of the subordinate commands and units. They are usually organized for deployment into task forces. The subordinate commands in the navy are:

- COMFORSUB, for submarines
- COMFORSBAR, for amphibious forces
- COMFORAER, for navy aviation
- COMFORDRAG, for the minesweeper fleet
- COMFORPAT, for patrol boats
- COMFORAL, for the deep-sea fleet.

The coast guard has functional lines of subordination to the Ministry of Transport, Ministry for the Environment, Ministry of Agriculture (this ministry is also responsible for fisheries), and Ministry of the Interior because they also exercise maritime police duties. Specifically, they have full police authority in all ports and on all coasts, together with the other police forces. Coordination is sometimes difficult, but conflicts are avoided through the use of common operational rooms.

From all these forces are drawn the necessary units that are deployed when missions related to homeland security are to be carried out and, in cases of natural disasters, to support the National Civil Protection Service.

The air force consists of about 45,000 pilots and support personnel. The operational structure is based on the Air Fleet Command, located in Rome, which is responsible for operational preparation and support, and in some cases has direct command of the subordinate commands and units, which are normally organized for deployment into task forces. It should be noted that the chief of staff of the air force is the national commander of the air defense system, reporting in this particular role directly to the minister of defense. The subordinate air force commands are:

- Air Operations Command, co-located with the Fifth NATO CAOC in Poggio Renatico

- Fighter Division "Aquila," which includes five interceptor groups (flying Euro-fighters, F–16s, and Tornados)

- Fighter Division "Drago," which includes five attack, interceptor, and reconnaissance units (flying Tornado IDS, Tornado ECR/SEAD, AMX, MB.339)

- The First Air Brigade, based on surface-to-air missiles for the air defense system

- The Ninth Air Brigade "Leone," which includes all search-and-rescue units

- The 46th Transport Air Brigade, based on three transport groups, two of C130–Js, and one with G–222s.

In addition, helicopters are widely distributed in most units. These units contribute the needed air assets in cases of missions related to homeland security or natural disasters.

Paramilitary Police Forces

Carabinieri. As was mentioned in the previous section, the fourth military service within the Ministry of Defense is the *Carabinieri.* They are fully recognized as an independent service and possess the full status of a police force as well as that of a military force. They report to the chief of staff for defense regarding their military duties and to the Ministry of the Interior in relation to their tasks in the areas of policing, public order, and public security. They also provide special units to the Ministry of Health, Ministry for the Environment, Ministry of Culture, Ministry for Social Policies, Ministry for Agriculture, and Ministry for Foreign Affairs to carry out compulsory regulatory activities related to the application of their ordinances.

The *Carabinieri*'s primary military duties are:

- homeland defense and homeland security, and safeguarding the nation's free institutions, the same as all the other armed forces

- military police and security tasks for all the other armed services

- judicial military police tasks for the military justice system

- providing security for Italian embassies and military attachés' offices.

Their police duties are all those that are foreseen for the state police.

The total strength of the *Carabinieri* is about 120,000. Their organization partially reflects the structure of the army (same ranks, same disciplinary code, same denomination of units, and also a similar command structure). The operational structure is adapted to the accomplishment of their distinctive tasks, having a territorial organization that covers the entire territory of the nation through the capillary presence of their 5,000 stations (*Carabinieri* stations are located everywhere, in rural areas and small villages as well as in all cities). They also have a mobile component of about 20 territorial battalions distributed in all regions, which serve as a strategic reserve. In addition, the *Carabinieri* also have a mobile brigade that includes one parachute regiment, two infantry-like battalions, and a special forces unit. This brigade provides the Italian component for the MSUs (military specialized units) deployed in peacekeeping missions and can also be assigned to provide security for special events and support to law enforcement missions. The special forces component is trained to carry out special weapons and tactics tasks, to protect special targets, to free hostages, and to intervene in cases of aircraft hijacking, ships, and so on.

In case of the implementation of specific homeland security measures, the territorial battalions and the mobile brigade are the first line of reinforcement in manpower and capabilities that may possibly fill gaps that the state police forces are not able to fill. In cases of emergencies due to natural disasters, the 5,000 *Carabinieri* stations distributed throughout the nation are part of the warning and alert system and provide an immediate response within their limited capabilities until the national civil protection organizations take over and other forces begin to carry out assistance and rescue operations. Again, the territorial battalions and the mobile brigade are also immediately available to the National Civil Protection Service, if required.

Guardia di Finanza. The *Guardia di Finanza* is a militarized corps, but they report directly to the minister of finance. They possess the fully recognized status of a police force and of the customs police, which they exercise in four areas: financial and tax, customs, judicial, and security.

The last area is of particular relevance to homeland security because the *Guardia di Finanza* has the responsibility to guard the external borders of the country, to contribute to maintaining public order, and to carry out law enforcement activities (together with the state police and the *Carabinieri*), and to counter terrorism and clandestine immigration. After the introduction of the Schengen Accords, according to which citizens enjoy freedom of movement within the European Union (EU), the *Guardia's* attention was partially shifted from the traditional tasks of securing the nation's borders (all Italy's neighbors belong to the EU) to securing Italy's maritime borders.

The total strength of the *Guardia di Finanza* is about 80,000 men. The commander of the *Guardia di Finanza* is always a three-star army general. The organization partially reflects the organization of the army (same ranks, same disciplinary code, same denomination of units, and also a similar command structure). Their operational structure is adapted to the accomplishment of their tasks, with interregional and regional headquarters and a headquarters for special units, which is also responsible for managing the air and maritime components. This last element is particularly significant, consisting of 6 patrol boats, 84 coastal vessels, 74 speed boats, 115 very high-speed boats, and 194 minor boats that operate under the auspices of the navy. The *Guardia di Finanza* has also a large canine unit, with more than 350 teams capable of searching for drugs and explosives.

They contribute to homeland security according to the capabilities described above, and they are particularly concerned with those measures that have been decided on at the international level to combat terrorism, which require inspections of all freight entering the country across both land and maritime borders and on all ships entering Italian ports or cross-ing territorial waters. They also contribute to assistance and rescue efforts in cases of emergencies due to natural disasters.

National Response Plans and Programs

During the Cold War, emphasis was placed on those response plans concerning a full-scale war situation, where all resources needed to be coor-dinated to provide maximum support to the armed forces. In more recent years, on the other hand, international terrorism has emerged as the main threat to the states of Western Europe, a threat that falls under the respon-sibility of the Ministry of the Interior. The Ministry of the Interior is then responsible for facing all possible domestic contingencies, with the support of the Ministry of Defense and the other ministries, each with its own par-ticular capabilities and responsibilities. The overall coordination is always in the hands of the government, within the Ministers' Council, which can activate the Military-Political Nucleus if the circumstances are considered extraordinary. In an emergency or temporary situation, the responsibility remains at the level of the Ministry of the Interior, both in terms of coor-dination and the general planning for such circumstances. There are three areas where specific planning is carried out, with different forms of involve-ment of the military:

- The first concerns homeland security as such. The Ministry of the Interior, with the cooperation of all the other ministries, has compiled a list of sensitive targets that could be subject to terror-ist attack. The list is the basis for the deployment of the military in support of the police forces and *Carabinieri* units on protection missions. The list is regularly updated at the provincial level, under the supervision of the local prefect; then a national list is elaborated.

- The second area concerns cases of CBRN attacks.

- The third area is planning for cases of natural disasters. For such cases, a general plan exists, which is the responsibility of the National Service for Civil Protection. Within this plan, the military has ensured different levels of possible support according to the gravity of the situation. To this end, they have elaborated some basic planning outlines, which include the subdivision of the national territory into areas of responsibility under the various operational commanders, the designation of the commanders of every area of responsibility, and the identification of the necessary forces for the first phase of the emergency response. For the second phase of the emergency, which involves a more structured intervention, the elaborated planning lines provide security, logistic support, and medical assistance. There are also two specific plans concerning two areas in which disasters could be expected. The first one is an evacuation plan for the population living around the Vesuvius volcano, which seismologists believe could erupt in the near future, with serious consequences in the area. The other plan concerns the Messina Strait, which is an area where earthquakes or the Etna volcano could cause a major disaster.

Protection of Critical Infrastructure

In cases of a terrorist threat, the military plays a specific role providing support to police forces for the protection of critical infrastructure elements that have been identified in the list of sensitive targets. The list includes all kinds of possible targets, such as agriculture and food systems, water networks, energy grids, telecommunication sites, information technology systems, banking and finance networks, and chemical and hazardous materials industries. Other institutional sites that are included are governmental sites, prefectures, embassies and consulates, and political party offices.

This protection is normally carried out by army units and is based on mobile patrolling and permanent guards. The army general staff has recently issued a new publication with detailed instructions on how to carry out this security task. This manual indicates:

- The general elements of the juridical norms to be observed in the execution of this mission. In most cases, the soldiers deployed are granted the special status of police agents, which allows them to carry out basic police activities, like stopping, identifying, and searching persons and cars.

- The procedures to be applied at the company (or equivalent) level for the (material) execution of the mission.

- Other instructions detail the level of force protection to be acquired for the security of the personnel carrying out the mission.

Special attention is given to the rules of engagement, due to the fact that these activities are performed in the domestic, friendly civilian environment.

Military personnel of all levels have been trained to balance requisite firmness with the need not to provoke resentments among civilians and to stimulate consensus and participation. In more backward and underdeveloped areas of the country, the presence of young soldiers—well trained, disciplined, efficient, smart, and, most important, devoted to their country—has been a welcome surprise for a number of citizens, with a positive effect on the success of the mission. Surveys that are regularly carried out to test the reaction of local and national public opinion have normally shown that these activities are well received by the absolute majority of the population.

These operations to secure Italy's domestic territory, when they are carried out according to military techniques, also represent an exceptional form of deployment for military units, which are basically trained to accomplish missions that are substantially different in nature. The army did not foresee to form any specialized unit in the area of such missions, although the frequency of these engagements, the large requirement of troops, and the need to rotate the soldiers have raised the decision to train artillery, engineer, armored, and logistic units as light infantry units as well. The light infantry training for these units has been limited to weapons handling, area interdiction techniques, setting up of roadblocks, protecting sensitive targets, and handling suspected individuals. Furthermore, each unit that has been identified for deployment on such missions undergoes a period of specific training before deployment. In the area of equipment, new acquisitions have been made, such as light body armor, shields, combat batons, material for roadblocks, special helmets, and so forth. The long experience gained in accomplishing this task has been entirely positive for army units, and it has been found that, with an appropriate rotation of personnel, it does not negatively impact on other priority missions.

Border and Transportation Security

Border Security Support

As has already been mentioned, the Italian army has been assigned on a number of occasions to contribute to border security. This has always happened on a temporary basis, and under particular circumstances, since border security is the primary task of the *Guardia di Finanza*. Only when clandestine immigration requires intense vigilance over certain segments of the nation's borders will the army—stronger in manpower than any other force—be called in, covering the critical areas around the clock. Due to their specific preparation, the army units have been successful and have in fact become so good at such missions that it has always been difficult to disengage. The activity is carried out following the principles described above. Soldiers are either granted the status of public security agents, which allows them to execute police essential duties, or each patrol or section includes one or two *Carabinieri* or police officers. The modalities can vary, but they are usually based upon techniques adopted by military forces engaged in battlefield interdiction or territorial control.

Air and Maritime Security

Air security is ensured by the air forces according to the criteria described in previous sections, both as part of the routine air defense system and in the exceptional case of a terrorist threat. The other military services can contribute on an occasional basis with assets that are present in certain areas but that are not included in the security organization itself. The maritime borders, which are under the responsibility of the *Guardia di Finanza* and the coast guard, do not normally require much support from the military proper, but the navy has also sometimes been asked to contribute, eventually placing one or more light ships in critical areas.

Interdiction of Illegal Immigrants and Materials

The case of illegal immigrant and material interdiction falls under the scheme for the prevention of clandestine immigration. However, this activity is mainly carried out in airports and seaports and is conducted by the *Guardia di Finanza* and by the state police forces. In particular, the *Guardia di Finanza* is engaged in the two projects mentioned above that are sponsored by the U.S. Government. The first one is the Container Security Initiative, which is targeted at preventing the traffic in materials usable for terrorist actions or to build weapons of mass destruction. It implies the intensification of controls over freight moving between ports of the European Union and the United States. In Italy, such measures already cover the ports of Genoa, La Spezia, Gioia Tauro, Livorno, and soon also Naples. A similar project is the Proliferation Security Initiative, aimed at interdicting the transfer—by air or sea—of weapons of mass destruction, missiles, and related technologies.

Highway Security

Only a special department of the state police, the *Polizia Stradale*, usually carries out the task of policing Italy's major roadways. It regularly patrols all highways by car and motorbike, as well as monitoring them by helicopter. When the temporary reinforcement of security measures is required, then the military can be assigned—following the established procedures—to contribute to the security of the more critical installations, such as bridges, tunnels, and flyovers. This job can be accomplished either through permanent guards or by patrolling. They will report to both the police operations room and their normal chain of command.

Rail Security

In most of the described cases of the deployment of military forces in support of the Ministry of the Interior for law enforcement purposes, the security of railways and rail stations is included. Differing from the case of highways, the Rail Police carries out its duty only on board of trains and convoys and in the main railway stations. The military reinforcement is then asked to provide security along the lines and to the main installations, such as bridges, tunnels, and power stations. As far as rail stations are concerned, the military can augment the security provided there through patrols and inspections inside and around the facilities.

Defense and Response to Catastrophic Threats

The primary responsibility to respond to a catastrophic threat falls on the National Civil Protection Service, even if there is some overlapping of responsibility with the Ministry of the Interior. The Civil Protection Service is also responsible for coordinating the appropriate response to major attacks, including CBRN attacks. The planning for such emergencies, along with responsibility for consequence management, is carried out by a special operational group that is part of the Civil Protection Service. The military is not initially involved. All the activities set up to face the emergency are carried out by fire brigades and the police. The warning of the attack will normally come through the police or *Carabinieri* operations rooms. The first step is to identify the concerned area. This is a task assigned to special fire brigade units. They are present at the provincial level and carry out the initial reconnaissance of the area, using special equipment, including protective clothing, mobile laboratories, and decontamination kits. A security cordon manned by police officers closes off the area. Outside the area, decontamination centers are organized, and an evacuation plan dealing with the extraction of the inhabitants from the affected area is immediately implemented. The military does not play a particular role, but within the framework of their participation in activities carried out by the National Civil Protection Service, they can be asked to provide support with their CBRN battalions and their medical and logistic units. If the emergency also requires the military to contribute to the law enforcement function, their intervention will be requested following established procedures.

Civil Support

The military can provide other forms of support to the civil government, in a variety of domestic contingencies. This includes the activities that would be foreseen in cases of:

- military assistance to the civil authority, such as disaster relief, fire-fighting, and essential services

- military support to law enforcement, such as training support, intelligence, explosive ordnance disposal, and drug interdiction

- military assistance in civil disturbances, including riots and insurrections

- support for providing security for national special security events, including elections, conventions, and athletic events.

In the cases described above, the military would provide support according to the procedures approved by the national regulations. No exclusions of the military from any possible areas of intervention for civil support are stated in principle.

Conclusion

In all democratic countries, the responsibility for homeland security is a function carried out by civil authorities. Ensuring law and order is a responsibility carried out by police forces, which are expressly dedicated to the accomplishment of this delicate function, one which requires particular instruments, special training, and adequate procedures. The same applies in cases of natural disasters or consequence management. When such events occur in Italy, the National Civil Protection Service takes responsibility.

In extraordinary situations, in emergency cases, and other unexpected events, on the other hand, the armed forces can be asked to provide support to the civil authorities, and their military capabilities can be easily exploited to fill gaps in a very wide range of activities in support of those civilian organizations which are primarily responsible for accomplishing their institutional tasks in those areas. Nevertheless, the contribution of the armed forces must always be envisioned as a temporary one.

In Italy, the armed forces have a long tradition of cooperation with civil institutions, and the existing laws are well established to allow a most productive interaction between all the available forces, above all the military. Their capability to contribute to the solution of problems linked to extraordinary or emergency cases is well proven and will continue to be even more valuable in the foreseeable future.

Chapter 6

A Neutral's Perspective: The Role of the Austrian Armed Forces in Homeland Security

Johann Frank

The Austrian Armed Forces (AAF) have historically played a significant role in accomplishing security tasks in the domestic sphere. These tasks, extending beyond territorial defense, form an integral part of the constitutionally defined spectrum of possible military missions, and extend back to the times of the Austro-Hungarian monarchy. These tasks are categorized as law enforcement assistance and disaster relief operations. According to Austrian legal regulations, military activities within the national territory in principle require that "the lawful civil power request its [the military's] co-operation."[1]

On the basis of such a request, however, a relatively wide range of military action is possible. The Security and Defense Doctrine adopted in December 2001 provides the political and strategic guidelines for adapting Austria's security policy to the challenges of the post–Cold War era. It includes plans to further develop and adapt the Cold War–driven concept of Comprehensive National Defense to the new risks and challenges posed by a multipolar security environment. A concrete operational model based on this doctrine, including a new definition of the tasks for the AAF in the framework of a modern homeland security strategy, does not yet exist. Simultaneously, due to the change of paradigms, Austrian security-political priorities have changed from reactive defense to proactive and multinational stabilization. This functional priority placed on external tasks requires a clear concentration of resources, which causes problems for homeland security tasks due to the low level of defense expenditures. The reorganization of the national security sector will therefore have to include a reassessment of the financing of national security tasks. While the international profile of the AAF is becoming clearer, the process of defining the military role domestically has been initiated only recently. It is quite obvious that the national policy of deployment of the AAF must be embedded in a comprehensive national concept, and should take into consideration all relevant developments at the regional level (namely, the European Union [EU]). However, due to its capabilities and special expertise, the AAF is able to make valuable contributions to cope with the new domestic security risks. The qualitative improvements of the transformed AAF (*Bundesheer 2010*) will lead to further enhanced military capabilities, especially concerning readiness, command and communication, and defense against nuclear, biological, and chemical attacks.

Domestic Employment of the Armed Forces

Historical and Conceptual Developments

The Austrian Armed Forces have three constitutionally defined tasks: ensuring national defense, rendering law enforcement assistance, and conducting disaster relief operations following catastrophes of extraordinary magnitude. The way in which national defense is realized is also constitutionally defined, and is referred to as Comprehensive National Defense (CND), which was adopted in 1975 under article 9a B-VG of the Federal Constitutional Act. As stipulated, CND must guarantee national sovereignty, the inviolability and unity of the federal territory, as well as "in particular maintain and protect [Austria's] everlasting neutrality." CND includes military, psychological, civil, and economic national defense. It is, in essence, a comprehensive defense concept following the examples of Sweden and Switzerland.[2] The embodiment of the CND approach is the Defense Doctrine,[3] which was adopted by all parliamentary factions on June 10, 1975, and defines in more detail the various elements of CND as well as contains a mandate to develop a National Defense Plan. The National Defense Plan, which was adopted on June 19, 1984, represents the first articulated overall concept for Austria's security with regard to all internal and external threats.[4] The fact that nonmilitary threats and risks form an integral part of Austria's security concept lent CND a very modern appearance at the time of its drafting. The individual CND areas—military, mental, civil, and economic national defense—are coordinated by the Federal Chancellery, and the respective security goals for each area are defined on the basis of a comprehensive threat scenario.[5]

Fundamental differences among the political parties regarding security issues, which ultimately manifested themselves in diverging assessments of neutrality and the North Atlantic Treaty Organization (NATO), prevented the adaptation of CND and the National Defense Plan to the new geopolitical and security environment of the 1990s. CND and the National Defense Plan are, therefore, still valid relating to legal form and, with regard to their civil dimension,[6] also binding in point of content.

Only the area of military national defense was adapted to the geostrategic situation and given new dimensions, in several steps of structural adaptations. In the course of shifting the priorities of Austria's security policy from reactive comprehensive defense to proactive and multinational environment stabilization, the defense task of the AAF gradually changed from territorial defense (under which rubric the military was intended to field a 300,000-strong force after mobilization), to a flexible, border-oriented protection and defense structure (the force organization in 1998 stood at 110,000 soldiers) to the "militarily domination of its own territory and guarantee of national sovereignty" in 2004, which still needs to be defined in more detail.[7] Planned contributions to international crisis management are increasingly becoming an integral part of the concept of Extended National Defense. However, the tasks of providing disaster relief and law enforcement assistance have remained unchanged and can, in fact, be traced back to the times of the Austro-Hungarian monarchy. The traditionally broad spectrum of domestic military assistance tasks is not least due to the fact that Austria does not have any civil defense forces or paramilitary units.

The new Security and Defense Doctrine (SDD), which was passed by Parliament on December 12, 2001, represents a significant step toward the further development of Austria's security policy.[8] The SDD includes plans to further develop CND into a concept of Comprehensive Security Precaution (CSP),[9] which foresees the Europeanization of the AAF with regard to the international spectrum of military tasks and, at the national level, recommends the development of a concept for a grand strategy and substrategies for dealing with the new range of security risks and threats. However, due to early elections on the one hand, and the appointment of the Austrian Armed Forces Reform Commission (AAFRC) on the other, the original timetable for developing these new strategies in the areas of foreign policy, defense policy, internal security, economic policy, agriculture, transport, infrastructure, finance, education, and information by the end of 2002 could not be met. Their finalization was envisaged for the second half of 2005. While the CND was organized on a purely national level, and mainly oriented itself on a passive threat-reaction concept, the CSP orients itself conceptually on the principles of prevention and European solidarity. However, what remains unchanged is the underlying principle of comprehensive security. According to Austrian constitutional regulations, the final responsibility for the aforementioned substrategies remains with the individual ministries, while the Federal Chancellery has a coordinating role only. One of the key challenges will be to ensure interministerial cooperation in a national as well as an international context.

In Austria, homeland security tasks are, therefore, still subsumed under the rubric of the applicable aspects of CND's civil national defense on the one hand; on the other hand, the adoption of the substrategies, which was expected in 2005, will assign several updated responsibilities for homeland security to various ministries. However, due to the absence of political regulations, as well as the principle of economic efficiency and the limited perception of international terrorism as a threat, the development of a comprehensive, interministerial homeland security strategy would seem only to be possible in the course of a first CSP review process. Until then, homeland security on the national level will remain conceptually underdeveloped, and will only in specific cases—and therefore insufficiently—be coordinated between the ministries.[10]

Security and Defense Doctrine, Grand Strategy, and Substrategies

The new Security and Defense Doctrine is a political-strategic conceptual guideline for adapting Austria's security policy to the new international security environment, which has not yet been realized to a large extent.[11] The emphasis and the direction of the discussion focused on the definition of Austria's future international profile and military commitment. The issue of homeland security did not receive adequate attention, however, and was addressed only in parts after the events of September 11. Despite a number of promising starting points, such as the installation of a National Security Council and the recommendation to develop comprehensive substrategies for all areas relevant in some way to security issues, there is to date no clear political direction as to how homeland security challenges are to be dealt with on the national level. Thus, the mission for the AAF with respect to their domestic tasks remains in place for the entire new threat spectrum, without being embedded into an overall national homeland security concept or defined priority requirements. In addition to "guaranteeing a military defense capability of operational, enforcement-capable strength" and "developing the capacity to participate in a common [European] defense," the SDD, in very general terms, recommends that any future defense policy "ensure assistance operation capacities, in order to provide disaster relief, support the Federal Ministry of the Interior in case of terrorist threats, control the borders, and protect sensitive infrastructure."[12]

In the course of the AAFRC's work, the future tasks of the AAF were redefined and received new emphasis. In the final report, the national and international tasks are presented as two equivalent pillars. However, a functional prioritization of the international tasks is derived from the fact that international requirements are to determine the future structure and capabilities of the AAF. The new organization of the Austrian military is to be implemented by 2010. With it, Austrian defense policy will undergo a paradigm shift, de facto attributing a secondary status to the domestic tasks of the AAF. The main reason for this development is to be found in the nation's limited financial resources. With defense spending of approximately 0.8 percent of the gross domestic product, international operations of the scope intended (at the brigade level or equivalent) can only be managed if Austria's military resources are clearly concentrated. Domestic tasks, therefore, also have to be covered under the international capability and capacity profile. Moreover, such tasks will either increasingly have to be taken over by other institutions, or require supplementary funding.

The shift of focus originates from a risk and threat assessment that operates on the premise that wars between Western European nations can be ruled out for the foreseeable future, and that threats to Austria's security can be expected only in the case of failed international stabilization measures. No strategic importance is attributed to the threat of international terrorism. Terrorism is considered to be a subconventional risk[13] and implicitly, therefore, primarily a police task. With this position, Austria's security and defense policy is following a Europe-wide trend of considering as politically relevant only those risks that can be managed fairly well with the resources at hand. The role of the AAF in fighting terrorism is seen as being rather restricted in Austria, limited to consequence management measures and clearly defined assistance operations.

Nevertheless, the domestic responsibilities of the AAF, as set forth in the relevant government documents, add up to a very broad spectrum of tasks. The issue of homeland security is mentioned in several passages of the final report of the AAFRC. In connection with the threat and risk analysis, it states:

> The Reform Commission recommends attributing an important role to the Austrian Armed Forces, within the framework of providing assistance in police security operations as well as within the framework of national crisis management, in protecting vital civil information and communication technology infrastructure or having backup systems in place, respectively, in the event of disaster or threat.

> The Commission further recommends [...] keeping sufficient forces available that can be deployed simultaneously with the contingents deployed abroad, for assistance operations at home, in case of natural or man-made disasters or a terrorist attack as well as for assistance operations in support of the law enforcement agencies.[14]

With respect to the future force organization and the needed operational capabilities, the report states: "The Commission recommends [...] to provide ready forces for tasks at home of 10,000 personnel within the frame of the operational organization/troops. If need be, as for instance in assistance operations, these forces are to be reinforced by call-ups, activating the conscript postponement clause, and particularly by committing militia forces."[15]

The substrategy document entitled "Defense Policy" (not yet adopted)[16] defines homeland security–related tasks as follows:

- contribute to maintaining full sovereignty of the nation's territory and air space, as well as to protect the Austrian population and strategically important infrastructure

- aid in law enforcement assistance operations that, particularly with regard to nationwide tasks, rely on an increased use of technology. Adequate capabilities to provide assistance are to be further developed in the new risk areas, such as terrorism, proliferation, and organized crime as well as information, communication, and technology security, including the necessary intelligence capabilities. This also includes the capabilities to protect constitutionally established institutions, the democratic rights of the population, and maintain order and security in general.

- develop the ability to cooperate with civil communication systems and support them in maintaining national communication on the basis of an independent information and communication technology component
- provide assistance in the wake of natural or manmade disasters in Austria
- conduct special operations at home.

Legal Authority for Deployment

This section deals with the current legislation governing domestic operations by the Austrian military. Article 79 B-VG of the Federal Constitutional Act enumerates all the tasks of the AAF. These are:

- military national defense (paragraph 1)
- assistance in law enforcement (paragraph 2)
- tasks of disaster relief (paragraph 2).

The general legal interpretation works on the premise that military national defense is to be considered the "primary and original core task" of the Austrian Armed Forces.[17] Due to the changes in the geostrategic environment in recent years, international AAF operations—as long as they do not cover tasks of international humanitarian assistance or disaster relief explicitly—are also seen as being part of Extended National Defense. In the event of a military national defense operation or a military-led domestic security operation (see below), special competencies and command and control responsibilities as well as rules of engagement and legal regulations apply. The structure of the Austrian military and its capability profile are derived from its original core task. How relevant a possible primary AAF national task competence would be to the military's structure would have to be decided on the political level and assessed against the background of a concrete situation, as well as in light of nationally available resources.

Law Enforcement Assistance

The tasks summarized under the term *law enforcement assistance* are outlined in the Federal Constitution as follows:

The AAF, insofar as the lawful civil power requires its cooperation, has furthermore:

1. Also above and beyond the sphere of the country's military defense:

   a. To protect the constitutionally established institutions as well as their capacity to operate and the population's democratic freedoms;

   b. To maintain order and security inside the country in general (Article 79, para 2 B-VG, Federal Constitutional Act).

Law enforcement assistance, therefore, serves two protective purposes: the protection of constitutionally established institutions, and the maintenance of order and security. A constitutionally acceptable request occurs when assistance is requested to provide immediate protection for:

- administrative bodies directly established by the Federal Constitution or recognized as such on the federal or provincial level of execution

- the highest organs of jurisdiction

- proponents of sovereign power, such as authorities on the federal, provincial, and community level.

Whether the phrase "to protect the democratic freedoms of the population"—which was added at a later date (1975)—also includes the protection of the basic constitutional principles[18] or only covers institutionalized organizational structures is a matter of some controversy.[19]

The second form of assistance refers to "the maintenance of order and security inside the country in general." This used to be an independent military task under the defense legislation of the Austrian part of the Austro-Hungarian monarchy and, therefore, could be carried out even without being requested by civil authorities. However, with the defense legislation stipulated in the Constitution of the First Republic (1919–1920), this changed, and military support for law enforcement operations has to be requested by civil authorities. According to current legal understanding, the tasks of maintaining public order and security include all measures aimed at countering general threats to objects of legal protection, which by their character cannot be limited to a specific administrative area (as is the case, for instance, with the inspectorates for fire safety, industrial regulations, or construction regulations). Derived from the wording "in general," the assistance purposes were extended to include subsidiary interventions within the framework of police-administrative tasks to thwart domestic threats. All in all, however, AAF law enforcement operations primarily serve to maintain public order and security as well as provide initial general assistance within the framework of countering threats to objects of legal protection. In addition, assistance operations to counter imminent threats in the field of security administration are possible as well. These would include measures in the areas of passport control and immigration, alien registration, surveillance of border crossings into and out of the federal territory, the entire field of weapons, munitions, ammunitions, and explosives, as well as monitoring the press and matters concerning the foundation of associations and gatherings, insofar as such measures do not merely serve to execute administrative procedures but rather are necessary to counter imminent danger.[20]

Independent military intervention for the aforementioned purposes is permitted without request in the event that either the responsible authorities and bodies are prevented from acting by force majeure, and the danger of irreparable damage is imminent; in the event of a violent attack; or in the event of violent resistance against AAF units. This constitutionally granted authorization may be regarded as kind of a state-of-emergency regulation.

The procedures of requesting and obtaining approval for military law enforcement assistance, which requires simple-majority legislative approval, are set forth in Section 2 of the 1990 Defense Act. The authorities and administrative bodies that are entitled to request military assistance in their respective areas of responsibility, provided they are unable to accomplish the tasks assigned to them without AAF assistance, include authorities and bodies on the federal, provincial, and community level. This accounts for a very broad legal framework for AAF law enforcement assistance operations. Organizations and authorities that are entitled to request AAF assistance within their respective areas of responsibility include:

- law enforcement bodies—the Ministry of the Interior, provincial security directorates, district administration authorities, the federal police directorates, mayors, and other community entities

- criminal courts, state attorneys, and criminal and administrative law enforcement authorities, in order to protect their activities or maintain the necessary order for carrying out their tasks.

Should an AAF assistance operation require more than 100 soldiers, a directive is needed from the federal government. In cases of imminent danger, the Minister of the Interior (in accordance with the Minister of

Defense) can make such a decision, followed by an immediate report to the federal government. An assistance request by civil authorities has to state the expected scope and duration of assistance to be provided.

The "100-men-clause" was introduced by a 1966 amendment to the Defense Act (Federal Law Gazette, No. 185/1966). Rejecting the request is justified if:

- the request is made by an unauthorized person/body

- complying with the assistance request would be in breach of penal code regulations

- the request evidently does not comply with the legal preconditions

- other urgent AAF domestic deployment does not permit compliance with the request.

Troop deployment for law enforcement assistance and the use of weapons are regulated under Section 33 of the General Service Regulations for the Austrian military. This paragraph applies to law enforcement assistance operations as well as disaster relief operations. It contains the principal obligation to carry out such operations as much as the capability and deployment modalities permit. The requesting authorities and bodies are expected to define the primary objectives of the assistance operation, while the order to carry out such an operation and the issuance of actual orders are exclusively the responsibility of the military commanders, who have to seek agreement with the civil authorities. In urgent cases, independent or requested authorization of assistance troops below the 100-man limit is the responsibility of the garrison commanders, the provincial military commands within their area of responsibility, and the Land Force Command, particularly if the units to be deployed are located in more than one command area, or if the operation extends over more than one federal province. In cases of imminent danger, the decision (immediately followed by a report) is made by the highest-ranking commander, the garrison's duty officer, or the unit's duty officer.

In assistance operations, soldiers act on behalf of the respective civil authority and thereby assume the legal status of the respective civil body. For the duration of the assistance operation, the soldiers assigned have the same competencies as the originally responsible administrative organization. These may, however, be modified in specific cases by the respective federal or provincial legislator.

The use of weapons by assistance troops is only permitted with the explicit consent of the requesting authority, and only after the respective commander has been heard. This restriction on the use of weapons is only suspended in the event of a direct attack against the troops, or in cases of imminent danger. Though the duration of an assistance operation is not specified, unlimited use of military assistance would contradict the principle that every administrative unit should have to carry out its responsibilities by itself.[21]

Personnel and material costs (such as the costs of military material used, or accommodation and food) are charged to the AAF. Only the procurement expenses for equipment assets exclusively serving the specific purpose of the assistance operation are to be covered by the requesting civil authority.

The Relationship between National Defense and Law Enforcement Assistance

Aside from national defense, the Austrian military may also be asked to assume primary responsibility for certain domestic tasks. The question of distributing responsibilities between the civil authorities and the Ministry of Defense is technically regulated, insofar as the core task of the AAF is the defense of Austria against dangers from outside. Countering domestic dangers is the primary task of the civilian legal powers. In principle, the AAF only becomes active in these areas upon request from and subsidiary to the relevant authorities. The shift of the global security paradigm has, however, blurred the line between interior and exterior security, and has thereby led to a lasting change in the concept of military national defense. This, in turn, has again brought up the question of the distribution of competencies between the ministries responsible for security. Objectively, however, the situation in Austria presents itself as follows.

As long as there is no direct military threat from outside to objects of legal protection, the Austrian armed forces will only act in a subsidiary, assistance-providing function. The transition to the military assuming primary responsibility is made only if the constitutionally established institutions and their ability to act as well as the democratic freedoms of the population are threatened from outside, or if events at home that are linked to exterior threats need to be countered, and this can apparently only be done by military means. The solution of the distribution of responsibility is a political decision made by the federal chancellor.

Disaster Relief

Under Section 2, paragraph 1, sub-paragraph (c) of the Defense Act, the AAF can be employed in disaster relief operations—i.e., following natural or manmade disasters of extraordinary magnitude—if the legal civil power, being unable to cope with the situation with its own means, chooses to draw on them. This also includes taking the most urgent measures to restore administrative and economic activity. In the broadest sense, this may also include measures to restore critical infrastructure; it is immaterial whether the damage or destruction were caused by terrorism or natural catastrophes. Disaster relief assistance can also be provided during a military national defense operation (for example, assisting in an evacuation of the civilian population or securing/recovering cultural property).

Authorities on the federal, provincial, and community level—federal ministries, provincial governments, district authorities, and municipal counselors—are all entitled to request military assistance, but these civil authorities have to check if the preconditions for requesting assistance exist. Normally, the request is submitted to the garrison commander, the provincial military command, the Air Force Command, the Land Force Command, the Ministry of Defense, or directly to the minister. Independent military intervention, on the order of a military commander (regardless of the echelon), is only permissible if the civil authorities are prevented from requesting military assistance by force majeure and any further delay would cause irreparable damage to the nation.

An assistance request is to be rejected if it is made by an unauthorized body, if complying with it would be in breach of penal code regulations, if the request evidently does not match the purpose of the disaster relief operation, or if the troops are needed to carry out other tasks related to national defense. In case of doubt, the request for assistance has to be complied with, and the decision about whether to continue the operation or break it off has to be made by the superior command.

If assistance is provided upon request, the deployed units and soldiers are executive organs of the requesting authority. The commander contacts the requesting authority in order to get a sufficiently accurate picture of the situation and additional information about the type and scope of assistance to be provided in order to achieve the assistance objective defined by the requesting authority. The military commander plans the operation and issues the orders. The operation ends when the requesting authority or body calls for it.

In order to ensure the best chances for the success of an operation, adequately trained and equipped units are to be employed. Particularly suitable for such domestic efforts are engineering and nuclear, biological, and chemical (NBC) defense units for technical operations, as well as medical units. If there are not enough trained active personnel available, conscripts may be called up, according to Section 35, paragraph 3 of the Defense Act. As an alternative, the conscript postponement clause of the Defense Act (Section 39, paragraph 2) can be activated. For operations following avalanche catastrophes, special avalanche platoons are set up in the affected provinces. For NBC defense operations, each province has, in addition to the units' NBC defense capabilities, one NBC defense platoon; nationwide, there are an additional three NBC defense companies. The civil protection regulations also apply to the troops under deployment. Air units are used for saving human lives as well as for transport and reconnaissance tasks.

If units from different parts of the armed forces are deployed, a suitable commander has to be selected to lead the entire force that is engaged in the assistance effort. In cases of disasters of major scope and duration, the assistance troops are led directly by the provincial military command or the Land Force Command respectively, and the Joint Command and Control Staff/Ministry of Defense. For such an eventuality, ready disaster relief staffs are installed in these commands. Each of these consists of a commander and a staff of branch officers, tailored to the specific type of assistance operation. As a rule, the operational staff includes one engineer officer, one NBC defense officer, one technical officer, and one air operations coordinator. The tasks of those staffs include operational planning, issuance of orders, liaison to the civil authorities on the federal and/or provincial level (in particular to the federal and provincial alert centers, the police, and first responder organizations), coordination of military and civil assistance personnel, coordination of equipment and materiel, branch-specific guidance, operational control, and supply efforts.

The interpretation margin of the currently valid law seems to cover the broadest possible spectrum of AAF domestic tasks. From the legal point of view, there is no reason why the AAF could not be used for the protection/restoration of critical infrastructure, the fight against terrorism, or transport protection.

Use of Weapons within Air Defense

According to the *Militärbefugnisgesetz*, air defense and security duties reside under the responsibility of the Ministry of Defense. Beside interception operations by fighter planes, antiaircraft defense systems on the ground can be employed. The use of airborne weapons is regulated as follows. Fighter planes that are on patrol at the moment are led to the unidentified flying object via the air traffic control center. After hostile intentions (or the misuse of civilian planes for terrorist attacks) have been confirmed, the commander of the two-plane element informs the control center in Pongau about the registration mark of the aircraft in question. The radar-control officer informs the duty officer of the control center. This officer then reports to the responsible officer of the army aviation command, who then gives the order to shoot after he has received authorization from the minister of defense, or the chief of the defense staff if the minister is not available.

Historical Precedents

Before 1990, the Austrian Armed Forces had conducted 23 operations. This number increased between 1990 and 2001 to 63, with 13 of those occurring domestically. Except for the military operation at the border to the former Yugoslavia, the other 12 operations were within the spectrum of law enforcement assistance and disaster relief. The number of working hours expended in the aftermath of disasters grew from 37,000 hours in 1995 to more than 330,000 hours in 1999. This section will provide illustrations of one law enforcement operation and one disaster relief operation; at the close of the section, an assistance operation of the modern type will be presented.

Law Enforcement Assistance Operations

Since 1955, there have been two major law enforcement assistance operations in Austria in which the military has provided assistance: the South Tyrol Operation and the Burgenland Operation.

The first, conducted in 1967, was a border surveillance operation at the Italian border. It came in response to a continuous series of terrorist attacks in Italy that started in 1961. The fact that the offenders moved from Austria to Italy (or vice versa) before or after the attacks, or were supported by persons living in Austria, led to considerable bilateral tensions between Austria and Italy. The personnel resources of the security organizations in charge of regular border control were not sufficient to ensure complete border control coverage. Thus, on July 11, 1967, the federal government decided to conduct a law enforcement assistance operation with the aim of "reinforcing law enforcement authorities" as well as "preventing illegal traffic of passengers and goods from Austria to Italy and vice versa, in particular with the aim of preventing or clearing up terrorist attacks." The AAF troops involved—primarily infantry units—were subject to the directives of the Minister of the Interior. Stopping, searching, and arresting suspects, as well as the use of weapons, were explicitly regulated in a detailed directive issued by the Ministry of the Interior.

The law enforcement operation in Burgenland became necessary after the collapse of communism, when freedom in Eastern Europe led to a considerable increase in the number of illegal border crossings, which once again overstrained the law enforcement agencies. The AAF assistance operation, which was decided on September 4, 1990, was initially limited to 10 weeks, but has been regularly extended since then, generally for a year at a time. The continuation of this operation will not change until the accession of Austria's Eastern neighboring countries to the Schengen Agreement. The objective of the operation is to prevent illegal border crossings by means of border surveillance as best as possible. To date, more than 280,000 soldiers have served in this assistance operation, detaining and handing over more than 80,000 illegal border crossers to the civil authorities.[22]

Disaster Relief in Galtür

On February 23, 1999, an 800-meter-wide avalanche destroyed large parts of the Tyrolean village of Galtür, and 31 people died. The AAF was asked by the Tyrolean provincial government to provide assistance. The mission order included search and rescue, logistic support for villages isolated by the avalanche, and the evacuation of tourists.

As the national helicopter capacities were not sufficient, an additional 27 foreign helicopters (from the United States, Germany, Switzerland, and France) were used. Until the end of the mission, on March 13, 6 avalanche-mission platoons, 3 infantry companies, and 16 Austrian military helicopters were employed in order to rescue 22 people and transport 17,000 persons and 75 tons of supplies.

Post-9/11

After the first anthrax-contaminated letters surfaced in the United States mail, insecurity also spread within the Austrian population (as well as among the authorities), and led to the discovery of an increased number of "suspicious substances" in Austria's postal system. Due to the lack of national capacities to verify and, if possible, minimize damage, the Ministry of the Interior, on October 13, 2001, asked the AAF to "provide law enforcement assistance in order to ensure the necessary NBC-defense measures as part of the physical and medical protection of the population."[23] In addition to Austria's standing NBC defense forces, the alert status was raised for air units to provide specimen transport, for experts of the Armament and Defense Technology Agency's chemical labs for sample analysis, as well as for parts of the military medical service in order to ensure rapid medical treatment. The operational control was based on the principle of "on-site cooperation, with central steering."[24] Following arrangements with the Directorate General for Public Security and the Ministry of the Interior, all assistance requests received by the police were submitted directly to the Ministry of Defense's Operational Center, which issued orders for the respective operations. Operational control was in the hands of the respective provincial military commands. Between October 14, 2001, and December 9, 2002, the military was involved in a total of 414 operations related to the anthrax scare. With the exception of one, all samples taken turned out to be negative. One sample from the U.S. Embassy proved anthrax positive, which led to further extensive sample taking from 92 mailbags, as well as decontamination and disposal measures by NBC defense experts.[25]

Types and Capabilities of Forces

The Austrian military, with its present structure and capabilities, is the result of several internal reforms and adaptations to international developments. The most recent reform took place in 2002. At present, there are six large commands, nine territorial military commands, and three infantry and two mechanized brigades. In the wake of this most recent reform, the personnel strength after mobilization has been reduced from 110,000 to 55,000. The actual personnel framework of the AAF without mobilization includes 35,000 military personnel (conscripts and professional soldiers) and 9,500 civilian employees. There are no paramilitary or special civil defense forces in Austria. In the future force structure of the AAF, projected to be in place in 2010, a contingent of 10,000 soldiers for domestic operations is foreseen; in cases of emergency, reinforcement through mobilization is possible. Within his legal powers, the defense minister can mobilize up to 5,000 militia troops. Above that level, a decision by the government is required. Mandatory national service will be reduced from 8 to 6 months by January 2006. The tasks for the relevant commands, and the basic duties regarding homeland security, are outlined below.

The majority of the land forces are under control of the Command of the Army (*Kommando Landstreitkräfte*). The main task of the army is to hold, attack, observe, and protect areas and objects. In addition, the army command is also responsible for training the troops and providing assistance to civilian authorities domestically. The territorial military commands in particular are deployed in cooperation with the civilian authorities in their respective provinces. The Army Aviation Command (*Kommando Luftstreitkräfte*) controls and employs the majority of the aircraft of the AAF; its main task is controlling Austrian airspace and assisting in troop transport.

The current force structure of the AAF includes three infantry brigades, two mechanized brigades, two reconnaissance battalions, one antitank battalion, six artillery battalions, three engineer battalions, three antiaircraft battalions, three army aviation regiments, three NBC defense companies, and several combat service and combat service support elements. The number of territorial militia-type infantry battalions will be reduced by one-fourth in the coming years, from 36 to 27.

In cases of assistance operations, the organization of the engaged military forces follows a needs-driven approach, which means that composition of the forces and capabilities is adapted to the particular situation. Although the successful accomplishment of these missions can only be achieved through the close cooperation of all branches, specially trained and equipped forces—especially NBC defense and engineering units—are used more frequently than others.

The NBC defense system in the Austrian military includes all measures necessary in order to minimize threats in the case of the use of nuclear, biological, or chemical weapons, as well as after the release of hazardous material from civilian sources. NBC defense troops support civil authorities through detection operations, situational analysis, decontamination missions, and urban search and rescue operations (including fire fighting tasks and water purification). The NBC defense troops are currently organized into three companies, six territorial NBC defense platoons, and five platoons at the army airfields. The research, training, and competence center is the NBC defense school. Increasing the quality and quantity of Austria's NBC defense capabilities is one of the most likely results of the current reform process of the armed forces.

Besides combat support, one major mission of the engineer troops is disaster relief. The tasks for such scenarios include two elements: the rescue phase and the recovery phase. The first phase includes the rescue of people, animals, and goods, as well as the prevention of further damage. The recovery phase aims at the restoration of the functionality of private and public infrastructure. Therefore, Austria's engineering forces are kept at high readiness, and should be able to conduct three disaster relief operations simultaneously.

As the primary responsibility for internal security and disaster management rests with the civilian authorities, the capabilities of the AAF should be considered as being complementary to the civilian forces. After the gendarmerie and police have been pooled under a new authority, there will be about 28,000 policemen available in total. Austria does not have any special civil defense forces. The civilian force providers are the voluntary fire brigades, the Austrian Red Cross, the Worker's Good Samaritan Federation, the Johanniter Accident Assistance, the Maltese Fraternity, and the mountain rescue brigade. Theoretically, around 350,000 persons could be mobilized on a voluntary basis.

National Response Plans and Programs

National Crisis Management

The Austrian national crisis management strategy was established in the wake of the 1986 Chernobyl reactor catastrophe. In principle, it is designed for dealing with all extraordinary crises, dangers, and disaster scenarios. It is based on the following facilities and instruments: the coordination committee, two operational centers, the national and provincial warning and alert centers/services, the radiation early warning system (with 336 detection points nationwide), a central computing system,[26] as well as alert and operational plans (such as a radiation alert plan, a refugee frame plan, and medical plans). These national measures are supplemented by international information-sharing and disaster relief agreements, particularly within the framework of the European Union, as well as by exercises at home or within the framework of the EU and NATO/Partnership for Peace.

The technical equipment, and in particular its international network, is in urgent need of updating.[27] The SDD intends a reevaluation of the instruments of national crisis management. While detailed alert and operational plans for nuclear and conventional damage scenarios have been developed on the basis of the experiences from the Chernobyl incident, no framework plans for terror scenarios involving biological or chemical agents have been developed thus far. Within their own area of responsibility, the provinces, districts, and communities develop their own disaster control plans, danger catalogues, and case-related framework plans, and each administrative level has operational staff ready at short notice. Moreover, the provinces themselves operate information technology–based warning and alert systems. In order to ensure the unity of command and standardized communication between all first responder organizations in an operation, manuals as well as training and exercise concepts are being developed for some areas.

Military Operational Plans

Due to the provinces' authority in areas concerning disaster response, the provincial military commands play an important role. As an example for military operational planning, the case of the Province of Lower Austria will be used as an illustration.

The operational concept governing the provision of military assistance in cases of disasters is based on modules.[28] The military operational modules are: Command and Control/Command and Control Support, Engineering, Radioactive Contamination, Chemical Threats, Logistics, Medical Logistics, Special Use, Alpine Operations, Search and Rescue, and Special Alert. This tailor-made strategy has been designed not only to counter the existing threat scenario, but also to ease the consistent pressure of personnel reductions and permit the full use of capacities by means of a flexible response structure.

The Command and Control/Command and Control Support module includes:

- establishing the command and control capability of the disaster relief operational staff of the provincial military commands

- ensuring press and information services
- providing support for deployed assistance units with command and control personnel and assets
- ensuring communication with civil authorities
- providing support for civil authorities with command and control personnel and experts.

The Engineering module is responsible for:

- preventing or minimizing damage to property and infrastructure by supporting the construction of protective structures
- rescuing persons and animals
- preventing/minimizing environmental damage
- assisting in the reconstruction of necessary infrastructure.

The Radioactive Contamination module covers:

- conducting local and regional detection operations
- marking, closing off, and controlling radioactively contaminated areas and objects
- controlling critical facilities on a case-related basis (such as schools, hospitals, etc.)
- performing decontamination operations
- taking and transporting samples
- advising civilian decisionmaking staffs.

The Chemical Threats element encompasses:

- marking and closing off areas on a large scale
- assisting in evacuations from contaminated areas
- transporting samples
- performing decontamination operations
- providing support to minimize environmental damage.

The Logistics module includes:

- providing logistic support for assistance troops and civilian aid workers

- supporting civil authorities in providing emergency supplies for the affected population
- making military infrastructure available
- supporting the authorities in managing large numbers of refugees.

The Medical Logistic module specifically covers:

- providing medical support to deployed assistance troops
- forming disaster relief platoons from military medical facilities
- supporting civil authorities with cross-country and/or armored ambulances
- supporting authorities after the outbreak of epidemics
- reinforcing civil facilities with military medical personnel
- providing psychological care for deployed personnel, affected persons, and their families.

The module known as "Special Use" includes:

- deploying assistance companies with light engineer equipment
- deploying in personnel-intensive assistance operations
- securing evacuated and quarantined areas, as well as recovering material goods
- constructing emergency shelters.

The Alpine Operations module is responsible for:

- alpine operations in winter (avalanches) and in summer (search and rescue)
- reinforcement/relief of civilian aid workers in longer-lasting operations in Alpine terrain.

The Search and Rescue module carries out:

- search and rescue operations (conducted by the NBC defense corps and supported by the engineer corps) following moderate and heavy damage
- search and rescue operations in contaminated objects and areas (conducted by the NBC defense corps)
- removal of debris following search and rescue operations.

The Special Alert module consists of:

- assistance in developing civil alert plans

- preventive preparation of assistance troops for special danger situations at high readiness status.

Protection of Critical Infrastructure

The task of securing critical infrastructure has implicitly been part of the traditional responsibilities of the Austrian Armed Forces (within the framework of Military Support to Civilian Law Enforcement Agencies[29]), and was redefined in the new definition of the military's responsibilities.[30] This military support can be mobilized either in cases of an external threat—and will then be led in parallel with a military defense mission—or as an independent operation in cases of public disturbance.

As required by the documents outlining the plans for such efforts, the objects worth securing are classified into different levels of protection, according to national and regional significance. Only objects of maximum value, the breakdown or destruction of which would lead to an enduring and persistent impairment of public life, are subject to an unconditional obligation to secure. Objects of maximum value are:

- the national and federal assembly; regional assemblies; the federal government; the federal president and ministers; regional governments; and the High Court

- facilities of energy supply companies

- information and communication networks

- facilities for providing the population with vital goods (water, medical supplies)

- facilities for the maintenance of vital transportation infrastructure.

The actual classification is made according to the proposals of the Security Policy Directorates of the provinces, in agreement with the Ministry of the Interior and the Ministry of Defense. For every object requiring security, special "object security sheets" and emergency plans are drafted. The precise mission for the military forces carrying out object security missions will depend on the civilian authority demanding this security. It will certainly contain a threat analysis, an object security data sheet, and a mission statement.

The missions assigned by civil law enforcement agencies could, for instance, include the following operations and tasks: protection of objects (surveillance and control, including defense), border monitoring, protection of traffic infrastructure and transports, support of the police in the implementation of checkpoints on roads, support of the police in the management of demonstrations, and escorting missions, which are generally conducted by special forces.[31]

When conducting these missions, military forces basically have to obey the principles set out for the military task of "protection." This kind of mission can be invoked both in cases of a threat against the forces posed by asymmetric warfare in the context of a military operation, and in cases of defense against attacks by irregular forces—that is, military support to civilian law enforcement agencies in the fight against terrorism. All these military actions have to occur on the condition that public life will continue to follow peacetime principles. In cases of an area (as opposed to object) security operation, a brigade can secure an area of around 1,200 square kilometers (km), guard 40 objects requiring protection, defend 15 facilities, or protect 45 to 60 km of state borders. The main actors in this force-intensive type of mission are infantry combat forces, reconnaissance forces, and special operations forces. Pioneer forces are primarily used for hardening the infrastructure. NBC protection forces are kept in a state of readiness for consequence management and search and rescue operations. The range of tasks carried out by a single soldier can include identity checks; checks, searches,[32] and arrest of persons; roadblock construction; stopping and checking vehicles; and escort duties.

In cases where the military is providing support to civilian law enforcement agencies, the soldiers have in principle the same powers as the civilian authorities. However, the soldiers' actual responsibilities should be defined precisely in the administrative directive. If the soldier accomplishes an eminently military task, such as a safeguard duty, the Military Powers Act (*Militärbefugnisgesetz*) applies. In any other cases, the Police Powers Act [33] (*Sicherheitspolizeigesetz*) is applicable to the members of the armed forces. The use of weapons in a military support mission is only authorized for purposes of legal self-defense (defined in §3 of the penal code), overpowering of unlawful resistance, forcing a lawful arrest, preventing the escape of an arrested person, or defending against a threat.

Border and Transportation Security

Border Security

The political liberalization in the former communist states of Eastern Europe led to a tremendous increase in illegal border crossing and, consequently, to a massive rise in the crime rate in regions that border these states. Following a 1990 decision by the federal government, the Austrian military has been assisting the civil authorities in controlling the nation's borders for about 14 years in order to prevent illegal immigration. Since 1990, the mission—which was originally limited to 10 weeks—has been extended 16 times, and the operation was expanded toward Austria's border with Hungary and the Czech Republic, as well as parts of the Slovakian border. Under the framework of separated assistance, the AAF has operated at the EU's Schengen border since October 1, 1997, using specially equipped helicopters.

In total, more than 280,000 soldiers have been deployed on such missions thus far. On average, about 2,200 soldiers are deployed at the borders, approximately one-fourth of which are professional soldiers who serve for about 6 weeks once a year. The majority of the personnel are conscripts from throughout Austria. In total, more than 80,000 illegal border crossers have been caught, and the preventive effect is calculated to be 80 percent. Despite the status of the neighboring countries as EU members, the mission will be continued until at least 2006. As the force is mainly made up of conscripts, all discussions about shortening the term of mandatory military service or implementing a professional army have a bearing on this operation. At present, a large number of illegal border-crossers are from Central Asia, Eastern Europe, and the Middle East, as well as a number from Africa and the Balkans. The main route that they follow goes through Slovakia. The irregular migrants are brought close to the border by human trafficking organizations. They then try to cross the border on foot in places where complete control of the border is difficult to exert, due to rough terrain. Once inside Austria, other smugglers pick up the majority of the immigrants, who are then taken into the country's interior.

The leading command for this operation is the territorial military command of Burgenland. It is the objective of the military command to work to curtail illegal immigration in close collaboration with the civil law enforcement forces. The deployed military forces are structured into two assistance contingents, Assistance Commands North and South, including nine companies in total. Both assistance commands control the federal border according to the objectives of the responsible political authorities (*Bezirkshauptmannschaften*). The primary geographical priority at present is the Slovakian border. In the conduct of the military operation, several important aspects are to be taken into consideration:

- fulfilling the tasks formulated by the regional-district authorities, in close cooperation with the civil law enforcement agencies

- avoiding border violations by Austrian soldiers through clear iden- tification of the borderline

- adapting to the permanently changing behavior of the illegal immi- grants through shifts between different modes of military operation

- preventing reconnaissance of the Austrian deployment profile through the constant change of patrolling elements

- picking up immigrants who have succeeded in crossing the border by rapid covering of prepared positions in "reception lines" in the rear echelon area of operation

- rapidly transferring apprehended individuals to the Austrian law enforcement authorities—never to foreign border guards.

During border service, soldiers carry their weapons in half-loaded status. The authority, powers, and duties of the soldiers are outlined in a special leaflet issued by the Ministry of the Interior. These include the right to stop, control, search, and arrest people, as well as to use weapons if nec- essary. The use of weapons is only permitted for self defense or emergency assistance. In case a suspect escapes from a unit's control, the platoon leader must immediately report to the next civil law enforcement office. When an unidentified person is stopped, the first procedure of the soldiers is to search for weapons, in order to ensure their own safety. Money and other objects of value must not be taken away. Then, if possible, the identity of the border-crosser has to be clarified in order to hand over the person to the relevant civilian authorities.

Based on practical experience, the practical preparation for this type of law enforcement operation consists of training beyond the standard mili- tary education. These standardized exercises include stopping of illegal bor- der-crossers, searching the terrain, handover of border-crossers, patrolling, and contact with large groups of infiltrated people.

Transportation Security

Some illustrative data may help demonstrate the complexity of transportation security: Austria's railway network includes around 10,700 km of track and 260 tunnels; the motorway system has over 2,000 km of road; 15 percent (350 km) of the Danube River is reserved for commercial use, heading toward 4 major harbors; Austria's airport infrastructure consist of 6 major airports and around 90 airfields.

The responsibility for transportation security is split up between several administrative bodies. Because of privatization, nonofficial actors are gaining increasing importance in terms of transport infrastructure. Besides the regular duties of airspace control, the AAF also assists the Special Forces in cases of emergencies or accidents that involve dangerous goods (especially nuclear, biological, or chemical elements). Securing critical transport infrastructure during peacetime is not explicitly excluded from the military's sphere of responsibilities, and in general is legally possible. In any case, any use of weapons may only be justified in situations of self-defense or emergency assistance.

The military police units are responsible for the supervision of military discipline and internal security, including military traffic control. They are not comparable with paramilitary forces like the Italian *Carabinieri*, because they are neither specially trained nor equipped for more demanding security tasks like riot control or the apprehension of war criminals.

Domestic Counterterrorism

The role of the Austrian military in terms of counterterrorism is based on constitutional preconditions, because all activities of the AAF need constitutional authorization. In principle, the main duty of the AAF is military national defense, which is focused on the defense of the nation from external threats. Defense against activities inside the country is possibly included here as well, if these activities are connected with threats from outside and an efficient response requires military measures and means. Examples of an internal threat being connected with an external actor can include an external group providing logistical support or operative guidance for groups engaged in political violence or international terrorist activities inside Austria, especially when they are organized on a large scale, weapons of mass destruction are involved, or air-supported operations are planned or conducted. Especially effective military forces for such operations are the Special Forces Command, NBC defense troops, as well as the military intelligence services.

The Special Forces are meant to cover those tasks that are not executed by conventional army elements. They are pooled together under the Special Forces Command. They include, among others, the so-called *Jagdkommando*, paratroopers, combat divers, bodyguards, and counterterrorism units. The Special Forces Command can also support civil authorities in the fight against terrorism. Parts of the command can therefore be used for special intelligence missions, arresting extra-violent persons, destroying weapons, ensuring personal security, securing critical infrastructure, fighting terrorists, and conducting hostage-rescue missions.

The two military secret services are the *Heeresnachrichtenamt* and the *Abwehramt*. The duties of the *Heeresnachrichtenamt* are set out in §20 Abs. 1 of the *Militärbefugnisgesetz*, and include acquiring, processing, analyzing, and presenting information on foreign countries or international organizations or other bilateral institutions that are relevant to any aspects or activities of the military. Although the *Heeresnachrichtenamt* mainly focuses on external developments, their analyses might result in valuable information concerning domestic counterterrorism. However, this aspect is primarily the responsibility of the *Bundesamt für Verfassungsschutz und Terrorismusbekämpfung* of the Ministry of the Interior.

According to § 20 Abs. 2 of the *Militärbefugnisgesetz*, the *Abwehramt* is responsible for military self-protection through acquiring, processing, analyzing, and presenting information on activities that might threaten the security of military institutions and operations. Due to its special knowledge and expertise, the *Abwehramt* can make a valuable contribution to the security of information and communication technology.

Other Civil Support Tasks

On the basis of the aforementioned legal authority and its existing capabilities, the Austrian armed forces might contribute to an even broader spectrum of domestic missions. Military assistance to explosive ordnance disposal (EOD) and drug interdiction efforts are conducted on a case-by-case basis. The most demanding EOD mission was destroying and decontaminating more than 100 mustard gas–filled artillery shells from the First World War in 1997–1998.

The military's canine unit includes around 250 dogs at the moment. They are used for securing military property at the highest security level (radar stations, airports, munitions storage, and closed areas) as well as for detecting drugs and explosives. However, the latter purpose has become increasingly challenging as a consequence of the increasing abuse of drugs and the rise in the number of terror alerts. These dogs are used by special units such as the *Jagdkommando* and the military police, as well as on missions abroad. Another important field of civil support in which the AAF is involved is providing training facilities and military experts for relevant civilian courses, especially in the field of disaster management and staff training for senior police officers.

Military support for national special security events has not been a significant factor in the past. But the forthcoming Austrian EU presidency in 2006 and Austria's hosting of the European Football Championship in 2008 have initiated a process of evaluation of the future role of the AAF in supporting such events.

Notes

[1] Federal Constitutional Act, Article 79, para. 2 B–VG.

[2] See Felix Ermarcora, *Österreichische Verfassungslehre* [Austrian Constitutional Law], vol. 2 (Vienna: Braumüller Verlag, 1980), 41ff.

[3] The "Defense Doctrine" is not a law, but rather a parliamentary recommendation to the federal government that honors and implements it as an "administrative maxim."

[4] See Hubert Kempf, "*15 Jahre umfassende Landesverteidigung im Bundeskanzleramt* [15 Years of Comprehensive National Defense in the Federal Chancellery]," *Austrian Military Journal* 2, no. 2 (1998), 98.

[5] *Psychological national defense* describes the population's information and motivation regarding CND; *economic national defense* means the prevention of economic disruptions and the maintenance of economic capabilities, while *civil national defense* includes the protection of the population and the ability of national institutions to function. *Military national defense* means border protection during conflicts in neighboring states, defense against military attacks, law enforcement operations, and disaster relief.

[6] *Civil national defense* encompasses measures of disaster relief, self-protection, warning and alert services, shelter construction, and medical provisions, as well as radiation protection. The responsibility for civil protection lies with the public authorities, civil and military organizations, as well as the citizens. The overall coordinating responsibility lies with the Federal Ministry of the Interior. Matters of disaster control are principally the responsibility of the provinces. Actual implementation of the laws is effected in the form of disaster control plans on the provincial, county, and community level. The federal government only takes responsibility under certain circumstances:

· extensive threats on the national or international level

· regional threats that bear the danger of escalating into an extensive threat and are of such great intensity that consequences of national scope may be expected

· insufficient manpower or material resources for disaster control in the affected area

· need of expertise and information not available to the responsible authorities on short notice

· creation of insecurity within the population.

[7] Friedrich Hessel, "*Strukturentwicklung des Bundesheeres von der 'Wende' 1989/90 bis zum Jahr 2003* [Structural development of the AAF between the 'turn' of 1989/90 and 2003]," *Schriftenreihe der Landesverteidigungsakademie* 6 (Vienna, 2004).

[8] Austrian Security and Defense Doctrine, General Considerations and Resolution by the Austrian Parliament (Vienna: Federal Chancellery, 2002); available at <www.bka.gv.at>.

[9] In the Austrian context, the term *homeland security* can best be interpreted as an equivalent of *Comprehensive Security Precaution.*

[10] Gustav Gustenau, *Sicherheitspolitische Aspekte der Homeland Security aus österreichischer Sicht* [Security-political aspects of Homeland security from the Austrian perspective], *Vernetzte Sicherheit*, Volume 3 (Hamburg: Mittler Verlag, 2004), 134–147.

[11] Gustav Gustenau, "*Ein Paradigmenwechsel in der österreichischen Außen- und Sicherheitspolitik? "Zur Ausarbeitung einer neuen Sicherheits- und Verteidigungsdoktrin* [A paradigmatic shift in Austria's foreign and security policy?—On the elaboration of a new security and defense doctrine]," in *Jahrbuch für internationale Sicherheitspolitik 2001* [*Yearbook for International Security Policy 2001*], ed. Erich Reiter (Hamburg: 2001), 955–964.

[12] Austrian Security and Defense Doctrine, General Considerations and Resolution by the Austrian Parliament (Vienna: Federal Chancellery, 2002); available at <www.bka.gv.at>.

[13] "*Teilstrategie Verteidigungspolitik*," *Entwurf* ["Sub-Strategy Security Policy," draft] (status as of January 2005).

[14] *Bericht der Bundesheerreformkommission—Bundesheer 2010* [Report of the Austrian Armed Forces Reform Commission—AAF 2010], 49–50.

[15] Ibid., 51–53.

[16] "*Teilstrategie Verteidigungspolitik*," Details on the military implementation and the required force structure are to be elaborated by 2005–2006 in the planning document "Management 2010."

[17] Karl Satzinger, "*Assistenzleistungen und Hilfeleistungen des Bundesheeres im Rahmen sicherheitspolizeilicher Aufgaben sowie ihre Rückwirkungen auf die militärische Organisation und Ausbildung* [Assistance and support operations of the AAF within the framework of law enforcement tasks and their implications for the military organization and training]," publication elaborated within the framework of the Higher Quartermaster and Legal Advisor Course (Vienna 1998), 1.

[18] The basic principles of the Austrian Constitution are the republican principle, the democratic principle, and the principle of law and order.

[19] See Satzinger, "*Assistenzleistungen und Hilfeleistungen*," 14.

[20] Ibid., 18.

[21] See Walter, *Österreichisches Bundesverfassungsrecht* [Austrian Federal Constitutional Law], 403.

[22] Source: <www.bundesheer.at/cms/artikel.php?ID=1101>.

[23] BMLV, *Operationsabteilung GZ. 67.200/028-5.7/02* (MoD/Operations Division, 2002).

[24] Norbert Fürstenhofer and Erwin Richter, "*Die Welt vor und nach dem 11. September 2001. Terror und Massenvernichtungswaffen* [The World Before and After 11 September 2001. Terrorism and Weapons of Mass Destruction]," in *Österreichische Militärische Zeitschrift 2/2002* (Vienna 2002), 175.

[25] See Hermann Lampalzer, "*ABC-Terrorismus—eine neue sicherheitspolitische Herausforderung. Beurteilung der Bedrohung und Reaktionskonzepte auf europäischer und österreichischer Ebene* [NBC-terrorism—A new security-political challenge. Threat assessment and response concepts on European and Austrian level]," MA thesis, University of Vienna (2003), 117–120.

[26] This computer backup system can, in case of a crash or other system failure, cover for one or more federal computing centers.

[27] Gustav Kaudel, *Staatliches Krisenmanagement in Österreich* [National Crisis Management in Austria] (Vienna: *Österreichische Gesellschaft für Landesverteidigung und Sicherheitspolitik* [Austrian Society for National Defense and Security Policy], April 1997), 22.

[28] Franz Schmidinger and Werner Suez, "*Militärkommando Niederösterreich: Das Katastrophe-neinsatzkonzept* [Provincial Military Command/Lower Austria: Disaster Relief Concept]," *Truppendienst,* no. 2 (2003), 125–130.

[29] In Austria, civilian law enforcement agencies are primarily under the responsibility of the Ministry of the Interior.

[30] See *Report of the Reform Commission of the Federal Army, 3.1.3,* and *Sub-strategy on Defense Policy,* Draft (January 2005); <www.bmlv.gv.at/facts/management_2010>.

[31] Compare Military Command, "Service regulations for the Federal Army [*Truppenführung. Dienstvorschrift für das Bundesheer*]," August 2004, 139.

[32] Search of persons includes the search of a person and their clothes with the aim of discovering certain objects.

[33] In this context, the following provisions appear most significant: §16 (intelligence-gathering), §21 (defense from danger), §22 (prevention of potential attacks), §36 (denial of entering as certain area), §48 (securing of persons and things), §49 (exercise of authority of command and coercion).

Chapter 7

The Soviet Legacy: Transforming Bulgaria's Armed Forces for Homeland Security Missions

Nikolay K. Dotzev

> *War is much too serious to leave to generals.*
> —George Clemenceau[1]
>
> *National security is much too serious to leave entirely to civilians.*
> —John M. Collins[2]

At the Istanbul Summit in June 2004, the member states of the North Atlantic Treaty Organization (NATO) confirmed that collective defense remains the main goal of the Alliance. The nations "remain fully committed to the collective defense of the people, territory, and forces" of the Alliance's member states, which stated, "Transatlantic cooperation is essential in defending our values and meeting common threats and challenges, from wherever they may come."[3] The processes of defense transformation have to ensure that the means match the ends, that the available capabilities match the missions.

A number of processes that have the character of a military revolution affect the latest developments in military affairs. Militaries undertake new additional missions and tasks. The Bulgarian armed forces are fully involved in these processes.

National Policy on Deployment of Military Forces in Domestic Contingencies

Bulgaria's Military Strategy defines three broad missions that encompass the relevant tasks for the Bulgarian armed forces: "Contribution to the national security in peacetime; contribution to peace and stability in the world; and participation in the defense of the country."⁴ These three missions were slightly modified by a Strategic Defense Review, and once again reconfirmed in a policy framework document.⁵

Extraordinary Cases: Armed Attack on the Nation

The participation and role of the Bulgarian military in the process of crisis management and defending the country against an armed attack on the nation, including chemical, biological, radiological, nuclear, and explosive attacks, is very clearly described in the Military Strategy. The armed forces should be prepared to face "military threats" in specific actions in the event of "deliberate violation of borders, large-scale sabotage and other activities, use of another country's armed formations and direct military aggression; mass epidemics and damage as a result of bacteriological, biological and chemical contamination."⁶ But they also have a role to play in cases of violations of "security and public order like organized crime, terrorism, and ethnic and religious tensions."⁷

Emergency Consequence Management

In peacetime, the armed forces can participate in operations in cases of crises of a nonmilitary character within Bulgaria's borders. They can conduct preventive activities or provide direct support and protection of the population and the national economy in the event of natural disaster, industrial failure, or other catastrophe. When a state of emergency is declared, they can participate in operations against the proliferation of weapons of mass destruction, illegal trafficking in weapons, and international terrorism, guarding strategically important sites and interdicting terrorist activities.

Temporary Support to Civil Authorities

Units and formations of the armed forces can participate in operations against the traffic in drugs, people, or weapons. The military can also aid in guarding objects or sites that are potential targets for terrorist attack. Because these tasks are primarily the responsibility of the Ministry of the Interior and the civil law enforcement agencies, the military would only participate when the civil authorities' efforts and resources are insufficient or are spent, and the sovereignty and security of the country are threatened. The armed forces contribute to the collecting and processing of information on potential security risks and threats; operations to deter and neutralize terrorist, extremist, and criminal groups; protection and support of the population; and providing support (as appropriate) to other state bodies and organizations.

Traditional Missions

The Bulgarian military develops and maintains capabilities of "collection, processing, and analysis of information necessary for the purposes of early warning and support to making political and military decisions on issues related to the military aspects of national security."[8] They provide capabilities and contribute to the control of Bulgarian airspace and territorial waters.[9]

Air force units help ensure the security of Bulgarian airspace, and navy ships and units implement maritime surveillance and interdiction tasks. The armed forces participate in the process of air traffic control jointly with the respective state authorities, as well as in the control and safeguard of the sea. Duty forces and assets are ready to act against airspace violators and safeguard the air and maritime sovereignty of the country, provide surveillance and control of the traffic at sea, and offer forces and assets for response to vessels that violate the country's maritime sovereignty.[10]

Historical Precedents

Postwar: How Military Forces Were Employed from 1945–1990

It might be useful and interesting to start the history overview a bit earlier than many 20th-century histories do, and go back to the period after the First World War. In 1919, the Bulgarian armed forces were exposed to heavy international restrictions with regard to manpower strength, quantities of armament, equipment, and heavy weapons systems. At the same time, the country's population and economy were suffering tremendous difficulties that were considered a national catastrophe. Prime minister Alexander Stamboliisky, leader of the party of the Bulgarian Agrarian Popular Union, passed a law through the parliament establishing a new "obligatory labor conscription," mobilizing men over the age of 20 and women over the age of 16 for public construction projects; this effort became one of Stamboliisky's most famous and admired reforms.[11] Even though it was announced as a temporary measure aimed at rebuilding the country after the war, and particularly at reconstructing vital infrastructure and economic installations, the "labor corps" (based on "labor conscription") outlived Alexander Stamboliisky's government by about eight decades.

In the period from 1945 to 1990, the "labor corps" developed further and split up into a series of armed and paramilitary formations subordinate to the different ministries, including the Ministry of Infrastructure and Construction and the Ministry of Transportation and Communications. They were building, maintaining, and, in some cases, guarding important infrastructure installations such as powerplants, large administrative or cultural buildings, bridges, roads, and even blocks of flats. The Ministry of the Interior also had its own troops, which consisted mainly of internal forces and border guard troops.

Another tradition also began from a lesson learned during Alexander Stamboliisky's government. He became a victim of a military coup d' état, which was later followed by yet other coups. That was seen as a reason to keep the armed forces out of internal security issues as much as possible, and particularly out of any political struggles.

Post–Cold War: Examples from 1991–2001

The period 1991–2001 was a period of transition. Changes took place in the state government, the political system, and the economy. The military faced questions about the role of the armed forces in a liminal period, when the guarantees of collective defense were not in effect, since the Warsaw Pact had collapsed, but Bulgaria had not yet become a member of NATO. The armed forces are constitutionally obligated to maintain their readiness to provide reliable defense of the country; at the same time, however, they began implementing changes and moving toward a "new qualitative status."[12] The Bulgarian armed forces implemented a reform plan with key parameters that have no equivalent in the history of the country.[13]

Similar processes of changes took place with regard to the forces, troops, and formations subordinate to other ministries. The labor corps was terminated, along with the practice of labor conscription. The troops belonging to the Ministry of Infrastructure and Construction and to the Ministry of Transportation and Communications were disbanded. Within the Ministry of the Interior, a civilian border police service replaced the border guard troops, and the Internal Forces were transformed into a form of gendarmerie.

Post-9/11

Since the terrorist attacks of September 11, 2001, the world is no longer the same. The importance of the availability, deployability, and usability of a capable military force was especially strongly outlined as a result of these tragic events. Bulgaria had begun to act as a real ally to the Atlantic Alliance long before it was invited to become a NATO member. Bulgarian troops have taken part in the operations in the Western Balkans, and at present Bulgaria is also providing host nation support and transiting of people and equipment for Kosovo Force and Stabilization Force (SFOR), and now for European Union Force. With the formation of the global coalition against terrorism, the country has contributed in different ways, ranging from providing political support, to opening its airspace and providing an airfield for coalition forces, to sending a mechanized platoon to Afghanistan and an infantry battalion as part of the Polish multinational division in Iraq.

Legal Authority for Deployment

The main law of the country—the Constitution of the Republic of Bulgaria[14]—defines the role of the armed forces: to "guarantee the sovereignty, security, and independence of the country, and protect its territorial integrity." Together with the constitution of the country and the Law of Defense and the Armed Forces in the hierarchy of fundamental documents, some other documents have a special role relating to the possible use of the military in domestic contingencies. These include the National Security Concept, Military Doctrine, Military Strategy, Joint Operations Doctrine, Operations Other Than War Doctrine, Special Operations Doctrine, the Doctrines of the Services, and Tactical Level Documents.

The National Security Concept provides a definition for security as a situation when "the major rights and liberties of the Bulgarian citizens are protected," along with "the state borders, territorial integrity, and independence of the country."[15]

The Military Doctrine[16] defines the primary goals in the area of defense. The first goal is to "guarantee the independence, sovereignty, and territorial integrity of the country against threats of a military, armed, or terrorist nature," and also the "protection of the population in times of natural disasters, industrial accidents, catastrophes and hazardous pollution."[17] The doctrine takes into account the risks to Bulgaria's security and territorial integrity that result from "destabilizing effects of more limited military and/ or armed formations and/or terrorist groups."[18]

According to the Law of the Ministry of the Interior and the rules and regulations governing its implementation, this ministry is tasked with the responsibilities related to providing internal security. The participation of the armed forces in the implementation of tasks related to providing internal security is done "under conditions and in order established by the Constitution and the Laws. The legally established mechanism guarantees that the tasking of the Bulgarian armed forces is in the interest of the society and for the protection of the national values."[19] It is based on the provisions of the Military Doctrine and the Law of Defense and the Armed Forces. According to these documents, during peacetime, in an emergency situation (or when a state of emergency is declared), the military shall provide support to the civil law enforcement agencies against the proliferation of weapons of mass destruction, the illegal traffic of weapons and people, and terrorism. The military takes part in guarding strategically important sites, and in operations directed at stopping terrorist activities. A state of emergency could be declared with a decision by the National Assembly (the parliament), or with an edict by the president when the parliament is not in session. Either the decision or the edict should specify the tasks, the number of troops involved, the period of use, and the command and control arrangements for the armed forces' units and formations that are involved. Some of the tasks described by the laws can also be implemented when a state of emergency has not been declared.

The Minister of Defense can authorize the participation of units and formations of the armed forces in the mitigation and resolution of the consequences of natural disasters, industrial catastrophes, and dangerous pollution on Bulgarian soil. The Minister of Defense and the Chief of the General Staff have to sign a special order for such authorization.

The military personnel implementing these tasks are instructed to strictly obey the provisions of the constitution and the laws. Limitations of the rights of citizens, freedom of movement, or violation of the sanctity of their property are permissible only as an exception and in cases of the highest emergency. The law or the act of declaring a state of emergency describes these exceptions.

Types and Capabilities of Available Forces

The protection of the country and its population is realized through different types of forces and assets for domestic contingencies. This pool includes "forces and assets, established for direct implementation of the protection tasks and also forces and assets of ministries and departments, economic and scientific organizations, executing their basic functions, part of which sometimes have defense implications."[20] For the protection of the civilian population, forces are provided from the Agency of Civil Protection; formations belonging to the Ministry of the Interior and the Ministry of Defense; personnel and assets of the Ministry of Health; and resources from other ministries and organizations, central and local governments and administrations, nongovernmental organizations, and volunteers.[21]

It is very important that the government have capabilities for fast and adequate reaction to terrorist attacks. Such a response would be faceted in nature; it would include "specialized detachments for rapid reaction in situations with hostages, to prevent chaotic massacres similar to the one in Beslan; technical teams; emergency medical personnel."[22]

Active Military Forces

Units of the three branches of the armed services maintain readiness for participation in different activities anywhere on Bulgarian soil. They are operational formations, and can be used only with the permission of the Minister of Defense and the Chief of the General Staff. Modular formations—created on the territorial principle, taking into account the location of the units—and combined detachments conduct specialized training to act in different situations.

Combat commando teams are prepared as part of the special operations forces. The specific structure of the special operations forces, along with their armament and special equipment, enables them to act in all kinds of conditions and allows flexible planning with a variety of options.

The Air Force Tactical Aviation Command can also bring to bear some of its special capabilities, such as aerial photography, reconnaissance and escort, transport of personnel and materials (including combat commando teams), and close air support. For the Air Defense Command, one of the biggest challenges is the detection, identification, and elimination of high-speed, small-size air targets, flying at low altitude, and coming into sight suddenly. The navy is able to contribute with their surveillance assets, aviation, and ships.

Paramilitary Police Forces

The Ministry of the Interior supervises a number of national law enforcement elements that have forces and assets with specific tasks. The Security Service specializes in counterintelligence and information gathering. The national police are an operational search and protection service for maintaining the public order and the prevention and investigation of criminal activity. The Counteraction to Organized Crime Service is dedicated to neutralizing the activities of local and transnational criminal structures. The Fire and Breakdown Safety Service provides fire control, firefighting, and search and rescue support on the national level. The Border Police guards the national border and controls the observation of the various legal regimes governing the nation's borders with its neighbors. The gendarmerie replaced the Internal Forces in 1997; it is a specialized guard and operational search service for guarding strategic sites and other objects of critical importance, fighting terrorist and sabotage groups, maintaining public order, and preventing crime. Its units are highly mobile police structures, and can act individually or in concert with other services to deal with crisis situations, maintain the public order in civil disturbances, and also serve as reserve of the Ministry of the Interior for guaranteeing internal security.

Some specific tasks are assigned to the specialized antiterrorist detachment. They may be implemented in interaction with other services of the Ministry of the Interior and armed forces units and assets, and include counteraction and neutralization of terrorists, searching specific regions, detaining terrorists and transferring them to the police, securing certain areas from terrorists, establishing contact with terrorist groups, and working for the release of hostages.

Reserve Forces

All forces and assets of the Bulgarian armed forces, regardless of which command structure or branch of service they belong to or their level of manpower, are obliged to participate in activities in cases of crisis situations within the boundaries of their garrisons.

The structure of the reserves is changing with the transition from conscript to professional armed forces. A concept for a national guard–type structure under the supervision of the local authorities is under development. It is aimed at filling the gap created while the reform process is under way. Moving operational units to the center of the country and closing a large number of garrisons left significant parts of the nation's territory without any military forces. Very often it takes an unacceptably long time to move the nearest military modular formation or unit to crisis and disaster areas.

Other

The Civil Protection Agency provides search and rescue teams, and deals with the mitigation of the consequences of natural disasters, industrial failures, and other catastrophic events. The national Agency for Refugees manages the verification, reception, and accommodation of displaced people, establishing temporary reception centers for foreign citizens seeking protection, along with other tasks. The Operational and Technical Information Directorate of the Ministry of the Interior is responsible for the important task of explosives disposal.

National Response Plans and Programs

While the availability of sufficient resources—both military and civil—is of critical importance, it is equally important for the government to have prepared "detailed plans for search and rescue, decontamination or quarantine operations. And most of all there must be an effective government structure and procedures for actions in crisis situations."[23]

The sharing of responsibilities for defense planning within the executive power is related to the implementation of government policy in the area of security and defense. This task is implemented through modern methods of defense resource management, concepts and programs for working in peacetime, and preparation of the national economy to work under conditions of a possible escalating crisis or in armed conflict. A system of crisis and wartime plans has been developed at all levels of the government—national, ministries and departments, organizations and companies, districts and communities—to insure the proper management of the nation's defense resources.

The General State Wartime Plan provides for the "proper distribution and management of the nation's resources in the interest of the defense of the country. This plan consists of a system of indicators and activities for all branches of the national economy."[24] The development of the plan is an integrated process. The Ministry of Defense coordinates the process of formulating and executing defense policy. The activities for the implementation of crisis and wartime tasks are managed through both central and local administrative bodies. The plan could be updated if the needs and requirements of the armed forces or the capabilities of the national economy change.

The armed forces' formations conduct operations for direct support and protection of the population in close interaction with the government authorities responsible for crisis management. The planning of the military's participation takes place as part of the integrated planning process at the national level and also for each part of the nation's territory, with the leading role taken by the central government administration, using common doctrines and procedures and focusing on the interaction among the different ministries and agencies. It covers the national-level activities, the preparation of the military formations to be deployed, the organization of the modalities of interaction between various groups and levels of administration, command and control arrangements, and logistic support. These plans are updated and coordinated annually.

The steps to be taken for the protection of the population, and the participation of the armed forces in particular, are described in "Plans for Interaction with the State Administration Authorities." This document outlines the methods of interaction between the different departments that participate in the "National Plan for Protection of the Population." For their part, the armed forces develop and maintain "Plans for the Protection of the Troops."

In cases of natural or industrial disasters, the Bulgarian military implements its "Plan for Potential Crisis Situations." Under certain procedure, troops may be assigned to participate in the protection of the population and to conduct search and rescue activities in cases of natural disasters, industrial failure, catastrophes, and dangerous pollution.

The Council of Ministers manages non-military crises and coordinates response activities. In the area of the crisis, the local government and administration authorities direct the effort. The senior commander, in accordance with the plans and the division of responsibility, exercises command and control of the participating military units. The command and control of the participating forces and assets require a unified command and control system. The National Military Command Center is the principal element of this system for the Ministry of Defense and the Bulgarian armed forces.

The exercise Joint Efforts 2004 took place in October 2004 with the participation of representatives, units, and personnel from the Ministry of Defense, the General Staff and the three services, the Ministry of the Interior, the Civil Protection Agency, and the Agency for Refugees. The goal of the exercise was to review the resources and capabilities that the state structures have for crisis prevention and management; to precisely define their responsibilities, functions, and tasks; and to assess their ability to act together. This, the first joint exercise of such a scale, was directed from the National Military Command Center.

Protection of Critical Infrastructure

The armed forces assist other ministries and departments by committing forces and assets for "protection and defense of strategic sites threatened by terrorist attacks, as well as during military conflicts in proximity of the state borders."[25] In cases of terrorist attack, the armed forces units guard strategically important civilian and military sites, limit and isolate the threatened region, provide security, and work to prevent the spread of rumors and panic.

Some good examples of capabilities that the Bulgarian armed forces have developed come from their participation in peace support operations abroad. A Bulgarian engineer platoon is building houses and doing substantial reconstruction of important infrastructure in Kosovo. In the process, it is developing useful capabilities that will definitely be employed when the platoon returns to its brigade in Bulgaria. A Bulgarian mechanized company is guarding the headquarters of SFOR (now NATO and European Union headquarters) in Sarajevo, and building skills in guarding strategically important infrastructure objects. Other units in Bosnia and Herzegovina, Afghanistan, and Iraq are being trained and gaining experience in area search, establishing and manning checkpoints, patrolling, and so forth. These are specific skills and capabilities that can be used after the 6-month period of the foreign deployment is up.

Border and Transportation Security

Land forces, with forces and assets belonging mainly to the Operational Forces Command, but also to the reserve commands, could contribute to a number of homeland security tasks. These include embargo operations, protecting Bulgarian territory from terrorist activities, preventing illegal immigrants from flooding through the state border, blocking and neutralizing paramilitary formations, and rendering assistance to the population.

The forces and assets of the air force, in coordination with civilian and military air traffic controllers, can conduct operations for the protection of Bulgaria's airspace. They include actions for guarding and defending the airspace (establishing borders and limitations of the regional airspace and restrictions for using it, coordination at the tactical level of military approaches) and providing security for civilian and military air traffic (reduction of air traffic in the area of the operation, introducing limitations and interdictions in the interest of the safety of civilian air traffic).

The Bulgarian navy, in coordination with other armed forces services and forces and assets belonging to other ministries (such as the Border Police) and agencies (the government agency responsible for controlling civilian shipping), conduct when necessary operations for control of Bulgaria's territorial waters and the protection of shipping.[26] Their aims are maintaining a favorable operational situation, ensuring the safety of shipping, protecting and defending seaports, conducting mine countermeasures, controlling the shipping lanes, preventing pollution, and inspecting ships in Bulgarian waters.

These are highly specific capabilities, which might not be needed every day. But the forces and assets that are providing them have to be properly equipped, prepared, trained, and kept at a relatively high level of readiness. The following two examples—one of air policing and one of controlling Bulgarian waters—provide an illustration.

An airshow took place several years ago in a neighboring country. The show finished a few hours earlier than anticipated, and a group of small aircraft of a different type from those participating in the show decided to go home immediately. They did not bother changing their flight plans and informing the air traffic control agencies. Bulgarian detection installations registered a significant number of "unknown targets" entering the country's airspace. Immediately, air defense fighter aircraft took off, established contact, and kindly invited the stray aircraft to land. These pilots were only harmless tourists. But what if among them were terrorists, who were equipped, trained, and had been preparing themselves for years for such an opportunity? And what if the fighters were not ready?

In a maritime example, a Bulgarian commercial ship sent a distress signal. An armed crewmember attacked the captain and took as hostages two other members of the crew. The incident took place out of the range of police vessels. The navy sent a combat ship with a helicopter, and the issue was resolved.

Domestic Counterterrorism

Units of the Bulgarian armed forces can participate in operations against weapons proliferation or terrorist activities when the efforts of the civil law enforcement agencies are not sufficient to control the situation and the security and sovereignty of the country are threatened. These operations may include actions against the proliferation of weapons of mass destruction, illegal trafficking of weapons, international terrorism, guarding strategic objects, and counterterrorist activities.

After the declaration of a state of emergency, the military assists the Ministry of the Interior in its counterterror efforts. These actions are based on special instructions for the interactions between the Ministry of Defense and the Ministry of the Interior.

The military can participate in the fight against terrorists actively or passively. The passive method includes measures like exerting strict control over the military's stock of weapons and preventing their illegal transfer to individuals, organizations, and other countries. The active method includes a wide spectrum of preventive work, countermeasures, and full interaction with the services of the Ministry of Defense, the Ministry of the Interior, and other national organizations and agencies.

Military units, mainly the special operations forces, provide support to law enforcement agencies in combating the proliferation of weapons of mass destruction and the illegal traffic in weapons. They implement intelligence and surveillance strategies and guard strategically important sites and convoys. In cases calling for direct action, they can participate in searches for and the collection of weapons and facilities for their production and use, as well as support the police units in such operations. Special operations forces, with their rapid-strike capabilities (especially in isolated regions), can also be used for direct attacks against terrorist groups and their supporting infrastructure, or for operations for release and evacuation of hostages.

Defense against and Response to Catastrophic Threats

Another important task for the military is participating in the prevention or mitigation of the consequences of nuclear, chemical, and biological contamination. The armed forces provide and maintain in permanent readiness capabilities for reaction in cases of nuclear, chemical, and bacteriological contamination, working in cooperation with the respective ministries and departments.

The protection of the civilian population and the national economy is part of a system of activities, both in peacetime and wartime, for the reduction of losses and negative consequences, and ensuring the necessary conditions for survival after a conflict. "The armed forces commit personnel and equipment to assist the population in emergencies, and especially in cases of disasters and catastrophes."[27]

Civil Support

In peacetime as well as in wartime, activities for the protection of the civilian population and national economy are a joint function of the state authorities, local governmental and administrative authorities, and various civilian nongovernmental organizations. They are managed by special bodies and implemented by specially established paramilitary and civil formations for the purposes of search and rescue operations and emergency restorations and reconstruction of the country during crisis situations.

The armed forces maintain a high level of readiness for humanitarian assistance and search and rescue activities, both on Bulgarian soil and abroad. They provide support to the population in many different situations. Modular formations are prepared for fighting forest and agricultural fires, for actions in heavy winter conditions, for relief of the consequences of devastating flooding, earthquakes, or industrial catastrophes, and also for unexploded ordnance disposal. The Minister of Defense in a special order every year assigns the forces and assets earmarked for participation in operations for protecting the population.

The armed forces conduct operations for protecting the population in cases of natural disaster, ecological crisis, epidemic, large-scale migrations of the population, radiation and chemical catastrophes, and other emergency situations. The command and control structures and formations prepared for action in nonmilitary crises, in interaction with other departments and agencies, local governments, and administrative authorities:

- observe the risk factors and extrapolate the crisis situation (reconnaissance and analysis)

- provide order and security in the threatened region (assist law enforcement authorities, ensure security of important infrastructure objects)

- provide assistance to the civilian population (drinking water and food supplies, medical assistance)

- conduct urgent demolition and restoration activities (evacuation of the population, livestock, and materials; specialized and sanitary treatment; decontamination; deactivation of hazardous materials; firefighting; clearing roads)

- resolve the causal elements of the crisis

- restore control of the situation

- contribute to the mitigation of the consequences.

For example, in early February 2005, severe snowstorms caused a disaster situation in many regions of eastern Bulgaria. After requests by the local governors, approved through the chain of command, units of the three services and modular formations were deployed around the clock, clearing out roads, pulling vehicles out of the snow, moving people to hospitals for life-saving treatment (including via navy helicopter), and delivering food and medical supplies to isolated villages.

Conclusion

The present spectrum of tasks for the military is larger than ever. It may be expected that the global and regional security environment will continue to present hard-to-predict challenges and the potential for dynamic changes. The military element will retain its important role in the homeland security system. It is a tool to maintain peace and stability together, along with diplomatic, political, economic, and other methods.

Traditionally, "the military do what the nation asks."[28] But they should be primarily asked to do what they are designed for and prepared to do best. The main task of the military is and will remain the defense of the sovereignty and territorial integrity of the country. The military are and will be more often asked to do things that are different or may seem different from the traditional purpose of a military force. Many tasks in peace support operations resemble the traditional role of the police. Search and rescue missions and support of the population have also become regular tasks for the military.

Military establishments are subject to changes. The military has to adapt its armament and equipment, structures, doctrines, and skills to new security challenges and domestic conditions. But they should not turn into a sort of police force in different uniform, or well-armed search and rescue teams and civil protection agencies. Although very important, these are supplementary tasks for the military, not its core purpose.

Notes

[1] Former French Prime Minister.

[2] John M. Collins, *Military Strategy: Principles, Practices, and Historical Perspectives* (Washington, DC: Brassey's, 2002), xvi.

[3] Istanbul Summit Communiqué, June 28, 2004, Press Release PR/CP (2004) 0096.

[4] *Military Strategy of the Republic of Bulgaria*, approved by the Council of Ministers in June 2002; available at <www.mod.bg>.

[5] Strategic Defense Review, "Policy Framework," adopted by the National Assembly on March 25, 2004; available at <www.mod.bg>.

[6] *Military Strategy of the Republic of Bulgaria*.

[7] Ibid.

[8] Ibid.

[9] Strategic Defense Review, "Policy Framework."

[10] *Military Strategy of the Republic of Bulgaria*.

[11] Stefan Gruev, *Crown of Thorns: The Reign of King Boris III of Bulgaria, 1918–1943* (Sofia: 1991), 109.

[12] *Military Strategy of the Republic of Bulgaria*.

[13] "Updated Plan 2004." Some of the key parameters are reduction of the military's peacetime strength to 45,000, and wartime strength to 100,000; significant cuts to the main armament systems and military infrastructure; increasing interoperability with NATO; professionalization of the force; establishment of a permanent reserve; and implementation of important modernization projects.

[14] *Constitution of the Republic of Bulgaria*, adopted by the Parliament (Grand National Assembly) on July 13, 1991; changed and amended on September 26, 2003.

[15] *National Security Concept of the Republic of Bulgaria*, adopted by the Parliament in April 1998; available at <www.mod.bg>.

[16] *Military Doctrine of the Republic of Bulgaria*, amended and added, *State Gazette*, issue 200 (2002); available at <www.mod.bg>.

[17] Ibid., Article 22.

[18] Ibid., Article 13.

[19] "Operations Other than War Doctrine 3.01," November 29, 2000, in *Doctrines and Concepts of the Bulgarian Armed Forces*, Volume 1 (Sofia: Military Publishing House, 2001).

[20] *Military Strategy of the Republic of Bulgaria.*

[21] Ibid.

[22] Brian Jenkins, "The Four Defenses Against Terrorism," *24 Hours* (Sofia, September 25, 2004).

[23] Ibid.

[24] *White Book of Security and Defense*, available at <www.mod.bg>.

[25] *Military Strategy of the Republic of Bulgaria.*

[26] Bulgarian territorial waters include internal seas, the territorial sea, the adjacent zone, the continental shelf, and the exclusive economic zone.

[27] *Military Strategy of the Republic of Bulgaria.*

[28] Harry J. Thie, "Planning the Future Military Workforce," in *New Challenges, New Tools for Defense Decisionmaking*, eds. Stuart Johnson, Martin Libicki, and Gregory F. Treverton (Santa Monica, CA: RAND National Defense Research Institute, 2003).

Chapter 8

The Role of the Ukrainian Armed Forces in Homeland Security

Petro Kanana and Alexey Telichkin

Ukrainian Policy on the Use of Military Forces

As a result of the disintegration of the Soviet Union and the end of the Cold War, North Atlantic Treaty Organization (NATO) countries have been transformed from major potential external threats to Ukraine into its potential allies. Do any threats to an independent Ukraine exist at all? And if so, what are they? Legislation adopted over the course of several years, including the *National Security Strategy* (1997), the law "On the Fundamentals of National Security" (2003), and the *Military Doctrine* (2004), has addressed these questions.

The law "On the Fundamentals of National Security" assumes that the potential threats to Ukraine may lie in the international, state security, military, border security, internal political, economic, social, humanitarian, technological, ecological, and informational spheres. The nature of these threats is defined by the historical experience of Ukraine, which suffered from two world wars; a great number of revolts, revolutions, civil wars, and other civil disturbances; as well as numerous natural and technological disasters. At the same time, in its modern history Ukraine has fortunately not been the scene of any large-scale terrorist attack. That fact explains why international and domestic terrorism are not regarded as actual threats to the country, but as potential ones (see below). The threats may be divided into military or nonmilitary, external or domestic.

Ukraine's national security is ensured by a number of actors, including the military, namely the country's armed forces, the so-called other military formations, and some paramilitary forces, which are incorporated within the military organization of the state. The primary mission of the armed forces is to counter external military threats by defending the state border, protecting Ukraine's sovereignty and territorial integrity, repulsing armed aggression, and protecting the air and underwater space of the country (Article 1, "On the Armed Forces" law). If necessary, the armed forces may assist other agencies to counter external, nonmilitary threats, for example, by protecting the state borders and maritime economic zones. There are strict legal restrictions on the armed forces in terms of their role in dealing with domestic threats. Their activities in this field are mainly limited to countering natural and technological disasters or, in some cases, combating terrorism.

The other military formations include border troops, civil defense troops, internal troops, and some others whose total strength exceeds 120,000 men, compared with approximately 245,000 of the armed forces. Their mission is to tackle some specific nonmilitary, mainly domestic threats, namely illegal migration, terrorism, public disturbances, and vital infrastructure protection, which requires the deployment of great numbers of manpower, special armament, and equipment.

Historical Precedents

Though Ukraine, as a member republic within the Union of Soviet Socialist Republics (USSR) until 1991, did not have its own armed forces, it played an important role in the military policy of the Soviet Union. Ukrainians formed a considerable part of the officer corps; there were three military districts on the territory of the republic; and the main bases of the Black Sea Fleet were located in Ukraine. In addition, the major heavy machinery plants of Ukraine to a large extent were devoted to defense production, producing tanks, missiles, aircraft, and other military hardware. In the republic there was also a network of military colleges, which were considered among the best in the Soviet Union.

Though the Soviet armed forces traditionally performed a broad range of tasks, in the post–World War II period there were only a few instances when the military performed their primary mission of defending the country (for example, armed conflicts on the Chinese border in 1968–1969). At the same time, under bilateral international agreements, the Soviet military was engaged in actions during the conflicts in Korea, Vietnam, the Middle East, and other wars, though their participation is still not too widely publicized. In the decades between 1960 and 1980, Soviet military specialists functioned as trainers, advisers, and suppliers in Angola, Ethiopia, Iraq, Mozambique, Nicaragua, Syria, and elsewhere. The Soviet army formed the bulk of the invasion force in Czechoslovakia in 1968. By contrast, the Soviet military involvement in Afghanistan in 1979 had a devastating effect on the public and army morale, mainly due to comparatively heavy losses and the absence of immediate success. This drop in public confidence was aggravated by a mass deployment of untrained and unprepared troops in helping to eliminate the effects of both technological (the accident at the Chernobyl nuclear plant in 1986) and natural (the 1988 earthquake in Armenia) disasters. In the late 1980s, the military was also engaged in police operations in several Central Asian, Caucasian, and Baltic republics. The culmination of the military involvement in politics was their participation in the attempted coup d'etat of August 19–21, 1991, in Moscow.

When the coup attempt failed, the parliament of Ukraine adopted a number of resolutions in order to elaborate a legal basis for the use of the armed forces in domestic contingencies and to create paramilitary forces that would report to Ukrainian republican authorities. On August 24, 1991, the parliament decided to place all the military units located on Ukrainian territory under its own command—thereby setting up the Department of Defense—and started building the armed forces of Ukraine as well as several major paramilitary agencies. The "Afghanistan" and "August *putsch*" syndromes determined the basic elements of the military build-up program: restriction of the armed forces' mission mainly to protecting the sovereignty and territorial integrity of Ukraine; distribution of the main functions of the protection of national security among different military forces and law-enforcement agencies; a ban on the armed forces' involvement in unconstitutional political affairs; a special procedure for sending military forces abroad; and a prohibition against foreign military bases on Ukrainian territory. Numerous terrorist acts in neighboring Russia caused by the war in Chechnya, as well as the events of September 11, 2001, led the Ukrainian public to regard terrorism as one of the major potential threats to the country, resulting in the adoption of the law "On Combating Terrorism" in 2003 and the corresponding changes in Ukraine's national security strategy.

Legal Authority

The legislation regulating the deployment of the armed forces in domestic operations may be represented as a three-tiered system. The first (basic) level is formed by the Ukrainian Constitution (1996), which established the fundamental guidelines of the functioning of the armed forces and determined Ukraine's defense, the protection of its sovereignty, territorial integrity, and inviolability (Article 17) to be the mission of the armed forces. It prohibits any deployment of the armed forces to limit the rights and freedoms of Ukraine's citizens, overthrow the constitutional order, or remove or hamper bodies of state authority (Articles 17, 64). It also establishes the range of powers of the president (Article 106), parliament (Article 85), and government (Article 116) in relation to the armed forces.

The second level consists of the legal acts that specifically regulate the functioning of the armed forces and other military formations: the laws "On the Armed Forces" (1991), "On Defense" (1991), "On the Border Troops" (1991), "On the Internal Troops of the Ministry of the Interior" (1992), and "On the Civil Defense Troops" (1999), among others. The third level is made up of the laws that indirectly regulate matters related to the armed forces, such as "On the Civil Defense" (1993), "On Participation of Ukraine in International Peace Operations" (1999), "On the Legal Regime of the State of Emergency" (2000), "On the Legal Regime of Martial Law" (2000), and so on.

Since 1991, the legal support policy of the Ukrainian armed forces has had at least three aims: to provide each aspect of military-related activity with a corresponding legal basis; to distribute the primary functions of national security among the different state agencies; and to prevent any potential intervention by the armed forces into the political life of the country. In particular, the legislation has confirmed the military as the lead agency in the sphere of the defense of the country; the civil defense troops as the lead actor in the sphere of responding to natural and technological disasters; and the Security Service as the lead agency in combating terrorism and other nonstate-based threats.

The legislation has also determined the highly centralized nature of the military forces command and control system. Under the Constitution (Article 106), the highest military authority is the president of Ukraine, who as the supreme commander-in-chief of the armed forces appoints the higher commanders of the armed forces and other military formations; determines the guidelines in the spheres of national security and defense; initiates the declaration of a state of war and makes the decision on the deployment of the armed forces in case of an act of armed aggression against Ukraine; and makes a decision on either a general or partial mobilization and declaration of martial law, or a state of emergency, or an ecological emergency area. Day-to-day command and control is provided by the commander-in-chief, whose position may be occupied either by the defense minister (if this person is a commissioned officer) or by the chief of the General Staff (if the defense minister is a civilian).

There are two laws that regulate the rules of engagement for the military. Articles 20 through 25 of the "On the Armed Forces Internal Service Statute" (1999) regulate the "military version" of the rules. A serviceman has a right to use his firearm to defend his health and life; to apprehend a person who is trying to escape after having committed a serious crime; to apprehend an armed person who represents a threat to servicemen; to repel an attack on an asset guarded by servicemen or assist in the liberation of the asset in case of its seizure; or to prevent an attempt to seize military weapons and equipment. The law "On the Militia" (1990) stipulates the "police version" of the rules, which are used by the Military Police and servicemen when performing law enforcement functions. For these individuals, use of a firearm is permitted to defend a citizen from an assault that threatens his/her life and health; to repel an assault on a policeman; to repel an assault on an asset under police guard or to liberate the asset in case of its seizure; to apprehend a person who is caught committing a serious crime and tries to run away; to apprehend a person committing armed resistance; or to stop a vehicle, if the driver's actions create a danger to the life and health of citizens or militia officers.

Types of Forces Providing National Security

The national security of Ukraine is provided by the armed forces, including the military, paramilitary, and specialized military forces. Currently, the armed forces of Ukraine consist of the army (51 percent of the armed forces' manpower), air force (32 percent), and navy (6 percent). In peacetime, the armed forces perform a number of tasks to counter nonmilitary external threats. In particular, the air force and air defense ensure the protection of Ukraine's airspace, while the navy is responsible for the protection of the nation's waters. These branches are also responsible for protecting Ukraine from potential terrorist attacks from the air and sea. The army, especially the engineering units, may be employed to counter natural or technological disasters.

According to Ukraine's current military doctrine, the armed forces should be transformed to meet the potential threats of today. The future armed forces will consist of three major components within the Advanced Defense Force: the Joint Rapid Reaction Force, the Main Defense Force, and the Strategic Reserve. The Joint Rapid Reaction Force's mission is to prevent and deter potential aggression and provide an immediate response to the country's security threats. In peacetime, their tasks are to protect defense-critical infrastructure from terrorist attacks, carry out antiterrorist operations to protect military assets or repel terrorist attacks from abroad, take part in international peace operations, and counter natural or technological disasters. The mission of the Main Defense Force is to repel acts of armed aggression. The main task of the Reserve Force is to reinforce the Main Defense Force.

Since 2002, the Military Police (its official name is the Military Service of Law and Order) have been functioning under the framework of the armed forces. The law "On the Military Service of Law and Order within the Armed Forces" (2002) serves as its legal basis. The mission of the Military Police is to provide law, order, and discipline among the servicemen; to protect military property; and to counter sabotage and terrorist attacks against defense-critical infrastructure. In cases of martial law or a state of emergency, the Military Police have the additional tasks of providing law and order within their zones of responsibility (for example, curfew) and combating terrorist activities directed at the assets of military infrastructure. In wartime, the Military Police do not perform a combat role but do provide support for the actions of the armed forces, in particular by combating the enemy's sabotage and reconnaissance groups and guarding prisoners of war. The strength of the Military Police must not exceed 1.5 percent of the total strength of the armed forces (Article 5). Its head is the chief of the main directorate of the Military Police, who reports to the defense minister through the chief of the General Staff. In some cases, the Military Police may be assisted by other servicemen. Even though they are members of the armed forces, the Military Police are subject to the same rules of engagement as the civilian police.

The military/paramilitary law enforcement forces include the Security Service, the border troops, and the internal troops. The Security Service is the state law enforcement agency, responsible for state security. Its tasks include protecting state sovereignty, constitutional order, and territorial integrity from the activities of foreign special services. In addition, the Security Service combats terrorism, corruption, organized crime, and other transnational and nonstate threats. The statutory basis of the service's activities is the law "On the Security Service" (1992). The service performs a number of functions, including information gathering and analysis; conducting counter-reconnaissance protection of defense-critical infrastructure; giving assistance in state border protection and in overcoming natural/technological disasters; and providing technical assistance to other law enforcement agencies combating crime and other threats.

The State Border Guard Service is a special-purpose law enforcement agency. Its legal basis is formed by the law "On the State Border Guard Service" (2003). The mission of the service is to ensure the inviolability of the nation's borders and to protect the sovereign rights of Ukraine in its maritime economic zone. In case of natural or technological disasters that may occur within the so-called border zone, the border guard must inform the corresponding state agencies and population. Within its structure, the service has the border troops (a 45,000-strong force), which functions as a special-purpose military force.

The internal troops (50,000 men) constitute a paramilitary police force (some authors regard them as the "other military force"), which acts on the basis of the law "On the Internal Troops of the Ministry of the Interior." Their main tasks are protecting and defending critical state infrastructure; overseeing penitentiary institutions; convoying special cargoes; combating crime; and protecting diplomatic missions. A list of the national critical infrastructure assets to be protected and defended by the internal troops is determined by the government. The troops are organized into formations of two major types: protection units and motorized police units. As to their armament and structure, they may be compared with the army's light infantry. The internal troops report to the interior minister.

The Ministry of the Interior within the structure of its regional departments has numerous rapid reaction police units, which, as a rule, are well trained and equipped, and as a result are quite effective in combating public disorders, riots, organized crime, and terrorist activities. Similar units exist in some other ministries as well (for example, the Ministry of Justice).

The Ministry of the Interior also oversees the State Protection Service, whose mission is to provide obligatory protection for some important assets, including state authority bodies, television and radio stations, archives, museums, urban infrastructure enterprises, and crucial railway and highway bridges. The legal basis of the department is the statute "On the State Protection Service of the Ministry of Interior" (1993). In addition, the Department of State Guard, reporting directly to the president, provides protection to high-level dignitaries.

The Civil Defense Troops are an example of a specialized military force whose mission—based on the laws "On Civil Defense" and "On the Civil Defense Troops"—is to defend the population in cases of natural or technological disasters. The troops are responsible for countering natural and technological disasters; fighting forest and brush fires; rendering assistance to the population affected by the disaster; evacuating the population; conducting radiation, chemical, and biological reconnaissance. It also provides explosives and ordnance demolition capabilities to the civilian authorities. The troops have all necessary means, including their own air force, to counter natural or man-made disasters. Being military by nature, the troops are a component of the civilian Ministry of Emergencies. Now, in accordance with the president's decree of December 13, 2003, the troops are being transformed from their traditional stance as a military force into a civilian operational and rescue civil defense service. The strength of the force should increase from its current strength of just over 10,000 to over 72,000 persons by the end of 2005.

Though many efforts are being taken to professionalize the armed services, the Ukrainian armed forces to a large extent are still manned by conscripts. In the particular environment of Ukraine, the system of mobilization has proven to be an efficient way to provide the military forces with reserves. A mobilization may be general or partial and may be conducted publicly or secretly. To counter natural or man-made disasters, a special-purpose mobilization may be conducted as well (Article 2, "On Mobilization Preparation and Mobilization"). The decision to mobilize is made by the president of Ukraine. To maintain the reservists' combat readiness, they may be called up for special training courses. Since the Soviet era, a great deal of attention has been paid to training the officers of reserve units by conducting special military courses of study at colleges and universities.

National Response Plans and Programs

Since 1991, there has been a strong tendency in Ukraine to elaborate formal national policies regarding the main types of contingencies that might involve the deployment of military and paramilitary forces and codify them in national legislation. These contingencies, among others, include cases of armed aggression, martial law, state of emergency, interdiction of illegal migration, natural/technological disasters, and countering terrorism.

The regulations surrounding the use of the armed forces in cases of armed aggression against Ukraine, natural/technological disasters, and counterterrorism will be addressed below. Martial law, which is regulated by the law "On the Legal Regime of Martial Law," may be declared by presidential decree (which must be approved within two days by the Parliament) in cases of either armed aggression or a threat of armed aggression, or a threat to the independence of Ukraine or its total or partial territorial integrity. Under martial law, additional executive powers are allotted to the state civilian authorities and to the military commands, including the General Staff, the army and navy commands, regional armed forces commands, and other military forces' commands. Should the area covered by the decree become a scene of combat action, martial law is provided directly by the military command. Though the military is the lead force in implementing martial law, the National Security and Defense Council of Ukraine may decide, with presidential approval, to employ the Border Troops, Internal Troops, Security Services, and other military formations as well.

A state of emergency, which is regulated by the law "On the Legal Regime of the State of Emergency," may be declared by a special decree by the president of Ukraine, which must be approved by the Parliament within two days, in cases of:

- extremely severe natural or technological disasters

- mass terrorist acts

- ethnic or religious conflicts that result in the blocking or seizure of critical infrastructure assets

- mass public disorder

- a coup d'etat attempt

- mass state border crossing from the territory of a neighboring country

- the need to restore the constitutional order and functioning of state institutional bodies.

This law determines that, in cases where a state of emergency is declared, some additional powers are allotted to certain military commands, including the Main Directorate of the Internal Troops of the Ministry of the Interior; the Security Service; the Main Directorate of the Civilian Defense Forces; and the Armed Forces Military Police. The armed forces or border troops may be employed only in cases of natural or technological disasters connected with human losses and requiring a great deal of urgent and large-scale repair efforts, or mass state border crossings from the territory of neighboring countries (Article 20). The chain of command in these cases is determined by the supreme commander-in-chief.

The policy regarding the interdiction of illegal migration is determined, first of all, by the "Program on Combating Illegal Migration in 2001–2004," approved by presidential decree on January 18, 2001. The main agencies that are involved in illegal migration interdiction include the Ministry of the Interior (the lead agency), Security Service, State Border Guard Service, State Tax Administration, State Department for Execution of Punishment, and so forth. The paramilitary forces (for example, internal troops) may be also used for joint patrols of border areas (with the border troops) to detect and detain illegal migrants.

Protection of Critical Infrastructure

There is no legislative act that determines a common policy for the protection of critical infrastructural elements. These questions are regulated by a number of acts, namely "On Internal Troops of the Ministry of the Interior," "On the Military Service of Law and Order within the Armed Forces" laws, "On the State Protection Service of the Ministry of the Interior" statute, and so forth. The means of protecting critical infrastructure depends on the type of asset—military or civilian—and the degree of its importance.

Military critical infrastructure assets are protected by the corresponding military force. The armed forces' critical infrastructure assets are protected by the military themselves and the military police. In particular, Article 2 of the law "On the Military Service of Law and Order within the Armed Forces of Ukraine" states that the military police take part in the protection of military assets and provide for the safety of the armed forces' property. In cases where martial law (Article 15 of the law "On the Legal Regime of Martial Law") or a state of emergency (Article 16 of the law "On the Legal Regime of a State of Emergency") is declared, the military command may take under its protection civilian critical economic assets.

Civilian infrastructure assets may be divided into four major categories: highest dignitaries (VIPs), strategic, important, and other. The protection of the premises of the administration of the president, the Parliament, the Cabinet of Ministers, the Constitutional Court, the Supreme Court, and some of the other sites associated with high-level dignitaries, as determined by the president, is provided by the Department of the State Guard (Article

9, "On the State Guarding of the State Authority Organs of Ukraine and Officials," 1998), a special task law enforcement agency that reports directly to the president of Ukraine (Article 11).

According to Article 1 of the law "Internal Troops of the Ministry of the Interior," the assets included in the category of strategic state-owned infrastructure (for example, nuclear and some other power plants; nuclear, chemical, and hazardous material enterprises) are protected by the paramilitary law enforcement forces of the Internal Troops. The list of these assets—which is confidential—is determined by an interagency commission, which consists of representatives of key state organs (Ministries of Interior, Economics, Energy and Fuel, Finance, Industrial Policy, Security Service, General Staff of the Armed Forces). The list must be approved by the Cabinet of Ministers.

The assets in the third category fall under the jurisdiction of the State Protection Service, reporting to the Ministry of the Interior. The list of these assets is determined by special regulation of the Cabinet of Ministers and includes the premises of the central executive power bodies; television and radio production and broadcast facilities; telecommunication systems; state archives; state museums, libraries, and other important cultural assets; the stock exchange of Ukraine; state banks; jewelry enterprises; assay offices; precious metal stocks; water-supply plants; sports and hunting weapons production plants; drug stores; mobilization stores; radioactive waste dumps; state department stores; and critical railway and highway bridges.

The policy governing the protection of other assets is defined by the heads of the respective agencies. Some agencies have their own armed protection units (for instance, the State Railway Department), while some enterprises have contracts with the State Protection Service, and others with private security firms.

Border Security

The legal basis for the state's activities in the area of border security is formed by the laws "On the State Border" (1992), "On the State Border Guard Service," and "On the Border Guard Troops." According to Articles 2 and 27 of the law "On the State Border," the protection of Ukraine's borders is provided by the State Border Guard Service on land, sea, rivers, and lakes, and by the armed forces in the air and underwater. The armed forces may also be engaged in operations in to support the protection of the state border and maritime economic zone on the grounds of a corresponding presidential decree, subsequent to its approval by Parliament (Article 1 of the law "On the Armed Forces"). In cases of armed aggression, the other components of the military organizations (Security Service, Ministry of the Interior, and Civil Defense Troops) may take part in the defense of the state border as well (Articles 4 and 12 of the law "On Defense"). The border guard servicemen, when performing their duties of land and maritime border protection, are governed by the rules of engagement stipulated by the law "On the Militia" and the Armed Forces Statutes (Article 21 of "On the State Border Guard Service"). However, it is forbidden to fire weapons in the direction of the territory of a neighboring country, except in cases of armed attacks, armed provocations, or armed resistance by border infiltrators.

Domestic Counterterrorism

Ukraine's state policy on combating terrorism is determined, first of all, by the law "On Combating Terrorism" (2003). The organization of the fight against terrorism is based on the principle of the distribution of the corresponding responsibilities among a number of actors: the Security Service (which serves as the lead agency, as set forth in Article 4, "On Combating Terrorism"); the Ministries of the Interior, Defense, and Emergencies; the State Border Committee; the State Department for Execution of Punishment; and the State Protection Department. The list of auxiliary agencies that can be engaged if needed includes the Ministries of Foreign Affairs, Health, Energy and Fuel, Industrial Policy, Finance, Transport, Environmental Protection, and Agrarian Policy; the State Customs Service; and the State Tax Administration. Besides these governmental resources, any other state or private agency may be engaged in counterterrorist activities.

The Security Service collects intelligence information, conducts electronic warfare operations, coordinates the efforts of actors in the fight against terrorism, investigates terrorism-related crimes, and provides protection of Ukrainian facilities overseas and their personnel. The Ministry of the Interior fights terrorism through the prevention, detection, and investigation of terrorism-related crimes and supports antiterrorist operations with personnel and equipment. The Ministry of Defense provides protection from terrorist attacks on assets of the armed forces; conducts the preparation and deployment of the ground, air, air defense, and naval forces in case of a terrorist attack from air or sea; and participates in antiterrorist operations at military assets. The Chechen war, however, showed that sometimes law enforcement agencies might need some heavy weapons (for example, tanks and helicopters), which are in possession only of the military. The Ministry of Emergencies provides protection of the population and the sovereign territory from technological terrorism-related contingencies, works to mitigate the effects of these contingencies, and conducts training of the population for such situations. The State Border Committee prevents terrorists from illegally crossing the Ukrainian border; combats the illegal traffic in weapons, explosives, poisons, and nuclear substances that can be used for terrorist activities; and provides protection of sea traffic within territorial waters during antiterrorist operations. The State Department for Execution of Punishment counters terrorist activities at correctional facilities. The State Protection Department counters terrorist threats aimed at VIPs or facilities under their protection.

The coordination of these various actors is provided by the Interagency Coordination Commission within the Antiterrorist Center, which is led by the Security Service and consists of the Head of the Commission; Deputy Ministers of the Ministries of Emergency and Interior; the Deputy Head of the General Staff; the Deputy Head of the State Penitentiary Department; and the Commander of the Interior Troops. Decisions on the conduct of antiterrorist operations rest with the head of the Antiterrorist Center, with written permission given by the head of the Security Service.

The president of Ukraine is to be immediately informed of any decision to carry out an antiterrorist operation. To provide direct command and control of the operation, an operational headquarters is to be set up. All the military and law enforcement personnel engaged in the operation are to perform their duties under the command of the head of the Operational Headquarters. If needed, a special legal regime may be declared to cover the antiterrorist operation.

Defense Against and Response to Threats

There are two main scenarios of catastrophic threats to Ukraine: armed aggression and international terrorist attack. The national policy on response to armed aggression is contained in two main legal acts: the law "On Defense" and in the nation's military doctrine. In the case of armed aggression against Ukraine, or the threat of armed attack, the president is empowered to make decisions about general or partial mobilization, the introduction of martial law in Ukraine or its separate parts, and the use of the Ukrainian military or other military formations. The president submits a petition on the announcement of martial law and the declaration of a state of war for approval by the Parliament. On the basis of the corresponding decision of the president, the armed forces and other military formations begin combat actions. Wartime is held to start officially at the moment of the announcement of martial law or the actual beginning of military operations and ends on the day that martial law ceases to be in effect. To provide strategic command of the armed forces, other military formations, and law enforcement agencies during this special period, the headquarters of the supreme commander-in-chief is to be set up (see Article 8, "On Defense").

Together with the armed forces, the defense of the country is also provided by troops of the Border Guard, the Security Service, the Ministry of the Interior, Civil Defense Troops, and other military formations (Article 12, "On Defense"). The tasks of the armed forces and other military formations depend on the actual stage of the conflict. In particular, they are responsible for implementing martial law and territorial defense efforts and protecting the population and critical infrastructure assets from enemy attack (Article 28, Ukraine's Military Doctrine). In the postconflict period, the armed forces and other military formations' tasks also include rendering assistance to the population and local authorities to counter the consequences of combat actions (Article 32, Ukraine's Military Doctrine).

The functions of the military forces in cases of terrorist attack from abroad are stipulated in the law "On Combating Terrorism." The military forces involved in combating international terrorism include, first of all, the armed forces, the Border Guard, and the Civil Defense Troops. The armed forces have three main tasks in the event of a terrorist attack:

- protect their critical assets, weapons of mass destruction, and other types of weapons, ammunition, explosives, and chemical and biological agents that are stored at military units from being captured by terrorists

- prevent terrorist attacks from air or sea

- participate in antiterrorist operations directed at military assets or, in the case of a terrorist threat from abroad, terrorist assets.

In addition, the navy is responsible for preventing any illegal trafficking of weapons by sea. There were some propositions that the capabilities of the armed forces (for example, military intelligence) should be used more actively to counter international terrorism, but these efforts were found to be unconstitutional. The Border Guard is responsible for preventing any crossing of the state border by terrorists and interdicting illegal trafficking in weapons, explosives, and chemical and radiological and other substances that can be deployed in carrying out a terrorist act. The Civil Defense Troops are responsible for protecting the population from a terrorist attack; evacuating the population when necessary; supplying the people who have suffered from an attack with food, water, medicine, and other essential items and services; conducting chemical, biological, and radiological reconnaissance; and providing decontamination services. If needed, the armed forces and other military formations may take part in antiterrorist operations.

Civil Support

Military Assistance to Civil Authority

The area where the military and civilian bodies cooperate most effectively is disaster relief. In 2003, there were 313 emergency cases registered in Ukraine (down from 362 the previous year), including 193 technological catastrophes, 111 natural disasters, and 9 social disturbances. As a result of these varied emergency situations, a total of 388 people died (in 2002 the death toll was 419). In cases of large-scale disasters, all the components of the military organization of the state—including the armed forces, other military formations, and law enforcement agencies—may be employed, though the Civil Defense Troops are the lead actor. According to the law "On Civil Defense in Ukraine," each citizen of the country has the right to be protected from the consequences of accidents, catastrophes, fires, and natural disasters. As the guarantor of this right, the state has created the system of civil defense, which aims at protecting the population from the dangerous consequences of accidents and technological, ecological, natural, and military catastrophes. The tasks of civil defense include:

- preventing emergencies of a technological and natural character and dealing with their consequences

- protecting the population from the consequences of accidents, catastrophes, and natural disasters

- creating analysis and forecasting management systems

- exerting observation and control over nuclear, biological, and chemical contamination.

The main civil defense forces consist of the Civil Defense Troops, along with specialized and paramilitary formations. Civil Defense Troops perform tasks related to the prevention and management of the consequences of technological and natural emergencies. In 2003, there were a total of 2,376 cases nationwide when these troops were called for assistance. Specialized formations are created to carry out specific tasks related to chemical and radiological threats, large-scale destruction caused by earthquakes, and emergencies in gas and oil fields. They are also responsible for preventive and restoration efforts, both inside and outside the country. Paramilitary formations of civil defense are created within individual regions, districts, government departments, and in private establishments and organizations, regardless of their form of ownership and governance.

According to Article 1 of the law "On the Armed Forces" and Article 9 of the law "On Defense," the armed forces may be deployed to handle situations related to natural and technological emergencies on the conditions determined by the corresponding presidential decree. (In practice, military units more often are deployed on the orders of their commanders, including the Minister of Defense.) The state civil defense system may function in three modes: normal mode, when the industrial, chemical, biological, and radiological situation is regarded as standard; advanced readiness mode, when any one of these situations has worsened; emergency mode, in cases of large-scale natural or technological disaster. In case of ecological contingencies, a legal regime of ecological emergency may be introduced by a presidential decree, subject to approval by the Parliament. To perform urgent large-scale search and rescue efforts, the armed forces and other military formations may be deployed at the president's discretion (Article 10 of the law "On the Ecological Emergency Area," 2000).

Military Support to Law Enforcement

The negative experiences that resulted from the deployment of the Soviet military in operations to manage ethnic conflicts in the late 1980s have had a number of consequences. First, since 1991, the Ukrainian armed forces' participation in law enforcement support activities has been allowed only in cases that are very specifically stipulated by law. The armed forces provide defense against terrorist attacks from the air and sea (Article 5, "On Combating Terrorism") and—should they be needed—assist the Military Police to keep law and order among servicemen within or outside military bases. The armed forces may be used to support public order, enforce curfews, and protect critical civilian infrastructure assets only in cases where martial law has been declared. The law does not stipulate that formations of the armed forces can be used to provide military support for law enforcement efforts of any kind—training, intelligence, explosive and ordnance disposal—except the Military Police, who are entitled to keep order among servicemen in public places (see Article 2, "On the Military Service of Law and Order within the Armed Forces"). Their contacts with civilian law enforcement agencies—namely, the civilian police—are rather restricted, limited mainly to information sharing (Article 8, "On the Military Service of Law and Order within the Armed Forces"). The Military Police may be employed to provide support for maintaining public order (in particular, to enforce curfew) only in cases of martial law or a state of emergency.

Second, the functions of military support for civil authorities that had previously been performed by the armed forces are now provided by "other military formations" and paramilitary forces. For example, the Civil Defense Troops, being a part of the Ministry of Emergencies, have enough specialists and equipment to be the sole agency responsible for providing explosive and ordnance demolition support (Article 2 of the law "On the Civil Defense Troops"). In 2003, civil defense engineers cleared 11,954 pieces of ammunition, including 806 bombs, 1,647 mines, and over 7,000 artillery shells. Similarly, the paramilitary professional and volunteer fire formations, which function within a separate department of the Ministry of Emergencies, are the leading bodies for providing fire security. In 2003, they extinguished 52,054 fires, saving 7,543 lives and property worth 883.9 million Ukrainian *hryvnia* (approximately $174.9 million USD) in the process.

Military Assistance in Civil Disturbances

The armed forces previously had been episodically engaged in providing armed assistance in cases of civil unrest. This responsibility is now entrusted to the Internal Troops or to paramilitary police forces. Since 1991, all the main law enforcement agencies (the Ministry of the Interior, Security Service, State Protection Service, and State Penitentiary Department) have created paramilitary rapid reaction forces to support their activities. The civilian police now have rather effective criminal intelligence bodies that serve to provide surveillance over organized crime, drug and weapons smuggling, human trafficking, and other large-scale criminal endeavors. As a result, the support of the armed forces is no longer needed to provide public security. For example, the responsibility for providing security at the Eurovision Festival held in May 2005 in Kiev was entrusted not to the Ministry of Defense, but to the Ministry of the Interior, the Security Service, the Civil Defense Troops, and the Border Guard.

Conclusions

This analysis of the role of the armed forces in homeland security functions in Ukraine leads us to six conclusions:

- The national security doctrine states that threats to Ukraine may be of a military, political, economic, social, humanitarian, technological, ecological, and/or informational nature. Currently, terrorism is not regarded as an actual primary threat to the country.

- The main national security support functions are spread among different military, specialized military, and paramilitary forces and law enforcement agencies (see table 1). That principle of decentralization has proven its efficiency, compared with the opposite tendency toward centralization that existed during the Soviet era.

- The armed forces' mission of protecting and defending the nation's sovereignty, territorial integrity, and inviolability is clearly codified in national legislation. Any deployment of the armed forces outside the stipulations of the law is prohibited.

- Any military involvement in the political life of the country is banned. This ban proved its efficacy during the political crisis in November–December 2004 connected with the presidential elections.

- There is a tendency in Ukraine to provide each aspect of military-related activity with a corresponding legal basis.

- Another tendency is toward a demilitarization of the forces that are responsible for providing functions in support of national security that are other than strictly defense-related in nature.

Table 1. Distribution of National Security Support Functions among Main Military and Paramilitary Forces and Law-Enforcement Agencies

Agency	Participation in Contingency Management						
	State Defense	Border Security	Terrorism	Disaster	Law & Order	EOD	Assets Protection
Armed Forces	Lead agency	Air, underwater	Military assets; air, sea threats	In case of state of emergency	Martial law	Military AOR	Military assets
Military Police	Territorial defense		Military assets	In case of state of emergency	Martial law		Military assets
Border Guard	Border protection	Lead agency	Border zone	Information exchange	Border zone		Border guard assets
Civil Defense	Territorial defense		Population protection	Lead agency		Lead agency	Civil defense assets
Security Service	Territorial defense	Assistance	Lead agency		Organized crime		Security service assets
Internal Troops	Territorial defense		Critical asset protection	In case of state of emergency	Critical asset protection		Critical asset protection
VIP Service	Territorial defense		VIP protection		Assistance		VIP protection
Protection Service	Territorial defense		Important asset protection	Assistance	Important asset protection		Important asset protection
Civilian Police	Territorial defense		Assistance	Assistance	Lead agency		Police assets

Chapter 9

Armies in Homeland Security: Romania's Experience and Practice

Iulia Ionescu

National Policy on the Domestic Employment of Military Forces

In Romania, the rules governing the domestic employment of military forces (along with those governing other strategic missions) are established according to defense policy objectives and priorities, strategic principles, decisions made by the responsible authorities, and on developments in the national and international security environment. Depending on the prevailing security conditions, missions are grouped as either peacetime missions, missions in crisis situations, or missions at war.

In peacetime, the Romanian armed forces are required to provide a credible defensive capability based upon organization, procurement, training, and cooperation. The main strategic missions during peacetime are:

- the establishment of forces to achieve a response at a specified level according to the objectives set out and the allotted resources

- the prevention of conflicts or participation in conflict prevention

- the preparation of the population, economy, and territory of Romania for national defense or to provide support to multinational operations

- the achievement of the military component of the Membership Action Plan, with a view to achieving interoperability and standardization objectives, as well as partnership and integration objectives

- cooperation in training within the framework of the Partnership for Peace and according to bilateral and multinational agreements concluded with other states

- participation in peace support and humanitarian missions
- providing support for the public authorities in civilian emergencies, as well as natural and other types of disasters.

Relating to the character of the crisis (internal or international) affecting Romania, the military may participate—according to the established legal provisions, and in cooperation with other state institutions—in the following actions: providing logistical support to the Ministry of Interior and local public authorities; preventing destabilizing actions; defeating terrorists and other illegally armed elements; controlling access to certain objectives of strategic importance; preventing proliferation of conventional arms and weapons of mass destruction; intervening for the protection of citizens and basic infrastructure; conducting intensive strategic monitoring and warning functions; achieving strategic security at the borders and objectives of vital importance; stopping arms and ammunition traffic; and confining and clearing the effects of disasters. The armed forces will be engaged in these types of actions according to government and local plans, whether at the regional or departmental level. These engagements will have a gradual and flexible character and will be carried out only after making the population aware of the dangers and the necessity of using the armed forces.

The military will use only the forces committed and equipped for such actions. The military will provide support in cases of natural disasters at the request of central and local authorities. To this end, the armed forces will establish bodies to cooperate with the civil protection forces and local public administrations. In certain cases, based on the decision made by the national command authorities, the military may also participate in this type of operation outside the nation's borders, with an aim to confine and alleviate the effects of disasters.

The Romanian military's participation in regional crisis management and response missions (which may also be conducted in peacetime) will be carried out only after the national command authorities approve these actions and allocate the adequate funds to them. The military's involvement will cease in a flexible and gradual manner to prevent the crisis from breaking out again.

The military forces will wind down their operations as soon as the responsible civil authorities are able to maintain control. In multinational operations, Romania will transfer the command authority of its units to the multinational force commander in compliance with the common agreed procedures approved by Romania's parliament.

During wartime, the missions assigned to the armed forces are established in keeping with the declared political objective and after the strategic situation has been clearly analyzed. The national command authorities establish the political objectives for any given military action. To achieve these objectives, the military forces may face enemies ranging from those using simple technologies in a new way to those using high technology and vast amounts of information. This range of potential conflicts is a challenge, requiring a force capable of mounting a rapid response. This means a force with a higher level of organization, doctrine, and training, endowed with modern combat equipment and an effective action potential.

Historical Precedents: Case Study

At the end of the 19th century, according to Romania's internal laws and regulations, it was legitimate and legal to use the armed forces against internal threats and dangers, including cases of social revolt.[1] As a general rule, all of these deployments had a dramatic impact at the political level, often bringing about changes of government and political realignments. On March 17, 1907, a state of siege was declared, and for the first time the law was applied for reasons of an internal crisis that jeopardized state security. The military was not only deployed in order to act as a peacemaker; they also deployed real armament against unarmed or lightly armed land workers. This was the first case of the Romanian military being criticized for not using their weapons against the population.

In the period between the World Wars, the army was used to address internal crises only when state security and the rule of law were endangered. After 1946, the armed forces were subordinated to the Communist Party. As part of this process, the Defense Council was created in 1965. Therefore, the armed forces were placed under double subordination: to the Communist Party and the state authorities. According to the Romanian Constitution of 1965, the president of the Defense Council was the president of the republic, who was also the supreme commander in chief of the armed forces. The activities of the Ministry of Defense were organized and controlled by the Communist Party's structures. According to State Council Ordinance No. 444/1972, regarding the organization and functioning of the Ministry of Defense, "the Ministry of Defense functions under the direct command of the Central Committee of the Romanian Communist Party" and executes the orders of the supreme commander of the armed forces (at the time, Nicolae Ceausescu).

The armed forces had direct representatives (military unit commanders) at the local level in the "Popular Councils" or "Local Defense Councils." But the army was not subordinated to the local authorities. This fact proved to be tremendously important during the 1989 revolution, when the armed forces were not forced to act against the population at the order of local Communist authorities.

The Communist regime created a special security force—the *Securitatea*, loyal to the Communist authorities—to control the population. In this context, new tasks were devised for the armed forces to fulfill during peacetime. Therefore, the concept of the soldier-citizen was implemented, fighting alongside the worker-citizen for the implementation of the 5-year plan. The army's resources (financial and human) were used to achieve some economic targets in the coal industry, construction, and agriculture. The military troops accomplished their duty to the party and country during the implementation of Ceausescu's plans (the Danube–Black Sea Channel, the Transfagarasan Highway, the People's House, and so forth). Therefore, the traditional missions of the military were corrupted, and the end result was the dramatic decrease of the Romanian armed forces' combat force and level of professionalism.

On the other hand, the army began to be highly politicized. In this respect, Communist Party membership became a mandatory requirement for military promotion. During the 1989 revolution, however, with few exceptions, the armed forces embraced the revolution and joined in the fight against the Communist regime.

Immediately after the revolution, the stability of the newly democratic state was dramatically affected by a series of internal crises. In 1990 and 1991, the government was dismissed in the face of miners' riots in Bucharest. In the context of a strongly negative image about the miners' activities in Bucharest, the capital city's population reacted when the miners decided in January 1999 to march against Bucharest in order to resolve their conflict with the government (caused by the implementation of economic reforms and the downsizing of the coal industry). According to the law, the Ministry of the Interior was responsible for resolving the crisis that ignited in Valea Jiului and for avoiding the miners' arrival in Bucharest. Given that the forces commanded by the Ministry of the Interior made severe tactical and command errors, the well-organized miners succeeded in breaking the blockade and advancing to Bucharest.

According to military analysts, the repeated announcements regarding the fact that the Ministry of the Interior's troops were not equipped with sufficient armaments could have served as a stimulus for the miners to become more violent.[2] At Costesti, the Ministry of the Interior organized another blockade. On January 21, 1999, a violent clash took place between the miners and ministry forces at Costesti. The miners' troops (over 10,000 people) once again defeated the police and gendarmerie forces. The military experts' report underscores the failures of the police and gendarmerie forces and the professionalism of the miners. The events showed that the miners were organized as a paramilitary force, that the riot was well organized, and that it was planned and possibly managed by some opposition political forces. It soon became obvious that the miners' protest had a strong political agenda (at the very least a change of government or a coup d'etat), with the foreseeable result of destabilizing the country and undermining the rule of law.

On January 21, the prefect of Valcea County and several police officers were taken hostage. Over 170 policemen were severely injured, and the miners seized an important quantity of armaments (primarily tear gas). Paradoxically, the Ministry of the Interior did not organize other security measures or blockades between Ramnicu Valcea (capital of Valcea County) and the next major city, Pitesti.

In his capacity as a politician, the defense minister gave several declarations regarding the ongoing crisis, but until January 21, 1999, the Ministry of Defense was not involved in managing the crisis. The General Staff permanently monitored the crisis and gave appropriate orders for the subordinated military units (especially for the ones in the affected areas) according to the law. In addition, the Operational Center for Crisis Situations (at the General Staff level) became fully operable.

On January 21, at the president's request, the Supreme Council for National Defense had an emergency meeting. The interior minister resigned, and the ministry was reorganized; a state of emergency was declared, and the Ministry of Defense/General Staff was given the responsibility to present a strategy for resolving the crisis. Keeping in mind the risk of possible U.S.-led coalition air attacks against Yugoslavia, the number of military units on high-alert status was increased. According to preliminary military data, the miners were not prepared for the armed forces' involvement in the resolution of this crisis. It was the first case in which the Romanian military used the experience they had gained during Partnership for Peace exercises and peacekeeping missions to solve a domestic crisis. For this operation, special units were designated, including reconnaissance units, mountain troops, and paratroopers. The military organized successive blockades on 12 communication routes, with special measures taken to secure the flanks. The troops involved in the crisis resolution effort were equipped only with individual armament and exercise ammunition. At the level of subunits, troops were provided with a minimal quantity of real ammunition in reserve. Bearing in mind the critical internal situation and the previous failures of state authorities in managing the crisis, the Ministry of Defense utilized tanks for blockades.

Simultaneous with the declaration of a state of emergency, the Ministry of Defense informed all the defense attachés accredited to Bucharest, the North Atlantic Treaty Organization (NATO) military authorities, and neighbor countries about the measures that were about to be taken by the Romanian military authorities. During the setting up of this operation, some police and gendarmerie forces were utilized to support the military. Unfortunately, a significant number of public order forces refused to carry the exercise armaments and ammunition designated for the mission.

During the organization of the mission, one of the most important dilemmas faced by the military concerned the possible juridical consequences of their participation in a case of internal crisis resolution, keeping in mind the fact that at that time a significant number of soldiers were on trial for carrying out their commanders' orders. Nevertheless, the military fulfilled its task, and starting on January 22, 1999, the government and the miners agreed to negotiate a solution. The professionalism of the military personnel involved in this deployment made a peaceful solution possible and helped avoid the outbreak of further violence. In this operation, the General Staff made use of 2,000 troops, 200 vehicles of various kinds, and less than 50 armored vehicles and tanks.

The General Staff Report concludes that democratic mechanisms were functional in Romania. Unfortunately, the miners' riot had a direct negative impact on Romania's integration into NATO. The 1999 riot was the turning point for initiating a genuine reform process both within the Ministry of the Interior and the Ministry of Defense, and also for launching the process of setting up a legal framework for regulating the involvement of state institutions in exceptional cases.

Legal Authority for Deployment

The political-military command of the armed forces in homeland defense in Romania is the responsibility of the national command authorities (the president, the parliament, the Supreme Council of National Defense, the government, the Ministry of Defense, and the public administration authorities having responsibilities in the national defense field). The president of Romania is the commander in chief of the armed forces and also the head of the Supreme Council of National Defense, an institution responsible for organizing and coordinating the activities of national defense. Based on the decisions made by the national command authorities at the strategic level, the General Staff is responsible for the operational and military command of the armed forces and for the operations carried out by it. The Supreme Council of National Defense conducts the central coordination of these types of activities and actions.

The National Military Command Center is in charge of the current operational command of military actions in peacetime; in crisis situations, the Operational Center for Crisis Situations is activated. In special situations, the General Headquarters are established by a decision of the Supreme Council of National Defense for the conduct of major military operations.

The joint task force headquarters, the Air Force and Naval Force Operational Commands, and the territorial operational commands oversee military actions at the operational level. For the conduct of special military actions with a highly independent character, or actions carried out in areas with unique geographical conditions, joint operational headquarters at the division level have been set up. The joint task force headquarters and tactical commands should be capable of carrying out operations anywhere on Romanian soil—as well as in Romania's area of strategic interest—as part of combined joint forces. The processes of organization, procurement, and training of forces; the logistical and administrative support of troops; and the current operational conduct of territorial military operations are performed by the armed services staffs, which in peacetime will have under their supervision all combat, combat support, and logistical structures. In crisis situations or in operations carried out outside the borders of Romania, the armed services will provide the joint task force headquarters or the tactical operational commands with the forces necessary to fulfill the missions assigned by the General Staff.

The territorial commands, which are responsible for the protection of Romanian territory, provide the training of the main and reserve forces. They conduct the transition from a peacetime to a wartime stance by gradually raising the level of combat readiness and by direct mobilization.

In peacetime, during crisis situations, and at war, the command of the Ministry of National Defense is assured by the minister. The Chief of the General Staff, the highest military authority, is the main military adviser to the president, the Supreme Council of National Defense, and the defense minister, and is responsible for the military command of the armed forces. To carry out these responsibilities, the Chief of the General Staff is advised by the Joint Chiefs of Staff.

In emergency situations, in cases of a threat to national security or the constitutional democracy, the Ministry of Defense organizes and conducts activities for providing logistic support to the Ministry of the Interior, if requested. In emergency situations, the General Staff organizes and conducts—according to previously elaborated plans of cooperation/intervention and to steps established by the Governmental Commission for Disaster Relief—the participation of armed forces in concert with other government forces and assets in confining and alleviating the effects of natural disasters and accidents. In siege situations, the Ministry of Defense is the main body responsible for coordinating the implementation of steps taken in the decision declaring this status.

Through the National Military Command Center (and the Operational Center for Crisis Situations), the General Staff exercises the practical conduct of military actions. At the territorial level, following a decision made by the National Defense Supreme Council, a military commander will be appointed in each county (and in the capital city). The responsibilities of the military commander are established in peacetime by the General Staff and are approved by the National Defense Supreme Council. The organizational structure of headquarters in both peacetime and wartime—and the standard operating procedures (SOPs) used to establish the concepts, plans, and documents for implementing them—will be similar to NATO SOPs. This process aims at improving military command and control at all levels, and at establishing the conditions for achieving interoperability with similar NATO and Western European Union structures.

According to the Romanian Constitution, when military forces are to be used in domestic contingencies, extraordinary measures are declared and used only in two cases: first, in cases of armed aggression against the country, when the president is authorized to take the appropriate measures for repelling the aggression; and second, in cases of a state of siege or emergency being declared on part or all of Romania's territory, when and if the parliament requests approval to use military forces, no more than 5 days after the forces are first deployed (Art. 92, para. 3; Art. 93, para. 1).

According to the law, the National System of Emergency Situations Management, coordinated by the interior minister, is responsible for managing emergency situations.[3] The armed forces support the forces of the Ministry of the Interior upon request and according to the approval and conditions set by the Supreme Council for National Defense. The military is to be involved only in supporting missions for which they are prepared and properly equipped. During a state of emergency or siege, the Supreme Council could increase the operational capacity of military units, including an increase in manpower.

Types and Capabilities of Available Forces

The forces designated for national defense and security are the armed forces and the protection forces. The armed forces include the army (under Ministry of Defense command); large units and units subordinated to the Ministry of the Interior; units belonging to the intelligence services of the state; and other defense formations organized in accordance with the law. The protection forces include civilian protection units and formations; the sanitary voluntary formations of the Red Cross; and other formations that shall be established by the law.

The Romanian government is responsible for the organization of activities and implementation of measures regarding national defense. The Ministry of Defense is responsible for the execution in the military domain of the fundamental conception of the country's defense. The military's capabilities should be sufficient to meet the requirements of achieving the whole range of the nation's strategic missions, including those organized in both peacetime and at war.

To face the challenges to its national security in the coming decade, the Romanian armed forces should use both their peacetime active forces and those that can be mobilized in wartime to augment the standing forces. The Romanian military functionally includes operational, territorial, and reserve forces. The operational forces include army mechanized, tank, artillery, mountain, and air transport troops; air force and air defense units; and navy formations and units, all fully manned and adequately equipped and trained. In times of crisis and war, they should be able to be subordinated to operational commands, aimed at setting up groups of forces necessary for conducting military actions both inside Romanian territory and abroad within multinational forces. The territorial and reserve forces include formations and units from each service. They are meant to conduct territorial defense, training and mobilization, as well as to support local authorities in civil emergencies. In crisis situations, they may take part in active structures subordinated to the joint task force headquarters for accomplishing the missions assigned to them.

During wartime, after their mobilization and a period of intensive combat training, the territorial forces may conduct actions, being either subordinated to the joint task force headquarters or to the territorial commands, depending on the situation. As far as action classifications are concerned, the armed forces include surveillance and early warning forces, crisis situation response forces, main forces, and reserve forces. The operational category in which each of these structures is included determines the priorities of the respective unit in distributing resources, personnel, equipment, and training.

A crucial requirement in achieving balance in the armed forces is ensuring that the first priority units have a high level of readiness and that the forces representing the bulk of the forces necessary in the event of war have a reduced and variable level readiness. The surveillance and early warning forces include specialized structures that are directly subordinated to the General Staff, to other central bodies of the Ministry of Defense, as well as to other armed services. They include reconnaissance and electronic warfare units and subunits, intelligence structures, forces used for command, control, communications, computers, and intelligence systems, as well as small, modular, and mobile combat units. These units are responsible for the identification of impending military conflicts and crises, the management of the factors contributing to the increase of threats against national security, and for preventing surprise attacks. These forces are, in general, at a permanent state of combat readiness.

The crisis situation response forces are responsible for participation in crisis management efforts, as well as for conducting the first response in cases of armed conflict. They participate in efforts dedicated to achieving Romania's military strategic objectives in peacetime, and they constitute the main deterrent element of the Romanian military. These forces are deployed to provide operational capability in the primary zones of operation. The forces that are deployed in crisis situations include:

- immediate reaction forces

- rapid reaction force

- commands, formations, and units named in the Individual Partnership Program.

The rapid reaction force will include formations and units of all armed services and will be capable of acting both independently and jointly. According to the decisions made by the national command authorities, a part of the reaction force will be used within multinational structures to prevent conflicts, manage crises, and in other international missions conducted under the aegis of the United Nations (UN) and the Organization for Security and Co-operation in Europe. The participant forces will be of an adequate size to ensure operational success and will possess action and deployment capabilities, as well as logistic support.

The main forces include peacetime formations and units, most of which are only partially manned. Though the basic personnel will include standing military troops, for the time being conscripts will constitute a significant percentage of the force. These forces will become operational in wartime only after being manned with human and material resources and after an adequate period of intensive combat training. In certain crisis situations, if the threat escalates in a very short time, the active elements in their structure may be included in the group of forces used for crisis management.

The reserve forces include formations and units established at mobilization. They have commands, training centers, and other units provided with structures and centers strictly necessary for operation in peacetime. At the time of mobilization, these centers establish combat, combat service, and logistics formations and units. The main forces and reserve forces achieve combat capability after their formation and intensive training.

Structurally, the Romanian armed forces consist of land forces, air forces, and naval forces. For conducting special missions, both at the central level and at the level of the individual armed service, special forces have been established. These forces are the ones that initiate, develop, and manage special operations in territory under the control of the aggressor.

National Response Plans and Programs

After the terrorist attacks of September 11, 2001, Romania adopted a package of legislative measures to improve its crisis management capabilities and to prevent and combat the use of the financial system in supporting terrorist activities. Moreover, the government also issued the *National Strategy for Countering Terrorism*, and subsequently created a center of coordination under the Romanian Intelligence Service to formalize the participation of all relevant institutions.

From a structural and legislative perspective, only cases of civil emergency (natural disasters and technological accidents) are regulated by these measures; states of emergency and siege states are still covered by Emergency Ordinance No. 1 (January 22, 1999). For the time being, a major threat against national security could be managed through the current system.

In the domain of public order, the crisis could take the form of a wide range of threats to the constitutional order, such as secessionist actions undertaken by political and ethnic parties belonging to national minorities, or the eruption of internal tensions of a political, ethnic, or religious nature into open conflict. The use of the military in responding to such a crisis is still a hotly debated subject among experts in the Romanian security community. A consensus was reached regarding the use of military forces in cases of armed aggression and states of siege. In cases of serious disturbances to the public order specific to a state of emergency, which also implies the use of force, the main responsibility for making a deployment decision belongs to the interior minister and the gendarmerie. In this case, military forces could be used only as "extraordinary forces," first when the other forces have failed to solve the crisis, and second for humanitarian rescue and evacuation missions.

When military force is used to end such a crisis, it is mandatory to prepare an action plan and to use technical means only within the limits of specific regulations. In desperate cases, individual initiative with respect to international and national regulations is encouraged (that is, it is forbidden to use force against children, pregnant women, the elderly, or against people who stopped their previous aggressive actions).

Protection of Critical Infrastructure

Activity in this field is organized according to the Law on Civil Protection and Defense against Catastrophic Threats. The experience gained during the management of local and international calamities determined the creation of a broader and more effective civil protection system at the national level. Civil protection is considered a part of national defense and includes all measures undertaken for securing the population, material belongings, and cultural assets in cases of war or disaster, as well as components of the process of preparing the national economy and territory for defense. The necessary measures are established by the chief of civil protection and are increased during the state of siege or emergency or in cases of general mobilization and wartime.

Until 1994, the chief of civil protection in Romania (the prime minister) ran activities in this field through the defense minister. The Civil Protection Command, a structure within the Ministry of Defense at that time, conducted the coordination and control of civil protection activities at the national level. At present, the Ministry of Administration and Interior is in charge of civil protection activities at the national level.[4] The Ministry of Defense primarily provides support to the activities of interior forces at the request of the interior minister.

Within the Governmental Commission for Defense against Disasters, the Ministry of Defense has organized the Central Commission for Nuclear Accident and Cosmic Object Collisions within the Civil Protection Command as a permanent secretariat.[5] According to national experts, Romania is subject to earthquakes, nuclear accidents, and chemical catastrophes.[6] The responsible authorities have elaborated specific plans for all four stages of response (prevention, protection, intervention, and rehabilitation) before, during, and after a potential disaster, as well as for long-term actions. The Ministry of Defense, Ministry of the Interior, the Red Cross, and units from other organizations provide the main intervention forces.

Domestic Counterterrorism

Immediately after 9/11, Romania initiated a series of national juridical documents to more explicitly legislate against terrorism (on the model of the USA PATRIOT Act) and to create an integrated national system for combating terrorism. To implement UN Security Council Resolution No. 1373 (2001), Romania adopted Emergency Ordinance No. 153 (2001), establishing an interministerial council to apply the resolution's requirements. The Ministry of Defense is a component of this council.

According to Regulation No. 36 (April 5, 2002), Romania's Supreme Defense Council has adopted the *National Strategy for Preventing, Deterring, and Combating Terrorism*, which lays the foundation for robust cooperation between 14 ministries and national agencies. Consequently, the National System for Deterring and Combating Terrorism has been initiated, and an institution with responsibilities in this field has been established, namely the General Directorate for Deterring and Combating Terrorism, which resides within the Romanian Intelligence Service.

The recent "White Paper on Security and National Defense" recognizes that:

> the main risks and threats to Romania's security and to that of the democratic community are rooted in the nexus of terrorism, proliferation of weapons of mass destruction, and unstable or undemocratic regimes. . . . Terrorism, including the biological and chemical types or computer linked terrorism as well as related economic-financial forms of aggression, are considered by Romania as major globalization-generated challenges to its national security.[7]

The proliferation of terrorist activities around the world determined the creation of the National System for Emergency Situations Management.[8] The main responsibility for the activities of this system is held by the National Committee for Emergency Situations, headed by the minister of administration and interior and under the coordination of the prime minister. Each ministry with responsibilities in this field will organize its own committee. The practical coordination is assured by the General Inspectorate for Emergency Situations, a permanent structure under the command of the Interior Ministry. The Ministry of Defense supports the activities of the General Inspectorate, according to the tasks established by law.

As a result of this new legislation in the wake of September 11, the missions of the armed forces have been extended to include participation in counterterrorist operations. First, special forces for counterterrorism were created within the Ministry of Defense, and a special operations branch/J3 has been created to coordinate them. Second, cooperation between national intelligence agencies and military structures has increased. Finally, Romania has allotted significant resources to increase its early warning and surveillance capabilities through acquisition of equipment for airspace management. The establishment of nuclear, biological, and chemical (NBC) protection units and mobile teams, along with the development of special training programs, have contributed to the improvement of Romania's NBC protection capabilities.

Civil Support

The Romanian armed forces have the responsibility to provide appropriate support to state and local authorities in case of civil emergencies. The military provides forces and logistic support to contain and eliminate the consequences of disasters of all kinds. When requested, the Romanian armed forces shall provide assistance to civil authorities in case of accidents at NBC facilities and installations.

Romanian soldiers can perform search and rescue missions in support of the civil population in accordance with available resources and in conjunction and coordination with other responsible agencies. In crisis situations, the forms of support provided to central or local authorities range from logistics to military. In civil emergencies or other special cases, the Romanian armed forces can provide material support free of charge (donations of tents and medical supplies) or can perform services that imply the use of manpower and equipment but under contracts established with other governmental bodies.

The Romanian armed forces wish to develop a genuine partnership with the public authorities, civil society, and the civilian population. Therefore, civil-military cooperation (CIMIC) is a component of the Romanian armed forces' current activities, whether they are providing civil assistance in preparing for combat or military assistance in economic or infrastructural rehabilitation. Currently, the First Territorial Corps includes the first CIMIC Group battalion able to fulfill specialized tasks at the national and multinational level. Furthermore, another CIMIC battalion will be developed according with national provisions and NATO standards.

At the request of the public administration, the armed forces can draft proposals and undertake studies of the means by which the military can help the civilian population in different crisis situations. The armed forces can support the public authorities in distributing humanitarian aid, or in other actions performed by the military to the benefit of the civilian population (providing transportation, food, shelter, or medical assistance). Another priority of the ongoing process of military reform is the alignment of military institutions to national efforts in supporting and expanding environmental rehabilitation and conservation. The Romanian armed forces also apply the national principles of lasting development and personnel healthcare by reducing the adverse impact of military activities.

Conclusion

Homeland defense is both a new and an old concept for Romanian military planners. Defending the country was the primary task of the Romanian armed forces up until 1989. One army stood ready for action against external invaders, while another one was acting against the inner enemy (the Romanian people themselves).

The new concept of homeland defense launched by American planners has resulted in a sound process of analysis and strategic thinking at the regional level in Europe. At the national level, the debate regarding the involvement of the armed forces in homeland defense has come to an end, with common agreement having been reached on the functions and roles of the Romanian armed forces. But the legislation for an integrated national crisis management system is still under debate. On the other hand, the new national security strategy is also under consideration. According to what is decided, the military doctrine will take shape. The Romanian military acknowledges the importance and the critical nature of developing capabilities in the area of homeland defense, but the legacy of Romania's difficult history should be taken into account when weighing the real danger of taking military measures against democratic freedoms and rights.

Notes

[1] Such as the peasants' revolt of 1907; the miners' revolt of 1929; the workers' revolt of 1933 in Bucharest, Ploesti, and Cluj; and the legionnaires' revolt of 1941.

[2] According to the General Staff Report presented to the Supreme Council of National Defense; published by Adevarul (February 6, 1999).

[3] Emergency Ordinance No. 1 (1999), published in the Official Gazette 1 (January 21–22, 1999); the text was updated in September 2004.

[4] According to Governmental Ordinance No. 47 (1994), regarding the defense against disasters; approved by Law No. 124 (December15, 1995) and updated on June 29, 2003.

[5] The commission is a central body headed by the prime minister and is composed of central commissions specializing in different types of disasters, organized within specific ministries and headed by the ministers.

[6] Col. Marin Moisescu, "Potential risks for disasters on Romanian territory," Romanian Military Thinking 7, no. 6 (1996).

[7] "White Paper," 2004, 2–3.

[8] The system was initiated by Emergency Ordinance No. 21 (2004), published in the Official Gazette 361, no. 1 (April 26, 2004).

Chapter 10

The Military's Role in Homeland Security in France

Denis Vaultier

Introduction

The purpose of the French defense organization is to ensure—at any time, under any circumstances, and against any kind of aggression—the security and integrity of France's national territory, as well as the life of the French population.[1] This vast defense concept considers any internal or external threat and also any emergency situation or crisis whether it originates in human, accidental, or environmental causes. It also covers military intervention outside national territory.

The three main components of France's defense—civil, military, and economic aspects—that rely on the civilian and military defense capabilities of the nation are operated by various state departments. All of these departments are under the command of the president of the republic and the prime minister, aided by specialized governmental offices.

The nation's defense schemes are carried out through a territorial-based organization, similar to France's territorial division, and also on the level of governmental planning, corresponding to different kinds of threats or crisis situations.

Three concepts are closely linked with that of the protection of France's national territory and population:

- homeland security *(sécurité intérieure)*, which is essentially enforced by the police and *Gendarmerie Nationale*, who protect the people and their property

- civil security *(sécurité civile)*, that is, dealing with crises and catastrophes, mainly involving the fire and rescue agencies

- defense on the national territory *(défense sur le territoire)*, involving exceptional situations and limited areas in which the military authority may exercise powers that under normal circumstances belong to the civil authorities.

As is the case in many nations, the classical armed forces (army, navy, and air force) provide homeland security by serving as a manpower and asset resource to the civilian services in providing help and support to the population. But the traditional branches of the military also play a role in homeland security in providing air defense in surveilling the nation's territorial waters and lands and, of course, in reacting to attacks led by enemy forces on French soil.

Yet one of the particularities of the French arrangement is the existence of military forces that are principally in charge of homeland security. These forces include first of all the *Gendarmerie Nationale*, which are in charge of public security on 95 percent of the nation's territory and also the firefighting units in the two largest French cities (Paris and Marseille), and the military units of the civilian protection agency (*protection civile*), whose missions primarily involve crises such as floods, fires, earthquakes, and technological disasters.

Political Organization

Homeland security and emergency crisis management are a part of the civil sector of the national defense organization. Most of the time they are directed by the minister of homeland security (*ministre de l'intérieur, de la sécurité intérieure et des libertés locales*), who is responsible for preparing and implementing civil defense plans. Within this broad area of concern, he is in charge of public order, protecting goods and persons, and ensuring the security of critical infrastructure and resources. He prepares, coordinates, and controls the implementation of the civil defense measures that are carried out by the other ministerial departments. His actions are carried out throughout the nation in cooperation with the military authorities; the ministry's work contributes to maintain the military's liberty of action by taking a portion of the security burden from their shoulders. To carry out his responsibilities and improve the operation of his many departments, he is supported by the defense ministry and the infrastructures of the armed forces, especially in operations dedicated to maintaining public order.[2]

To accomplish his homeland security mission, the minister has complete authority over not only the ministry's departments, including the national police (*direction générale de la police nationale*) and the civil defense and safety departments (*direction de la défense et de la sécurité civiles*), but also the national gendarmerie (which is part of the Ministry of Defense) and customs (part of the Ministry for Economy, Finance, and Industry).[3]

The minister's actions are based on an appropriate governmental planning process, which has been elaborated by interministerial working groups directed by the General Secretariat for National Defense (*secrétariat général de la défense nationale*) under the supervision of the prime minister. Finally, this action is led in the field by the prefects (*préfets*), high-ranking civil servants who, within the French administrative organization (made up of 7 defense zones, 22 regions, and 100 departments), have authority over all the local state agencies. These prefects are responsible for preparing and implementing the national government's decisions. Thus, the role of the minister of homeland security is crucial in all operations involving homeland security, as well as those concerned with crisis management.

Extraordinary Conditions: Armed Attacks

Attacks from outside France, whether they are conducted by identified foreign entities or situated in the context of serious internal troubles, should be dealt with by a global response of the defense system that would combine—depending on necessity—the actions of law enforcement forces as well as the armed forces in gathering intelligence; protecting civilian life and property, and particularly some sensitive facilities; and ensuring the security of the nation's territory. The extreme seriousness of such a situation may force the government to entitle a military authority with the responsibility of ensuring public order and conducting civil defense procedures.

Chemical, biological, radiological, or nuclear attacks (CBRN) currently concern France primarily in the context of a possible terrorist attack, and not from the perspective of global aggression from an external state actor, as was the assumption during the Cold War. In the contemporary security environment, the reaction to this kind of an attack would depend on the Ministry of Homeland Security.

Emergency Conditions

The terrorist attacks of September 2001 in New York and Washington, DC, along with the subsequent bombings in Madrid and London, have now made both public opinion and governmental policy sensitive to the evolution of the terrorist threat, which now seeks out mass effects in its actions.

These large-scale attacks aim at disorganizing the state by resulting in unacceptable human casualties and material losses, just as a natural or technological disaster might do.

In response, the government operates in a permanent security posture (*posture permanente de sécurité*), within the framework of a governmental plan of vigilance, prevention, and protection against threats of terrorist attack called the Vigipirate plan.[4] This plan outlines in detail the means and responsibilities of different actors, the procedures for communicating the government's decisions, the exercises' modalities, the threat levels, the alert levels, the security objectives, and a catalogue of specific measures planned by various domains of activity. Although classified, this document is fairly widely distributed; it represents a highly concrete, comprehensive, and complete tool for formulating the government's response to homeland security issues.

Taking as its starting point a permanent posture of security—which is the minimum basis for preventive measures against terrorist acts—the plan identifies four levels of alert. These four levels—yellow, orange, red, and crimson—correspond to the systems of reference in neighboring countries. The plan integrates specific recommendations from international organizations such as the International Naval Organization or the International Civil Aviation Organization and can be updated as these recommendations change.

The Vigipirate plan may impose several different levels of alert in any of the nation's domains of activity. It may also activate intervention plans and specialized emergency plans designed to face a crisis situation consequent to some event of this kind.

The support of the traditional military forces may be requested following a governmental decision. Nevertheless, within the nation's borders, the search for intelligence and the carrying out of counterterrorist interventions is the responsibility first of the homeland security forces, such as the *Gendarmerie Nationale*.

The management and resolution of a crisis remain under the authority of the prime minister, who devolves responsibility for these actions to the minister of homeland security. Nonetheless, it must be emphasized that the prime minister may give these responsibilities to the minister of defense in the areas that are placed under his or her authority and also to the minister for overseas territories as far as overseas departments and territories are concerned.

Temporary Conditions: Support to Civil Authority

Any intervention that is decided by the prime minister permits the integration of the capabilities of the armed forces in defense systems, subordinate to the administrative authority and often placed under command of the interior security forces, such as the police or the gendarmerie. This is especially the case when, under the rubric of Vigipirate, the government estimates that a threat justifies the call for the armed forces in order to reinforce the security forces in their control mission. These joint actions take the form of combined patrols in public places, railway stations, airports, and popular tourist sites.

These military troops, who belong to the classical armed forces, do not have a specific legal framework governing such patrol work, and the hypothetical use of their weapons is strictly limited to self-defense. When confronted with criminal actions in the course of their mission, these units have no specific judiciary function either, but only the obligation to act that is required by the law for all citizens that witness a crime or legal offense.

In case of exceptional events, such as the Group of Eight summit in Evian in June 2003 or the celebrations associated with the 60th anniversary of D-Day in Normandy and Provence in June and August of 2004, the armed forces are mixed in a joint system, under the command of the prefect and dominated by the action of both the police and the gendarmerie. Within this mixed command framework, military troops assist in the surveillance of certain locations, participate in searches for explosives, or conduct air and naval surveillance around the event.

Routine Conditions: Traditional Missions

The *Livre Blanc de la Défense* ("White Paper on the Defense Organization"), published in 1994, highlights four main strategic functions for France's defense organization: deterrence, prevention, protection, and power projection. The engagement of the armed forces in homeland security efforts essentially takes place within the framework of the protection aspect. In this regard, the gendarmerie are the most heavily involved group of the defense structure, thanks to their presence over all of the nation's territory (3,600 territorial units), the diversity of their formations (navy, helicopter units, riot police, mountain units, counterterrorist units, and the *Garde Républicaine*) and of their missions (conducting criminal investigations; maintaining public order; gathering intelligence; policing the roads; and protecting state agencies, the national armament industry, and the nation's nuclear weapons). This breadth of resources and missions allows the gendarmerie to be a key asset in the protection of people and property, of spaces and institutions.

France has no coast guard agency, so the French navy is in charge of controlling the nation's territorial waters, carrying out state actions at sea, and conducting the struggle against drug trafficking and illegal immigration. It performs these tasks with the help of the *gendarmerie maritime* (naval gendarmerie), the customs agency, and the agency for maritime affairs. It should be stressed that the function of *préfet maritime* (maritime prefect), who is in charge of the coordination of the different agencies dealing with maritime matters, is given to an admiral commanding the corresponding area. He has the same power as an inland prefect may have on terra firma.

The French air force is in charge of surveilling the nation's airspace and is responsible for the interception of aliens, as decided by the government. These missions are operated by the air command for defense and operations, whose commanding officer holds the title of High Authority for Air Defense (*Haute Autorité de Défense Aérienne*).

Legal Authority for Employment

The constitution of October 4, 1958, states that the president is the chief of the armed forces. The prime minister is responsible for national defense and carries out the nation's defense policy, according to the president's directives. Nonetheless, the rules governing the engagement of military forces in missions of homeland security—rules that have been defined since the 18th century—are aimed at preserving the separation of powers and correspond to very precise standards.[4]

Circular no. 500 (May 19, 1959), dealing with the role of the armed forces in keeping public order, says that the civil authority in charge of preventive actions directed at keeping order may ask for "reinforcements from the armed forces as far as the circumstances call for it."[5] This military intervention in a domestic crisis is organized in two modes: the requisition and the demand for cooperation.

A requisition is compulsorily used to initiate any armed engagement or attachment for the preservation of public order, even in cases of preventive action. This document is crucial, both formally and as a broader justification concerning the legality of the troops' engagement in peacetime on domestic territory. The requisition leaves the military authority responsible for the accomplishment and (under certain restraints) the choice regarding the assets to be deployed.

Three types of requisitions are used successively in most cases:

- general requisition (*réquisition générale*). This form aims at putting a certain volume of troops at the civil authority's service in a given area and for a certain time.

- specific requisition (*réquisition particulière*). This requisition specifically includes or excludes the potential for the use of force. It gives an exact mission (main effect).

- special complementary requisition (*réquisition complémentaire spéciale*). This requisition gives troops permission to use weapons.

The cooperation demand—which may be refused—concerns any other type of operations that the military may fulfill to the benefit of, or in reinforcement or replacement of, other agencies. There is no compulsory formal rule regarding its use (it has, nonetheless, to have an adequate motivation); a simple protocol is enough.

Concerning their use in maintaining public order, the armed forces are sorted in three categories:

- territorial gendarmerie units and units of the *Garde Republicaine*. These are units that fulfill missions daily that fall under the realm of maintaining of public order.

- mobile gendarmerie units, which are general reserve units at the government's disposal. They receive special training for order maintenance missions and are specially equipped with suitable assets, such as armored vehicles, CBRN intervention capability, and other special equipment.

- army, navy, and air force units, support units, and reserve gendarmerie units, which are all deployed at the discretion of the minister of defense. They are commonly used for the reinforcement of the first and second category forces or to guard critical assets, and in very last resort, for combat operations.

Operational command of the military forces is always in the hands of the forces' own hierarchy, but their control is the responsibility of the civil authority, who defines the missions, the main effect, and the duration. During operations dedicated to maintaining public order, the conditions concerning the use of weapons are always determined by the civil authority's requirements. The use of force on the troops' initiative is only acceptable when acts of violence are committed against the soldiers, or when there is no other way to hold ground.

Beyond cases of self-defense, taking the initiative in opening fire is possible for the military in cases concerning the defense of certain sensitive zones and under other predetermined conditions (for example, operations at a nuclear military site). Noncommissioned officers and officers of the gendarmerie may use their weapons under strictly defined conditions and in cases of offenses that justify it within the framework of their missions, even in cases other than in self-defense. This is a distinctive power belonging to this service that is neither granted to the police nor to the armed forces.

Historical Precedents

The armed forces and the gendarmerie have always participated in the defense of the nation, yet the missions they have been assigned have evolved over time, according to national or international events. The participation of the classical armed forces in homeland security, and especially in operations related to maintaining public order, is a phenomenon that has appeared and disappeared regularly throughout France's history. Nonetheless, the prospect of general purpose troops—obviously unable to operate appropriately under the circumstances—opening fire on a crowd seemed unbearable to the French people in the 19ᵗʰ century, just as it would at the beginning of the 20ᵗʰ century. It seems that, from this point on, respect for the law and for human rights finally rendered more obvious the necessity to use units that are specially designed and trained for the specific situations that troops are likely to confront in homeland security operations.

Post–World War II: 1945–1990

This long period can be divided into two shorter periods: from 1945 to 1962 and from 1962 to 1990. In the wake of World War II, France faced the conflicts of decolonization in Indochina, then the war of independence in Algeria. The French armed forces were principally engaged outside the homeland, whether in the occupation of Germany or of colonies in Africa or the Far East. The gendarmerie themselves, while still assigned the task of ensuring homeland security, also participated as operational units in some operations in these areas. Nonetheless, many of the operating modes that were used—however violent the combat actions—were beginning to resemble police operations: gathering intelligence while facing a diffuse enemy, settling outposts in the middle of the native population, enlisting local volunteers, and, above all, operating within the legal framework of action because these territories were at the time considered to be part of France.

The war in Algeria that followed the loss of Indochina coincided with a peak in the commitment of the armed forces in police-type missions. Indeed, in the face of the violence of the terrorist attacks of the Algerian National Liberation Front, the French government decided in January 1957 to grant the military the responsibility of keeping order in the city of Algiers. Paratroopers and foreign legion troops acted as police; they searched houses and questioned suspects, thus posing the problem of torture, which was committed to obtain crucial information.

These troops controlled the urban zone. This confrontation became known as the Battle of Algiers, which was a complete military success, but one with negative collateral effects. The unsuccessful coup of 1961, conducted by decorated military leaders that marked the rebellion of those who had physically devoted themselves to keeping Algeria part of France, painfully witnessed a confrontation between rebel military units and gendarmerie squadrons who were ordered to stop them.

The period between 1962 and 1990 saw a clear increase in the divergence between the gendarmerie and the armed forces in terms of professional culture. The gendarmerie, which are a highly professional agency, instilled their specific culture even more deeply by modernizing their criminal investigation techniques and developing the training of their antiriot units, drawing especially on the lessons learned from the students riots in May 1968. In 1975, a counterterrorist unit was created that was to become an international exemplar; the Intervention Group of the National Gendarmerie.

Under the command of a senior civil servant since 1947 (either a magistrate or prefect), the gendarmerie kept their distance from the army, on which they had depended for a long period. For their part, the armed forces were confronted with growing protests about the draft system and the obsolescence of their assets, the costs of which (mainly supported by France's nuclear autonomy) were less and less acceptable to the French public, who were not really concerned with the Soviet threat anymore. The armed forces often played a role as a substitution for industrial groups that had gone on strike or in the collection of garbage; they transported hay and water for farmers in need. Despite the lack of overseas operations, the armed forces, while having a presence in France and in neighboring territories (such as Western Germany), were not asked to play any significant role as far as homeland security was concerned. Instead, they were focused on preparing themselves for the threat posed by the Eastern bloc.

Post–Cold War: 1991–2001

This period is a crucial one from the perspective of France's national security, not only because of the collapse of the Warsaw Pact and the vanishing of a structured threat coming from the East, but also because the first Gulf War in the early 1990s stirred up a new level of north-south antagonism between Western countries and the nations of the Muslim world. For the armed forces, this was the beginning of a period—one that is still in progress—of enhanced engagement outside the nation's territory, in operations in the Persian Gulf, the former Yugoslavia, various trouble spots in Africa, and on United Nations and North Atlantic Treaty Organization missions. In the meantime, the manpower available to the French military was diminished because of the suspension of the draft and because of the professionalization of the military that followed.

Concerning homeland security, the increase of the terrorist threat was met with a range of responses, including the reinforcement of the police and gendarmerie system within numerous supporting military patrols under the framework of the Vigipirate plan. The gendarmerie also had to deal with an outbreak of terrorism in the Basque region, and above all in Corsica, where their units are still often shot at or bombed.

Post-9/11

The trauma of the terrorist attacks of September 11, 2001, had a remarkable impact on both public opinion and governmental policy. In particular, the French government became aware of the urgent necessity to federate all capabilities and to offer a coherent and homogenous system to face a threat that is virtually impossible to anticipate.

From this point on, the need for security became a priority preoccupation for the French. On one hand, it has taken form in the modernization and reinforcement of the nation's homeland security capability. This includes more manpower (6,500 more men for the police, and 7,000 for the gendarmerie between 2003 and 2007)[6]; more assets (5.6 billion Euros in funding for security programs over the same period); an increased level of cooperation between the police and the gendarmerie, under the authority of the home secretary (in coordination with the minister of defense for the gendarmerie); and a more advantageous legal regime governing the activities of these forces.

On the other hand, the typology of the terrorist threat—the response to which requires an analytical and planning capability, but also the technical and human assets already possessed by the armed forces—demands that the nation not neglect its classical military capabilities, who now wish to play a larger role in homeland security. There is no question of giving police power to nonspecialist forces (despite the fact that commanding officers on navy ships have specific criminal powers in order to note certain offenses to French law committed at sea). But surveillance of certain areas (unmanned aerial vehicles and electronic warfare), logistics capabilities (transport and communications), or even the use of special forces as support for the gendarmerie counterterrorist unit cannot be ruled out in this new security environment, which calls on states to draw on all their resources in shaping a comprehensive response to the terrorist threat.

As a crisis often accelerates a process, the search for improved convergence of all the capabilities that could be required in this effort resulted in a profound reorganization of the government's planning process between 2003 and 2004, especially in the governmental plan for vigilance, prevention, and protection known as Vigipirate, as well as in the specialized intervention plans that follow from it.

Types and Capabilities of Forces

The three branches of the armed services and the gendarmerie represent the main part of the armed forces capable of intervening both within and without the nation's borders. Despite the fact that France has no paramilitary forces—this force concept is not in use in France—other forces are designed to intervene and fulfill paramilitary-type missions.

Active Military Forces

The Gendarmerie Nationale. This force is 104,000 men strong, and its origins date back to the 13th century. The *Gendarmerie Nationale* have traditionally been in charge of ensuring the security of the nation's countryside. They formally belong to the Ministry of Defense but are effectively under the command of the Ministry of Homeland Defense, within the framework of this ministry's homeland security responsibilities. Their establishment within the Ministry of Defense was recently reaffirmed by the recent nomination (in December 2004) of a general coming from their ranks as their head. (They had been commanded by a top-level senior civil servant since 1947.)

The *Gendarmerie Nationale*'s missions are as follows:

- Public order. The task of maintaining public order is fulfilled by the territorial gendarmerie, which are in charge of 95 percent of French national territory, accounting for 50 percent of the population (the remaining 5 percent of the nation's territory—including most of the nation's large cities—is under the surveillance of the police). For that purpose, a territorial network of 3,600 units is in place, which permits the gendarmerie to work in close contact with the population, resulting in a remarkable level of intelligence collection.

- Restoring order. The 17,000 men of the mobile gendarmerie are battle-hardened and trained for power projection. They operate in France, in the nation's overseas departments, and abroad, in locations such as Bosnia, Macedonia, Ivory Coast, and Haiti. They are equipped with armored vehicles, and have the capability to act in a CBRN atmosphere.

- Counterterrorist intervention. Counterterror operations are built on the experience of the Intervention Group of the National Gendarmerie within a coherent response framework that prescribes which different gendarmerie units will be involved in aggregate actions (threats against nuclear sites or airborne terrorism) and which will participate in special forces–type responses (maritime counterterrorist actions with navy commandos).

- Criminal investigation. The gendarmerie record about one million crimes and offenses a year and possess highly competent investigative units as far as technical and scientific forensic police work is concerned. They also possess special investigative units dedicated to all types of fraud, as well as a terrorism investigation unit.

- Prevention, assistance, and rescue missions. The gendarmerie include mountain units, helicopter, and boat units that give them an intervention capacity in all types of environment.

- Surveillance of the territory. The gendarmerie play an especially important role in controlling road traffic, surveilling the seaside, and securing zones in commercial airports.

- Overseas police and military police. These are roles that are unique to the gendarmerie because they can depart with the armed forces in overseas operations. In cases of crisis, they can participate in combat operations.

Overall, the activity of the gendarmerie breaks down into 50 percent civil defense, 40 percent criminal investigation, and 10 percent military missions.

Army. The French army is 180,000 men strong, of which number 136,000 are actual military personnel; this group represents 40 percent of the nation's overall military personnel. The army has 90 battalions, whose main mission consists of settling crises and conflicts through engagement on the battlefield.

The army owns assets common to other Western armies, such as helicopters, engineering vehicles, CBRN decontamination assets, signals, and so forth. Some of these assets may be deployed in homeland security missions in case of disasters or major events. They actively contribute to the nation's internal security, under the rubric of the Vigipirate plan. The army has special forces who—despite the fact that they do not have the gendarmerie's experience in the field of counterterrorist operations—are able to deliver complementary capabilities to the Intervention Group of the National Gendarmerie in crisis resolution situations.

Navy. The French navy is a force of 60,000 men, of which 45,500 are military, representing nearly 15 percent of the nation's total defense personnel. Beyond the portion of the navy devoted to nuclear and attack submarines (10 ships), these forces take part in homeland security efforts by projecting state power at sea through the naval action force (72 ships); the fleet air arm (152 fighter airplanes); and the marine infantry, which includes a small number of commando units trained in maritime counterterrorist operations in support of the Intervention Group of the National Gendarmerie. The navy is particularly concerned with missions devoted not only to combating narcotics trafficking and illegal immigration but also to carrying out rescue and support operations in all of the maritime zones placed under national authority.

The navy shares these tasks with the *Gendarmerie Maritime*, which is linked with the navy and possesses 30 ships of its own; with the nautical units of the territorial gendarmerie, who work in coastal regions in cooperation with small naval units; with the customs department; and with the maritime affairs administration. The homeland security missions that are carried out at sea are the responsibility of the maritime prefects, who also are admirals commanding the naval forces in the concerned military area.

Air Force. A 70,000-man force (of which 63,500 are military), the French air force represents 16 percent of the nation's total defense manpower. The main components are air strategic command, which is responsible for France's nuclear arsenal; the tactical air command, which is responsible for ground fire support, air support, and power projection; the army's air transport capacity; and air defense.

This last component is responsible for the surveillance of French airspace to detect abnormal behaviors and overflying of restricted areas. They also operate interception capabilities with the help of missiles or fighter airplanes. The general commanding the air defense command is empowered as the top authority for air defense. He is in charge of interception decisions and is therefore a key element in the prevention of an airborne terrorist attack. He works in cooperation with the neighboring countries' air defense systems and with the civil air control system. As part of this counterterror effort, helicopter capabilities might be operated near the airports in order to prevent the use of man-portable air defense systems against civilian aircraft.

Last, the air force contributes—as does the army—to the Vigipirate system by conducting patrols in public areas. Depending on the threat, they also operate mobile detection and interception systems near sensitive sites or major events.

Other Military Units

The gendarmerie belong to the Ministry of Defense, but some military units are fully integrated under the command of the minister of homeland security, within the Civil Security and Defense Agency. These units include:

- The firefighters' brigade in Paris, which consists of 8,000 military troops drawn from engineering units and detached from the army. They ensure firefighting and rescue missions in Paris and its near suburbs, as well as for the Kourou space center and the military testing center in the Landes province.

- The navy firefighters' battalion in Marseille, which handles the same mission in the second-largest city in France, is made up of navy personnel.

- Intervention units of the civil security, who are detached from the army's engineers and who are in charge of interventions to the benefit of the civilian population on French territory as well as all over the world in case of serious events (whether natural or technological disasters).

- The military medical service's assets can also contribute to providing medical care for numerous victims, the deployment of field military medical facilities, or the analysis of biological or chemical material. Yet, as is the case for other military capabilities, their commitment to homeland security missions is subordinate to the nation's political priorities and their current operational readiness since an asset that is engaged in an overseas operation may not be available on the national territory.

Reserve Forces

The French reserve forces are 100,000 men strong, of which 50,000 are reserve troops of the gendarmerie. These personnel are either people who have left active service in the armed forces or the gendarmerie in the past 5 years and who are committed to serving compulsory reserve duty during this period or voluntary personnel who have signed a contract to serve in the reserves and have been approved by the Ministry of Defense. These people can be employed up to a maximum of 120 days a year, which represents a very useful form of support for the active duty military forces.

The reserves can be employed either inside active duty units or, less commonly, in full reserve units. These personnel can be mobilized rapidly, and it is not rare that some of them may spontaneously present themselves for service when an important event makes them think that they may be needed. On the one hand, they are used in homeland security operations as experts; as reinforcements to units engaged under the Vigipirate plan; or during particular events, such as large gatherings, holiday departures, and search and rescue operations. On the other hand, they are third-category forces, whose engagement in the maintaining of public order must be precisely defined.

It is interesting to note that, since 2002, the Ministry of Homeland Security has seen a level of interest in this flexible resource of force that the police have not witnessed. They obtained approval for the creation of a civil reserve, which proceeds from the same principle of service for personnel who have been retired for less than 5 years. As for the gendarmerie, these personnel possess some of their criminal investigation powers when deployed. This permits them to provide the benefit of an experienced reinforcement force instantaneously.

Inter-armies Territorial Defense Organization

Modeled on the administrative territorial organization, the Joint Territorial Organization of Defense reports to the chief of defense, who has authority over the army, navy, air force, and support services (including medical and fuel units). The armed forces deploy a joint headquarters in each of the main cities of the seven defense zones.

The general officer of each defense zone works in concert with the defense zone prefect and the general commanding the gendarmerie zone in ensuring the organization and participation of the armed forces in the civil defense of the defense zone and also in writing the defense plan for the zone. This officer is responsible for the protection of top-priority defense and military facilities. In case of an act by the Council of Ministers, this general also receives authority over the gendarmerie within the framework of operational territorial defense, at least as far as its deployment is concerned.

National Response Plans and Programs

The planning of prevention measures or crisis management programs on the national level systematically proceeds from an initial elaboration through interministerial work groups led by the secretary general for national defense, who depends on the prime minister's agencies. After its approval by the prime minister, each plan is reviewed by each specific ministry. The plans are also reviewed at the defense zone and department level, where the local implications of the plans are analyzed and transformed into orders by the prefects. Finally, each operator develops the orders that follow and the plans he is concerned with. The national government ensures that these measures are followed. The major innovations in the realm of planning after the events of 9/11 lay in the mandating the permanent adaptability of the response plans according to the lessons drawn from each event and in the development of a culture of exercises initiated by the central agencies and locally relayed in order to test the global coherence of those systems that formerly were subject to little central control.

The part of the governmental planning process that is most often talked about in the mass media is the recent reshaping of the PIRATE plans related to the prevention of and response to terrorist actions. This attention has been especially high because of frequent national training exercises that have been held in recent years. Moreover, the Vigipirate plan was entirely reshaped in 2003.

The specialized intervention plans that were approved by the prime minister in 2004 cover the different confirmed potential threat forms, including: chemical, biological, nuclear, air strike, naval, computing systems security, and attacks on French holdings in foreign countries. These plans are adaptable from one to another in case of combined threats. The various plans list the different resources that are available to be contributed to a crisis management effort of each kind. They also define the roles of each actor, the rules of engagement, the directories, and the exercise policies. The plans' distribution is classified, and their updating is permanent. Other plans provide a scheme for responding to pandemics or natural or technological disasters; plans are also in place for the medical treatment of numerous victims and the preservation of the resources and structures that are essential for the survival of the nation. The armed forces' role is precisely delineated in each plan. These guidelines are written in common in the presence of representatives of all the ministries and primary concerned agencies.

Protection of Critical Infrastructure

The infrastructural elements, establishments, equipment, networks, and structures whose damage or destruction—regardless of its cause—would pose a direct and significant risk to the capability of the military, civilian, or economic defense (either directly or indirectly), or whose damage or destruction would seriously harm the basic security needs of the population or endanger a portion of the population, are sorted into four categories:

- assets essential for the practice of authority of the president and the government or to preserve the machinery of the state (buildings or other structures)

- infrastructure critical to the operational capability of the defense system

- infrastructure related to the basic needs of the country such as energy, communication, transportation, and so forth

- technological structures and installations whose destruction could result in numerous casualties, as well as sites that represent genuine vulnerabilities in terms of protection of the civilian population.

These structures and sites thus benefit from particular measures and systems of protection, surveillance, and intervention that are executed by the law enforcement forces and (if necessary) the armed forces to ensure security and continuous operation. Security plans include two types of measures: those concerning protection (in place under normal circumstances and at the beginning of a crisis), and those of internal and external protection (when the operational defense of the territory is activated) that combine with one another and have complementary effects.

The internal protection measures are put under the responsibility of the appropriate functional authority. One exception is internal protection reinforcement measures involving the detachment of law enforcement forces (police, gendarmerie, armed forces, third-category forces), which may be taken when circumstances call for it.

External protection measures are the responsibility of the department prefects and are carried on by the police or the gendarmerie, depending on the location of the action. They include both permanent and reinforcement measures. The gendarmerie are involved in implementing the framework of these measures, and also through carrying out guard duties, in order to ensure the external security of certain structures and sites (this is a part of its general mission) while preserving the possibility to carry on interventions inside the site at the request of the functional authority.

As far as the defense of these sites is concerned, efforts should interdict any hostile elements' action that could be classified as acts of war or at least limiting their effects. Indeed, after the activation of the operational defense of the territory, the reinforcement of the internal defense measures is the responsibility of the armed forces and the gendarmerie.

The scope of action of the armed forces is often limited to that of the gendarmerie in the following fields of activity: agriculture and food supply, drinkable water, energy and nuclear power, technology networks and communications, computing systems, banking and finance, chemical industries, and other key domains, including national symbols. The gendarmerie possess their own scientific and technological investigative and detection assets in order to detect malfunctions in and attacks on the critical "life networks," such as food, water, and energy, and also on communication and information networks. Besides, the proximity of those units to the local authorities and the quality of their contacts with them lend added coherence to the territorial network. One potential form of engagement for the armed forces might consist in using their assets to reestablish temporary services, such as utilities, or to ensure the security of particularly threatened facilities. Finally, the protection of key national symbols (the presidential palace, the sensitive ministries, the senate, and the National Assembly) is essentially conducted by units of the *Garde Republicaine*, as well as those of the mobile gendarmerie (who are also responsible for protecting sensitive embassies such as those of the United States and Israel).

Border and Transportation Security

Transportation networks and the nation's borders offer vulnerable points where terrorists or organized criminals can focus efforts to undermine homeland security with illegal activities. Thus, they represent a governmental security priority, one to which it is difficult for the classical armed forces to make a daily contribution. Apart from the navy, which controls the nation's naval borders, the gendarmerie play the most important role in the armed forces' contribution to border and transportation security.

Border Security Support

In France, border control is the responsibility of the border police (*police aux frontières*) and the customs agency. Nonetheless, the gendarmerie—in continental France, but most importantly in the overseas departments—also take part in the struggle against illegal immigration at the borders and inside the nation's territory. Moreover, they carry out administrative police missions directed at foreigners involved in illegal activities.

The opening of the European borders, related to the June 29, 1993, Schengen treaty, has had a dual effect:

- increasingly free movement of people between the signatory countries through the suppression of systematic controls at border crossings

- the creation of a unique external border where entry controls are performed only when entering the Schengen area.

The borders of this area are often not those of France itself; thus, it is within the framework of multilateral cooperation that coordination in this domain is organized. Some centers for police and customs cooperation have been created in order to facilitate joint operations connected with the crossing of borders by law enforcement forces of a neighbor state. The participation of the gendarmerie in these centers, as well as in the European agencies for police cooperation, help solidify the contribution of the armed forces to border security efforts in France, as do their actions throughout the national territory within the context of their permanent missions and the work that is done at sea in concert with the French navy.

Air Travel Security

The area of air terrorism has received the most media attention since the 2001 attacks. If the air force takes part in the detection and the interception of an aircraft in flight, the gendarmerie are the most important contributor to:

- ensure the safety of the restricted areas in the main international airports such as Roissy Charles De Gaulle or Orly, thanks to the air transports gendarmerie (*gendarmerie des transports aériens*, or GTA), a unit that is at the service of the General Agency for Civilian Aviation (the border police operates outside of these areas to perform immigration control duties)
- ensure the security of sensitive flights (conducted by the GTA, reinforced by the gendarmerie mobile's armored vehicles)
- perform search-and-detection efforts for explosive devices and weapons
- control and secure freight, businesses, and people that enter the restricted areas
- collect intelligence and ensure public security outside the airports and in public areas, with territorial gendarmerie for the airports installed in their area of responsibility
- post armed guards (sky marshals) on board sensitive flights (conducted by the Intervention Group of the National Gendarmerie)

- conduct surveillance of pilot schools and flying clubs (performed by the GTA and territorial gendarmerie)
- control any suspicious aircraft that fly over a forbidden area that have been previously rerouted by the air force, conducted in coordination with the air command for air defense and air operations.

Maritime Security

Attacks against the *Limburg* and the USS *Cole* have shown that the maritime domain could represent a field of operation for terrorists. The hardening of the security measures applied to ships as well as harbor facilities, in particular taking the form of the international ship and port security measures, has increased the importance of state actions at sea that are likely to prevent the commission of an act of terrorism or to facilitate the settlement of any subsequent crisis.

The *Gendarmerie Nationale*, who are involved because of their maritime units' coastal guard missions and their experience in maritime antiterrorism operations with the Intervention Group of the National Gendarmerie, actively participate in this matter as well, along with the Ministry of Transportation Administration. Like the navy, they contribute to the evaluation and approval of the safety plans for ships and harbors.

The navy, which is also engaged through the action of the maritime prefects, engages their nautical and air assets in the surveillance of the French zone of interest in the struggle against drug trafficking and illegal immigration. They also equip maritime traffic surveillance centers and are also on the lookout for environmental offenses committed by unscrupulous ships. On the other hand, specific criminal investigations rest within the specifically delineated powers of the *Gendarmerie Maritime*, which are also deeply involved in the policing of fisheries and the surveillance of inshore navigation.

Interdiction of Illegal Persons and Contraband

As defined by a law dating from November 2, 1945, the policing of foreign nationals is broadly sorted into three main missions:

- border controls, including the control of the traffic over the nation's borders and the struggle against illegal immigration at the border
- the struggle against illegal immigration inside the nation's territory, through criminal investigation

- administrative police measures toward foreigners involved in criminal activities, especially detention and deportation.

The territorial gendarmerie units:

- control and surveil foreigners who remain on French territory

- provide information to the administrative authorities (prefectural services) about foreigners who solicit the issue of a visa for a prolonged stay

- conduct criminal investigations of offenses related to illegal trafficking in persons and goods and in the field of illegal labor immigration

- participate in various aspects of deportation operations, from the arrest of an illegal alien through his conduct to the nation's border (the gendarmerie is responsible for the management of the three administrative detention centers within France proper).

The roads and highways represent important vectors for the transportation of illegal immigrants. The gendarmerie's highway platoons and road units are often deployed to deal with illegal aliens. All the efforts that are carried out as part of the fight against illegal immigration dovetail with the government's continuing commitment to crack down on illegal laborers and human trafficking for labor.

Finally, in the struggle against itinerant crime, the government has created a central agency made up of both policemen and gendarmes, but whose main directive was issued to the gendarmerie. This type of crime, which is mobile and structured, uses borders and communication routes (essentially roads) to commit numerous offenses, including freight robbery, car theft, and hold-ups. Connections between this form of crime and the financing of terrorism are regularly established.

Highway and Road Security

The *Gendarmerie Nationale*, under the umbrella of their broader mission to secure the nation's roads, provide a permanent presence on 90 percent of the national road network. Their conduct of this mission creates a feeling of insecurity among criminals and terrorists, who are regularly detected during routine road controls. In addition, the territorial gendarmerie—reinforced in certain circumstances by the mobile gendarmerie—are in charge of supervising the transportation of any nuclear material, whether civil or military, moving across French soil. Construction sites, and especially tunnels, are the object of special care by the gendarmerie involved in these missions. The other armed forces are not concerned with these aspects of road security.

Rail Security

As with the nation's roads, the railway network (excluding Paris' commuter rail and subway systems) is in a large majority settled within the gendarmerie's area of responsibility. The risks connected with sabotage or terrorist actions are real; the gendarmes pay particular attention to the high-speed trains (TGV) that run at more than 300 km per hour. The territorial security network enables the gendarmerie to secure a TGV train and rescue the passengers as fast as possible. The canine squads of the gendarmerie also play a role all over France's railway network.

As far as the classical armed forces are concerned, their actions mainly consist of patrols in the railway stations within the framework of Vigipirate. Yet, in case of a disaster, the use of the army's engineering assets can be considered, perhaps in the form of a requisition in order to contribute to clearing operations.

Domestic Counterterrorism

The struggle against terrorism within the nation's borders is above all the concern of police and criminal procedures and thus resides within the capabilities of the police, the gendarmerie, and other agencies in the field of intelligence, investigation, and intervention. To take into account certain cultural differences, it seems useful to specify the sense that is given to the terms in France.

Antiterrorism (*contre-terrorisme*) efforts consist of planning and executing preventive and intervention measures connected with the terrorist risk. This element includes conducting an upstream analysis, benchmarking, audit, training, definition, and operation of action modes.

Counterterrorism (*anti-terrorisme*) efforts combine intelligence maneuvers with police and other law enforcement actions directed toward the recording of legal offenses, arrest of the criminals, and collection of evidence. This requires reactivity and the capability to coordinate and combine efforts.

Thus, the offensive action capabilities of the classical armed forces play a role only in the field of counterterrorism, outside our borders, whether in the case of the collection of terrorist intelligence (in the case of military operations) that could be of interest as far as the homeland security is concerned, or under the rubric of special operations aimed at the neutralization of identified terrorist networks.

On French soil, the engagement of the armed forces in the struggle against terrorism primarily involves the protection of the nation's territory (air defense, coastal surveillance, defense of sensitive locations, participating in Vigipirate, and securing CBRN military assets). Yet the information collected by the military intelligence agencies is taken into account in the evaluation of any terrorist threat. As far as the gendarmerie are concerned, on the other hand, they are particularly committed to combating terrorism within the nation's borders and are simultaneously involved in antiterrorism in the context of their capabilities listed in the previous paragraphs, and in the field of counterterrorism, due to their criminal investigation capabilities and the collection and analysis of intelligence that is carried out by their network. These units' action is coordinated by the counterterrorism office of the gendarmerie's headquarters, in relation with the national counterterrorism coordination unit, which is in charge of coordination at the state level between the various agencies involved in counterterrorist activities.

Catastrophic Threats

The governmental decree of June 21, 2000, established from that point on the concept of "defense on the territory," instead of that of "global military defense" that had previously been the prevailing concept in French policy-making. It covers two domains that are relevant to the strategic concept of "protection": the operational defense of the territory, on the one hand, and the contribution of the armed forces to civil security on the other.

In case of serious trouble inside the nation's borders, protection would take priority over missions of prevention and power projection. All the available forces are then likely to participate in protection missions, which must be capable of confronting a number of diverse threats simultaneously. The protection of military installations is one of the permanent missions that are subsumed under the operational defense of the territory. Global defense actions—that is, the deployment of troops on the ground—are aimed at reassuring the population, collecting intelligence, intervening to protect threatened sensitive facilities, and searching for, deterring, and neutralizing hostile elements.

As soon as peace is restored, the common missions of the armed forces are to:

- seek out, exploit, and transmit intelligence related to the security of the armed forces
- ensure the internal defense of military assets and facilities
- continue to participate in civil defense efforts, if their operational priorities allow it
- generate, analyze, and distribute defense intelligence
- ensure the internal security of sensitive civilian locations and essential services.

In case of a threat, the armed forces also have to:

- lead an intervention to secure threatened sensitive locations
- facilitate the buildup and movement of military forces on the national territory with particular respect to military road traffic
- participate in combat actions aimed at the destruction or neutralization of hostile elements.

In addition to these missions, the gendarmerie carry on their permanent public service missions in the administrative and criminal domains. Moreover, the *Gendarmerie Nationale* play an important role in conducting the operational defense of the territory. They are in charge of:

- searching for intelligence, using their active-duty territorial units, reinforced by reserve elements
- defending sensitive civilian locations and public utilities by mobilized units
- protecting the most important sensitive locations under threat.

The fulfillment of these missions also involves the use of active-duty and reserve units under the authority of the officer commanding the gendarmerie in the defense zone.

As set forth in the governmental decree of March 1, 1973, the *operational defense of the territory* is defined as: "In relation with the other forms of civilian and military defense, to participate in maintaining the freedom and continuity of action of the government, as well as the preservation of the essential organs of the defense of the nation."

Activated by the government's decision, in response to an external threat that has been officially acknowledged by a defense committee, or in response to aggression whose source is unknown, operational defense of the territory covers all of the military actions conducted on the ground and within the nation's borders carried out in order to ensure the security and integrity of the national territory. This situation does not constitute a separate legal regime because the public order powers are not totally transferred from the civil authority to the military authority. Instead, the civil authority maintains its own specific responsibilities. All of the military operations on the national territory are then placed under the command of the chief of defense at the government's decision; he decides on the operation of the military units in coordination with the three chiefs of staff and the director-general of the *Gendarmerie Nationale*. The operational defense of the territory is permanent as far as the protection of sensitive military facilities is concerned. In cases of extremely severe crisis, it can take the form of specific operating measures (defense plans) for the entire territory, which are rescinded as soon as peace is restored.

Civil Support

The actions led by military forces engaged in support of homeland security are carried out under the supervision of the civil authorities and under the rule of common law. In response to crisis conditions that result in the paralysis of one or more sectors of the economy and compromise the nation's ability to meet its basic needs, the use of the armed forces aims at ensuring the minimum functionality of basic public services through the operation of substitute facilities. (Civil and general security missions are included.) In spite of the global evolution of society, the privatization of the public utilities and the structure of the armed forces make this type of mission more difficult.

Defense Assistance to Civil Authorities

The anticipation of risks and the protection of people and property demand an appropriate organization and specialized resources. The organization of civil security rests at the same time on both the action of the state's structures and on the efficiency of the rescue systems installed across the nation with the help of local governmental bodies. Thus, civil security represents a broad scale of emergency response to the question of keeping the population safe. It extends from the accidents of everyday life to major disasters. In terms of the protection of the environment, it extends from brush fires to industrial pollution. Regarding the protection of property, it extends from the prevention of household fires to the mitigation of the effect of floods and other natural disasters.

Aside from the civilian units, a certain number of military units exist that are dedicated to civil security. They are reinforcement units that were created in response to the civil unrest of 1968 and are now deployed nationwide. These units represent a permanent professional force on a national scale with a high level of technical proficiency, capable of deployment at any site within France or abroad. They operate as a reinforcement to the resources of local communities, and they are placed at the service of the home secretary for the protection of the population against catastrophes in times of peace or war. In this context, the Paris firefighters and the Marseille navy firefighters should also be mentioned.

Defense Support to Law Enforcement

The military's provision of technical support in the various domains of law enforcement does not constitute one of its formally recognized missions, except in the case of the gendarmerie. As far as de-mining operations are concerned, the participation of the armed forces in the intervention system that has been formulated in case of CBRN explosive neutralization missions should be underscored. The gendarmerie operate canine squads for explosive detection, especially in air transport. The navy provides support in the struggle against drug trafficking.

Defense Assistance in Civil Disturbances

When social unrest or other disorders are seen as likely to create a climate of general insecurity and to undermine the functioning of the government and the ability to meet the needs of the population, the armed forces might be requested to perform the actions of police and gendarmerie forces and to participate in maintaining public order. They may act alone or inside joint systems, which is the organizational form that is preferred for dynamic missions.

As for operations devoted to keeping public order, the missions that can be given to the armed forces are surveillance or patrol functions aimed at reassuring the population or deterring hostile actions; securing the flanks behind the line of contact held by units specialized in keeping public order; holding ground as the contact line goes forward; escorting arrested suspects; demolishing obstacles; guarding facilities; and providing various forms of logistical support. In the countryside, military forces may also guarantee the free flow of traffic on roads (through demolishing road-blocks and holding seized hills), generate intelligence through ground or air observation, conduct surveillance of border areas, build detours, and serve as special escorts or joint patrols. The armed forces can also step in when the social or political environment deteriorate to a level where they pose a threat to the continuity of public order.

Support for National Security Events

The use of the armed forces on the occasion of events of a national scale has until now essentially been limited to providing support, medical services, and technical equipment (such as generators). The evolution of these functions over the past several years has seen a growing engagement of the armed forces as a complement to active-duty and reserve gendar-merie units that are massively deployed. These activities essentially involve providing area surveillance assets such as unmanned aerial vehicles, mine detection crews, or protection of secondary locations not to divert law-enforcement manpower. CBRN intervention assets (especially decontami-nation facilities) are also part of this contribution.

Notes

[1] Article L 1111–1 of the *Code de la défense* (former Article 1 of the Ordinance of January 7, 1959, on the general organization of the nation's defense).

[2] Article L 1142–2 of the *Code de la défense* (former Article 17 of the Ordinance of January 7, 1959, on the general organization of the national defense).

[3] Decree no. 2002-889 of 15 May 2002, concerning the powers of the Home Secretary.

[4] *Vigipirate* is the contraction of vigilance (*vigilance*) or *vigie* (watchtower) and pirate (*pirate*).

[5] *Code de la defense*, reinstating the principles mentioned by the law of July 10, 1791, on the connections of the civil power with the military authorities in fortified towns and military posts; the law of September 14, 1791, which provides for the institution, composition, rights, and duties of the police; as well as articles 21–23 and 33 of the law of August 3, 1791, which are not overruled by the present code.

[6] The authorities allowed to demand the service of the armed forces are the civil authority (prefects, for example); the presidents of the parliamentary assemblies in the places where they hold session; the judicial authorities in the surrounding places where they are competent; the military authorities in military installations or establishments; and the maritime prefects (within certain limits). Law no. 2002–1094 of August 29, 2002, referring to the orientation and the programming of the homeland security.

Chapter 11

The Fruit of EU Homeland Security: Military Policy

Brooks Tigner

Homeland security is of distinct U.S. coinage. As such, the term tends to sit uneasily with Europeans, partly because it comes from across the Atlantic, partly because it was conceived by an American administration whose rhetoric antagonizes many European polities, and partly because it contains vague but worrisome implications for personal privacy: it sounds Orwellian to European ears. But there is another reason—unvoiced in public debate and political speeches—as to why national and European Union (EU) policymakers do not like the term.

To secure one's domestic territory, in a global sense, against terrorist attack, as both U.S. and EU leaderships now aim to do, requires a mobilization of all available means to prevent those attacks or, at a minimum, an elaboration of policy that takes into account all those means. This would embrace the possible uses of military power to prevent or deal with the consequences of a terrorist attack which, in circular fashion, demands that policymakers review their military options if they are to produce effective policy.

But such a review is prohibited in a European Union of 25 national governments, and particularly among those with long histories of independent foreign and military action. Any hint in Brussels of an EU operational link to things military at the national level—be it for homeland security or any other purpose—remains official anathema in too many capitals, and especially in London where Euro-phobia often teeters on the hysterical.

So what EU policymakers have done instead is to readjust the terminology. They do not refer to homeland security. They refer instead to "security for the citizen" or "an area of justice, freedom, and security" for the European Union. Such wordplay offers both eschatological and pragmatic advantages compared to an ostensibly more hard-edged, all-encompassing "U.S.-tainted" concept of homeland security.

The eschatological advantage is that Europeans conceive the fight between good and evil in the world, as well as their political "mission" and approach to it, in ways that substantially diverge from those of the United States. Due to its own more recent and brutal history, the Old World has drawn its lessons. Thus, Europe is beyond an automatic reliance on brute force; it shies away from direct confrontation in favor of dialogue and positive incentives-based persuasion; it favors the collegial; it seeks the mantle of legitimacy conferred by multilateral versus bilateral solutions; it hands out generous amounts of untied foreign aid; and it is *always* careful to stress the need for sustainable growth and a fair division of wealth among nations as the keys to international stability and respect for human rights.[1]

This worldview rather neatly stands the European Union in sharp contrast to a United States that, rightly or wrongly, is increasingly viewed from abroad as a military bully in a china shop that smashes whatever it wants, whenever it wants, in the name of national security. It is a well-crafted, if simplifying, declamatory sleight-of-hand, but this line of thinking allows the European Union to float on the idea—illusionary or not—that the security of its homeland is not quite as susceptible to attack as that of the United States. Despite Europe's 30-year battles with domestic terrorism (Spain, Italy, France, Northern Ireland, and so forth) and the horrific events of the March 2004 bombings in Madrid, there is certain tendency among Europe's polity that if it can keep the terminology of its rhetoric fine-tuned just so, if it can twin this with the right beau geste of humanitarian and development aid, if it can manufacture enough dialogue with potential enemies, then it will defuse or at least minimize the terrorist threat to Europe.

As for the pragmatic advantage of its terminology, the EU preference for "security of the citizen" over "homeland security" is equally vague as a concept. But it is Europe's own concept, designed to accommodate an agenda that reflects the batch of homeland security policy goals, which 25 national capitals have agreed, if somewhat reluctantly, can only be achieved at the level of the European Union.

Together, these two terminological devices go some way toward explaining why the EU has ragged fissures in its homeland security policy regarding national militaries. A more prosaic reading to Europe's careful choice of words and slogans yields two concrete observations about its homeland security obligations and why these fissures exist.

One is the obvious fact that the European continent is surrounded on three sides—southern, southeastern, and eastern—by instability, poverty, dubious political regimes and cultural-religious societies that have too little in common with Europe's long and arduous march to secular democracy. Europe also possesses sizeable minorities that have not yet absorbed its historical values. In short, the Europeans have a great deal to worry about.

The other observation about the EU rhetoric of security is less obvious but just as mitigating in its effect for keeping the military out of a collective homeland security stance. The European Union is an institution riddled with policy gaps, split responsibilities, power struggles between national and EU authorities, occasionally ludicrous divisions of policy labor, legal restrictions of nightmarish complexity precluding rapid implementation of homeland security decisions, and, lastly, contradictions in doctrine that have a direct bearing on the use of military assets for purposes of homeland security across the European Union.

As a result of these two factors—fear of provoking potential enemies and the EU/national institutional atomization—there is no open and healthy discussion in Europe by its politicians, bureaucrats, diplomats, and especially its military hierarchies about how national armies should fit into the EU commitment to create security of the citizen. These actors dance around the subject, they make oblique references to scenarios that imply a vague future need for more coordination between national militaries, they explore and perhaps even agree on bilateral military arrangement or another, they cite historical and jargon-filled initiatives that have led nowhere, they work up a paper exercise or two; and they talk about working with the North Atlantic Treaty Organization (NATO). Above all, they equivocate, equivocate, equivocate.

If the concept of homeland security carries a somewhat distasteful flavor as a concept to the European public, then the military's place within that concept—or, more accurately, its denial of any role whatsoever within a comprehensive EU-wide homeland security policy—is Europe's dirty little secret, best kept in the cellar. Even on those rare occasions when its head has been raised, ever so slightly, at conferences and public debate, it is slapped down as a naive or premature concept and, above all, irrelevant in a European Union of presumably independent member states.

This is carrying political irresponsibility to breathtaking heights. To be fair, a terrorist-engineered event whose impact spreads across multiple frontiers in Europe would unavoidably create chaos, no matter how strong a civil emergency structure. But a response mechanism that cannot automatically rely on pan-European military support and logistics, that is not predicated on clear, predefined civil-military command chains that account for all of Europe's internal frontier regions will lead to anarchy. Europe is not prepared in this regard.

This is not to say the continent is doomed to ineffectiveness; it is not. There are cause-and-effect lags on both sides of the Atlantic. Indeed, in certain policy areas the European Union is moving faster than the United States, which cannot guarantee the inviolability of its own borders and which faces enormous logistical and administrative challenges in fusing over 20 national agencies and 180,000 government workers into an effective Department of Homeland Security. The EU's law enforcement agencies have a long, if informal tradition of working together, a cross-border practice that is now spreading to other national agencies and ministries of the 25 member states. For example, cooperation in setting up common databases among its judicial and border control authorities in the fight against terrorism is making good progress. The EU is also consolidating its coordination of civil-emergency response networks and identifying national inventories of medical supplies, transport equipment, and other stocks that can be shifted from one member state to another for disaster relief.

The problem in Europe is not one of threat perception. Its problem is "sovereignty deception"—the increasingly desperate maneuverings by member states to stave off federalism—and the attendant lethal risk of retarding agreement on collective and comprehensive EU policies that could prevent or minimize the effects of terrorist attack.

Sovereignty is a tired issue in Europe, but it is a tenacious one. Nonetheless, it is under slow but steady attack via the EU's inexorable, if sometimes imperceptible, march into policy domains that have been the exclusive remit of individual countries. Europe's national bureaucracies and its politicians know this. Some sense it instinctively and accept the inevitable; others scream and demand a clawing back of EU authority. Many member states are doing their best to prevent this, and, in the short term, they may succeed in winning tactical skirmishes. But in the long run, the force and logic of the EU's global responsibilities will shove them aside.

Europe's national militaries have been curiously mute in this whole debate surrounding Project Europe, be it homeland security or other topics with military implication. Whether they have chosen, or been told, to let their political masters do the dissembling or whether it stems from some internal expediency to protect their own national command sovereignty is unclear. But if Europe's military authorities continue to simply ride it out silently and see what—if—the politicians decide, they too will share the blame for not getting their cross-border house in order the day a disastrous event blossoms across Europe's homeland.

Fortunately, there are hints in Brussels that attitudes, both political and military, may be starting to change about the wide-ranging exigencies of homeland security and the military's necessary involvement in it. But the thinking in that direction is inchoate, hesitant, scattered, and still fraught with doubt.

The Evolution of EU Homeland Security

As in the United States, the fall of the Berlin Wall and the Cold War's end meant Europe could focus on the more "innocuous" problems of domestic security, such as organized crime, illegal immigration, drug-running networks, and money laundering activities. While the instability and tensions produced by the Balkan wars of the mid-1990s certainly contributed to—and continue to exacerbate—these headaches, the region's security defaulted to NATO militaries to sort out, leaving the European Union to spend the large part of the 1990s refining legislation to tackle its more "prosaic" domestic challenges and trying to push national law enforcement agencies to work more closely together. Driven in equal measure by a need to crack down on financial crime and a desire by its member states to squeeze undeclared tax revenues, for instance, the EU passed a series of directives to clamp down on bank secrecy and money laundering.[2] It also spent considerable energy encouraging more cooperation among national judicial authorities, though the effect of that campaign remained rather limited until the end of the decade.

Perhaps more significant from the point of view of shared domestic security was the decision in 1992 to create Europol, the pan-European police agency in The Hague.[3] This was a step in the right direction, though a limited one since Europol was not given the authority to request information from national law enforcement agencies; its role was merely to facilitate/coordinate requests coming from national authorities. But it prefigured more significant cross-border law enforcement developments to come. In the same fashion, but getting an earlier start in the late 1980s, the Schengen countries, named after the Luxembourg town where their agreement was signed in 1985, began allowing citizens to circulate freely within their collective territory. To enable this, they put together a common database of visa files, known as the Schengen Information System. This, too, would lay the groundwork for later EU decisions to exploit this database and link it to new ones for homeland security applications.

Despite the above formal moves, cross-border judicial and law enforcement cooperation in Europe throughout the 1990s tended to remain voluntary, ad hoc, and based on nonbinding political agreements. Information was provided and coordinated among national authorities according to a case at hand, though often not very quickly. Strategic intelligence agencies, both military and civilian, continued to go their own way and did not enter the policy picture.

Three events changed this. One was the agreement by EU leaders in Tampere, Finland, in October 1999 on a new agenda of home affairs objectives. Part of the reason behind this was a recognition that cross-border cooperation in home affairs and judicial matters was not working very well, or at least not fast enough to keep up with the EU's unfolding single market and the criminal elements taking advantage of its increasingly borderless internal structure. The other was the EU's looming enlargement in 2004 to take in a large chunk of Central Europe. Worries in EU capitals about the newcomers' porous borders was a major spur behind their decision to tighten cooperation.

The 5-year Tampere agenda laid down a wide array of objectives, both political and legislative, to tighten cooperation among the EU nations' judicial and law enforcement authorities, while guaranteeing civil liberties. These covered measures to create a common policy on asylum and immigration; integrated management of the EU external frontiers, including the formation in 2005 of an EU border management agency; harmonization of law enforcement instruments; and better use of Europol and other international fora to fight cross-border crime and regional terrorism within the union such as Spain's Basque separatist rebels.

Initial progress on Tampere was slow, however, until the second event came along—the September 2001 terrorist attacks—which catalyzed Europe's home affairs agenda, causing Tampere to accelerate dramatically. EU leaders wasted no time adopting an action plan for fighting terrorism, since it was evident the EU would not be able to cooperate effectively or quickly enough with the United States or other international interlocutors in matters of intelligence, surveillance, law enforcement, and other security imperatives unless it first vastly strengthened internal coordination among its member states. A second and perhaps more embarrassing spur was the fact that U.S. intelligence agencies traced many of the logistical links supporting the 9/11 attacks to terrorist operatives based in EU countries.

One consequence later to emerge from this reenergized Tampere program was a more assertive European Commission determined to deflect U.S. designs to impose, unadulterated, its homeland security imperatives on Europe, particularly via Washington's use of bilateral divide-and-conquer techniques. A good illustration of this was the Bush administration's moves in 2002–2003 to strike accords with individual EU nations to bind them to its maritime Container Security Initiative—moves blocked by the commission and replaced with an overarching EU–U.S. agreement.[4] Such defensiveness on Brussels' part, however, was more a tactical measure by EU authorities rather than one of substantive opposition. Both sides of the Atlantic largely agree on the ways their bureaucracies must work together to counter terrorism.

The third galvanizing event and the one with the most ramifications for Europe's homeland security agenda was the March 11, 2004, bombings in Madrid, which killed 191 and wounded another 1,800. As fate would have it, the bombings occurred in the same year the EU was due to review and update its Tampere agenda. The result was to accelerate that review and to produce yet another strengthened 5-year set of home affairs objectives, which was approved in November 2004.

Except for vague and incidental references to civil/military coordination for certain kinds of civil disaster, no mention of an explicit role for Europe's militaries in EU homeland security figures in either the EU's 2001 counterterrorism action plan or its two 5-year home affairs agendas, including the cascade of political initiatives and draft legislation that has flowed from these agendas. Again, the subject is politely avoided in Europe's policymaking parlors. A typical example of this blinkered approach is found in the member states' adoption in late 2002 of a program to improve cooperation across the EU to guard against and limit the effects of chemical, biological, radiological, and nuclear (CBRN) threats—risks that Europe's armies have long trained to deal with because of the Cold War. There is only a single reference to national military capabilities in the policy objectives listed in the document's operational annex,[5] and this reference is relegated to a footnote supporting, somewhat incongruously, a description of a CBRN conference organized earlier that year by Europol.

The stark fact of international terrorism since September 2001, and particularly its deadly impact in Europe in March 2004, has forced national and EU policymakers to start addressing, if gingerly, new strategic issues and to rethink older ones—issues that have military implications for homeland security, even if those implications remain unvoiced or played down in official public discourse for the time being. While a single chapter of a book cannot do justice to any analysis of the range of EU developments of the last 4 years that, together, are likely to coax a role for military planning in Europe's homeland security to gestation, the following is a modest enumeration of the ones that seem the most important in this regard:

- September 2001. EU leaders frame their broad action plan to fight terrorism. It calls for much tighter cooperation among national governments in judicial and law enforcement matters, intelligence-sharing, and the control and surveillance of their common external borders.

- October 2001. The European Commission sets up its Monitoring and Information Center (MIC) as a pan-EU rapid alert system enabling one member state to alert all others of natural and man-made disasters. This was followed in May 2002 by two complementary rapid alert systems, BICHAT (for biological events) and ECURIE (for radiological events).

- January 2001. Member states agree to create an EU Military Staff (EUMS) and an intelligence-analysis unit within the Council of Ministers.

- October 2003. EU leaders agree to create a Border Management Agency to begin operations by mid-2005.

- December 2003. The European Security Strategy is approved by EU leaders to frame its external security stance.

- February 2004. The Council of Ministers creates its so-called Athena financing mechanism to accelerate the release of joint member-state funding for EU-led military missions abroad.

- March 2004. The EU appoints Gijs de Vries (The Netherlands) to the new post of Counter-Terrorism Coordinator and tasks Javier Solana, the EU's top official for security and defense policy, to widen cooperation among national intelligence services across the European Union.

- March 2004. A high-level panel of European security experts urges the EU to set aside at least 1 billion euros per year from its budget to support security-related research projects, starting in 2007.

- March 2004. The commission unveils a sweeping draft port security directive to boost and extend the security of the EU's 780 most important ports.

- April 2004. Brussels and Washington sign an agreement on the U.S. Container Security Initiative.

- July 2004. The EU's European Defense Agency is officially anointed.

- September 2004. The European Parliament creates its first subcommittee on defense, reporting to the foreign affairs committee.

- October 2004. EU leaders sign the draft constitution, whose provisions include reinforced civil emergency cooperation among its member states, a solidarity clause based on mutual defense in case of attack on one or more nations, and a general expansion of the EU's legislative authority in the field of justice and home affairs.

- November 2004. The commission unveils a sweeping new policy that calls for the protection of critical infrastructure against terrorist attack across the 25 EU member states.

- December 2004. Europe's transport ministers endorse the launch of the development and operational phases of Galileo, the EU's navigation satellite network that will go live in 2008.

These are the EU's vertical and horizontal policy axes that lie on a complex institutional matrix.

Name That Rune: Military What?

As the above list suggests, EU homeland security initiatives are proliferating, and, in their ensemble, one could assume they suggest a coalescing civil-military strategy to confront threats to Europe's domestic security. Unfortunately, these elements do not intersect within the matrix—or not enough, at least, to produce a coherent homeland security policy with a bona fide military dimension. A brief analysis of each should help explain why they preclude this coalescence for the foreseeable future.

Action Plan to Fight Terrorism

As earlier mentioned, the EU's post-9/11 antiterrorism plan and judicial/law enforcement agendas do not address things military. Though Europol's authority has recently been shored up at the insistence of EU leaders, its right to lead terrorist-related investigations—and especially its right to demand information from national intelligence authorities—remains weak and overly dependent on the goodwill of Europol's member organizations. Its role is essentially one of coordination. Perhaps more worrying, it has no links, tangential or otherwise, to military intelligence sources about terrorist activity, and there are no plans to do so.

Monitoring and Information Center

The commission's 3-year-old rapid-alert apparatus is well-equipped and staffed to carry out its central function of triggering the public and private segments of national civil emergency networks for an integrated response to events across the European Union. It relies on the EU Joint Research Center for satellite applications and other technical support, for example, and has teams of experts trained to liaise with national and regional authorities for purposes of logistics, linguistic aid, and other forms of support. The problem, however, is that MIC is a voluntary civil alert network activated only at the behest of a member state. Moreover, it does not rope in national military assets or chains of command that could be deployed in support of a pan-EU disaster. This is a gaping hole in the Union's homeland security landscape, as one EU official very close to the issue recently confided: "EU leaders are aware of this and have tasked the commission to include national CBRN assets that could be deployed in an emergency. The commission is trying to do this, but it has virtually nothing to show for it."

The reason lies in the refusal of national military and political bureaucracies to entrust the commission with such information. Explains the official, "National security offices don't trust the commission's ability to prevent confidential data from leaking. The functioning of MIC cuts across many DGs [directorates-general] within the commission such as environment or consumer affairs and they are not secured structures."[6] As for national militaries, "they are extremely reluctant for strategic reasons to pass on to the commission information about their stocks of available CBRN equipment capabilities. And I don't think this is going to change very soon," said the official.

Similarly, MIC's subalert networks for biological and radiological events suffer the same problems. Governments and their high-security research laboratories and storage facilities are reluctant to reveal the size of vaccine and radiological protection stocks for either strategic reasons or fear of public reprisal if the stocks are too low or outdated. This does not offer the elements of a coordinated homeland security policy in these areas.

EU Military Staff

Though the staff carries out planning for out-of-area missions and elaborates scenarios based on the EU's security strategy, its contacts with NATO's far more seasoned operational planners—with whom it is supposed to have some kind of relationship—are superficial. Moreover, the EUMS remains secretive about the scope and direction of its work and, by coincidence or design, has produced no documents of substance for public scrutiny or debate. Its contributions to a more comprehensive homeland security policy with a well-defined civil-military element, to the European Defense Agency's future work, and to a revision of the European Security Strategy are potentially of great significance, but it keeps such a low profile that it is virtually invisible. The public could not be faulted for asking: what is its *raison d'être*?

As for the council's 4-year-old intelligence-analysis unit, Solana has been pushing since its inception to broaden the sharing among member states of data from the EU's major intelligence-gathering nations. A deep skepticism still prevails among the 4 or 5 major intelligence-gathering countries at the idea of seeing their information distributed to the EU's smaller member states and particularly to the 10 new members. While there is a certain justification on their part about the reliability of data security measures in these countries, homeland security demands a hermetic approach within the EU's territory to intelligence collection and analysis.

Border Management Agency

This EU agency raises a host of logistical and political problems, linked primarily to the fact that its official role will be merely one of coordination and that primary responsibility for actual border patrol/management remains national. This means each member state will look after its section of the EU's shared external frontier, with the Agency to distribute "alerts" about suspicious movements of people, border incidents, and requests from one member state to another for help. It will also train "flying squads" of border patrol personnel for dispatching from one region to the other as needed.

While the planned extension of the Schengen Information System II to include biometric data in visas and passports will greatly boost border-movement awareness among the member states, there remains the intractable problem that border and coastal patrol activities are organized differently in each member states and splintered across a hodge-podge of national agencies. Soldiers patrol borders in some EU nations, dedicated border police in others. Military policy may cruise one national coast, while naval or coast guard units do the same next door. Even within a given country, the navy may have responsibility for a port, but not littoral areas falling outside the port. "It's an octopus with a hundred tentacles across the EU," said a Swedish emergency response official. "It will take years and years to sort out a system where everyone is communicating with everyone else."

European Security Strategy

The strategy needs major reconstruction work. It is a broad-brush effort whose author, Solana, found himself forced to dilute its wording to produce a document politically palatable to 25 countries. As a result, it suffers two major faults, explains Jan Marinus Wiersma, a Dutch member of the European Parliament's Foreign Affairs Committee, who follows defense issues. "The strategy is wholly oriented toward external threats, which means it has no formal political, operational, or legal links to the EU's domestic security agenda," says Wiersma.

The other problem arises from the EU draft constitution's solidarity clause: "This is not reflected in the security strategy, either. So we will have this obligation for the member states to defend one another if attacked. But the attacks today are terrorist in nature, which are often connected to things external. Where's the logic?" he said.

Athena

The member states are looking at ways both to expand their common financial resources and to shorten their release further by cutting the time needed for a decision from 6 weeks to 20 days or less. The council's idea is a big step in the right direction, even if the amounts involved are still modest. But, again, it excludes any application of this principle to possible joint military operations dealing with a homeland security event within EU borders.

EU Counter-Terrorism Coordinator

De Vries is quietly but insistently raising the need to address homeland security in its fullest sense—military and civilian—at every opportunity in discussions within the council's Political-Security Committee, the EUMS, and the defense agency. But his office is woefully understaffed and his pleas are bumping into the hard walls of sovereignty deception.

Security-related Research Projects

The EU's goal of a research budget of 1 billion euros per year in 2007 is likely to be severely downgraded, according to EU and defense industry officials. One policy adviser to Günter Verheugen, the EU's Enterprise and Industry Commissioner responsible for security research, says a range of 400 to 500 million euros is more realistic, and there are fears among Europe's major defense companies who follow the debate closely that it may shrink even more. "Anything below 300 million euros would not be a serious approach to security research in the EU, when the United States is spending five times that," said one executive at the European Aeronautic Defence and Space Company (EADS).

Furthermore, due to concerns about public sensitivities, EU policymakers avoid, whenever possible, any acknowledgment of the budget's application to defense research, referring only to its possible "dual-use" dimension. This coy wordplay does no service to promoting dialogue about the defense and military aspects (and research needs) of homeland security.

Port Security Directive

This directive leaves it up to each national or regional port authority to strengthen security standards in and around its port facilities. Because so many actors are involved, coordination of the information networks necessary to link the 780 ports to their surrounding critical infrastructures is exceedingly complicated. Many of Europe's ports share territory with NATO naval facilities, but the EU and NATO have no official dialogue to coordinate against terrorist intrusion or consequence management.

U.S. Container Security Initiative

While the U.S. initiative aims to guarantee the security of all U.S.-bound maritime containers departing EU–U.S. designated ports in Europe, no civil-military interface is provided for in the agreement; reference to the military's involvement in threat reduction or consequence management within the ports is absent.

European Defense Agency

This organization stands to play an important role in supporting the development of homeland security, but its legal remit is yoked to things related to common EU foreign and security policies (that is, identification of equipment for forthcoming EU rapid reaction units, future military requirements) and to defense industrial issues (research priorities, program management, and so forth). It has no direct involvement in homeland security issues.

Subcommittee on Defense

The European Parliament subcommittee on defense, reporting to Foreign Affairs, is a positive institutional development and a necessary forum for generating ideas and voicing criticism of the EU's institutional and legal fault lines in the realm of homeland security. But, this being the European Union, it has no binding oversight whatsoever on defense and military matters, whether for homeland security or European Security and Defense Policy.

Draft Constitution

In a similar twist, the EU's draft constitution will reinforce civil emergency cooperation among the member states by shifting many areas of legislative initiative in the field of justice and home affairs from an intra-governmental footing (that is, falling outside the EU's legal framework) to one based on the European Union. This means the European Commission will have the right to initiate, and withdraw, binding legislation on the 25 member nations. However, the treaty does not make any formal linkage between the commission's soon-to-be-expanded justice and home affairs competencies in the field of homeland security and the external dimension to homeland security.

Infrastructure Protection

The commission's proposal for protection of critical infrastructure against terrorist attack across the 25 EU member states points to the same problems of sheer complexity as those of border management and port security, with the added element that the private sector in all its diversity will be involved as well.

Galileo

After several years of institutional hiccups, implementation of the EU's navigation satellite is getting off the drawing board. Though primarily commercial, it will reserve a slice of its operational capacity and broadband spectrum for military and intelligence needs. Europe's high-resolution technologies and applications for Earth observation are already functioning and available for homeland security ends, such as littoral and ship surveillance, chemical cloud analysis, or detection of certain kinds of illicit surface transport activity. While the EU does envisage usage of Galileo for certain homeland security tasks, control over the information that the system will produce breaks down into national authority. The thorn of sovereignty deception also manifests itself in today's absence of an agreed set of common security rules among EU countries to govern the future collection, distribution, exchange, and analysis of intelligence that Galileo will generate.

"We don't know what our governments are arranging among themselves or what they expect from our industry," said the EADS executive. "It's a blank space for us." Though Verheugen insists this is not a problem, flatly having asserted during the EU's February 2005 Earth & Space Week in Brussels that the satellite system's security arrangements will be fully worked out by 2008, Europe's defense industry remains skeptical. "That's not a lot of time for so many governments to get an agreement. I have my doubts," said the EADS executive.

Though woefully short of nuance, this plus-and-minus schema of EU initiatives points to a jumble of policy strands and interfaces that loop and double back on one another in endless and often impenetrable contortions. Like an old-fashioned switchboard with a slightly devious operator in control, the strands that fire a decision only connect according to an occasionally impulsive choice and sequence of institutional buttons. At any rate, the homeland security button for "military" suffers a short circuit to all the others.

Conclusion

The prospects for a military component in an EU-level homeland security structure are not promising without a number of major shifts in policy. Even assuming by some miraculous stroke of luck and political vision these changes were actually effected, the inertia of collective institutional forward movement in Europe is such that it would still require several, if not many, years before military planning is integrated into an EU homeland security policy in a way that is meaningful for preventing or dealing with the transfrontier effects of a terrorist incident.

What are some of the policy changes needed? An immediate priority is the EU's security strategy. Its content and legal footing orients it wholly toward threats external to the EU; this is patently misguided, given the obvious fact that terrorism knows no boundaries, internal or external. Regardless of the separate "pillars" or legal footings on which the EU's treaty rests, its security strategy needs linkages—legal and operational—between the EU's justice and home affairs competencies and its ESDP prerogatives. The institutional walls that block rapid liaison and information exchanges between the member states' judicial, law enforcement, intelligence, defense, and military establishments need to come down, accompanied, of course, by laws that protect privacy rights for the innocent. An outward-facing ESDP divorced from an inward-looking homeland security policy is a recipe for confusion and disaster. The member states would be wise to let Solana and de Vries immediately begin revising the doctrine in this direction—and to widen and deepen intelligence exchanges among the member states.

On a different operational level, EU leaders should compel their military bureaucracies to provide the commission's MIC alert center with nonstrategic information about the kinds of CBRN equipment and supplies, including vaccines, in their inventories to compile a complete picture of what is available across the EU as a whole. If national governments continue to point to the low security status of commission facilities as an excuse for not doing so, then the commission should upgrade the security of its buildings and data networks as quickly as possible to assuage the concerns of national governments and their militaries.

The EUMS should be tasked to analyze the consequences of a wide-ranging terrorist event within the EU (chemical, biological, disruptions to infrastructure) and their implications for cross-border cooperation between national militaries. It should be instructed to collect data on the available military personnel, equipment, and supplies in border areas between member states for deployment in support of civil emergency authorities; identify the most important demographic and infrastructure sites with a cross-border dimension (major power lines, water supply systems, cargo railway tracks, rivers) to be secured in such events; and, finally, predefine the military chains of command that cut across national frontiers as needed.

There is no reason why the council's Athena funding mechanism could not serve as a model for covering the joint costs of cross-border military deployments *within the European Union* in response to a homeland security incident. Nothing in the EU treaties prevents this. As a rebuttal, national capitals will argue that Athena covers only the common overhead costs of EU military missions abroad, leaving basic operational costs to "fall where they may" into the separate national budgets of a mission's participating member states.

But from that reasoning one cannot infer there will never be joint overhead military costs associated with emergency reaction to a transfrontier homeland security incident. On the contrary, one might ask, what prevents a EUMS paper exercise from identifying the necessary shared costs in advance, with the goal of financing them from common money just as Athena does for foreign missions?

Such a "homeland security Athena" mechanism could prove particularly valuable for a member state whose rapid reaction capability is too small or inadequate to deal with an incident. Secure in the knowledge that cost arrangements and command chains have been arranged in advance, this would enable it to immediately call on neighboring forces for consequence management support and relief. Indeed, one could argue that the rationale of joint overhead military costs for the EU's homeland security is a *greater* imperative than that for Athena, since Europe's reaction to a cross-border terrorist incident cannot be foreseen or planned months in advance as was done for the EU's military missions in Africa and the Balkans.

In a similar vein, the EU's Border Management Agency could be tasked to identify and test how well all the different border control authorities are working along the Union's shared frontier, and whether cross-border contingency plans exist for drawing on military forces in case of a severe threat to the EU's homeland security. Given the EU's ambitious designs to secure its maritime and inland ports and related inland infrastructure, such as power plants and transport networks, common sense suggests a need for close cooperation and information exchanges between port authorities, the Border Management Agency, coast guards and navies, and all the public and private parties with a stake in logistics chains that link Europe's hinterland to its ports. Even if the EU and member states have a master plan for doing this, which is very unlikely, it surely will need a rationalizing eye cast over it to make sure it is working. However, given the EU's "pillar" structure and sovereignty deception, no such eye seems possible for the time being.

In sum, a daunting and corrugated obstacle course spreads out before the European Union, a policy terrain that will take an enormous force of will to level before the military component of a pan-EU homeland security policy can be smoothly rolled out and joined to the evolving civilian one. Unless the 25 EU nations give serious consideration to accelerating their debate about the cross-border military dimension to homeland security, then they consign their continent to the whims of circumstance. As the EU official concluded, "despite all the member states' good intentions and declarations, I fear that only a terrorist catastrophe is going to force capitals to move as one on homeland security and the military issue." While the official's fatalism probably is not misplaced, there is always the possibility, however slim, that enough policymakers within the EU's hallways will start "connecting the dots" and realize that the military's side to homeland security demands more urgent attention.

A cautious pessimism suggests that this might happen, though whether it leads quickly enough to operational changes is another matter. Ironically, it was not a terrorist event, but a natural one, that has pulled EU thinking about the uses of military capabilities for homeland security in this direction. The colossal tsunami that hit southeast Asia on December 26, 2004, cruelly revealed how unprepared Europe and many other parts of the developed world were to deal with its consequences in terms of rapid civil emergency response. Quite naturally, it has raised the same question in the minds of many European policymakers: *What if a transregional disaster of this proportion were to hit our continent?*

Virtually all of the rapid deployment capability Europe possesses lies within its military domain. This sobering fact has started to sink in at the European Commission and European Parliament and, crucially, at the Council of Ministers, where the subject of civil-military cooperation at the level of the European Union is now being discreetly probed by Solana, de Vries, and others. The discussions are still whispered, with a nervous edge to them due to the political and institutional taboos that traditionally adhere to them. But the crucial thing is that the topic is being explored. And even a whispering awareness of such import is better than no whispers at all.

Notes

[1] A typical example of this rhetoric can be found in a December 2, 2004, statement featured on the official Web site of Benita Ferrero-Waldner, European Commissioner for External Relations and European Neighbourhood Policy. Noting that the EU and its member states are the world leader in development aid, accounting for 55 percent of all aid handed out each year, she declared: "Our priorities will be to tackle poverty, to promote sustainable development, to build democracies, support good governance and respect for human rights. Europe does not have to choose between tackling extreme hardship in Africa and helping developing countries take their next steps up the ladder. We have a duty to do both." See <http://europa.eu.int/comm/external_relations/news/ferrero/2004/poster_021204.htm>. More recently, on the eve of President George W. Bush's February 22, 2005, meeting with EU leaders in Brussels, Martin Schulz, leader of the 202-strong Socialist Group in the European Parliament, declared: "We are not in principle against military intervention where appropriate and in a UN [United Nations] context but the unique element of our European strategy is the stress we put on prevention and peaceful solution of conflict. A civil superpower must address global terror. This also means concentrating on the elimination of poverty, environment questions, human rights abuses, cultural and religious intolerance and providing help for the reconstruction of failed states."

[2] See Directive 91/308/EEC of the Council of Ministers, June 10, 1991, on prevention of the use of the financial system for the purpose of money laundering, EU Official Journal L 166, 28/06/1991, P. 0077–0083; and the subsequent amending Directive 2001/97/EC of December 4, 2001, EU Official Journal L 344, 28/12/2001, P. 0076–0082.

[3] For the history, structure, and functioning of Europol, see <www.europol.eu.int>.

[4] See European Commission press release of November 11, 2003 (IP/03/1565), announcing the agreement in principle, which led to formal signatures 3 months later. For a chronology of reporting on the developments leading to the agreement, see the author's stories for Defense News at <www.defensenews.com>.

[5] See Council document 14627/02 of November 21, 2002. Stating that the EU security and defense instruments are designed only for external use and not for application inside the European Union, the footnote's last sentence sums up the situation: "The use of national military capabilities and specialized units for support of the protection of civilian populations may only be provided, case by case, on a bilateral basis or through the Community mechanism."

[6] Indeed, the only venue within the EU executive's scattered facilities in Europe that meets the stringent security requirements of NATO is the top 12th floor of the Charlemagne building in Brussels, reserved for the European Commission's External Relations Directorate-General, where limited discussions and exchanges of documents take place between commission and NATO officials.

About the Authors

Carlo Cabigiosu was the Joint Operations Commander in 2001–2002, responsible for the military contribution to homeland security in Italy.

John L. Clarke is Professor of Leadership, Management, and Defense Planning at the George C. Marshall Center in Garmisch-Partenkirchen, Germany.

Nikolay K. Dotzev works for the General Staff of the Bulgarian Armed Forces as Head of the Liaison Team Department that deals with international relations and military cooperation.

Johann Frank is head of the Division for Security Political Analysis within the Austrian Ministry of Defense.

Iulia Ionescu is an expert adviser to the Romanian Ministry of Defense.

Petro Kanana is Executive Assistant to the Defense Minister of Ukraine.

Gerhard J. Klose served as the Principal Staff Officer for Domestic Operations on the Joint Staff of the German Armed Forces.

Thomas L. LaCrosse is Director of Civil Support, Office of the Assistant Secretary of Defense (Homeland Defense), U.S. Department of Defense.

Jonathan Stevenson is a Senior Fellow for Counterterrorism at the International Institute for Strategic Studies, London.

Imre Takács is a Senior Staff Officer in the Hungarian Ministry of Defense.

Alexey Telichkin is head of the International Law Enforcement Department, National University of Internal Affairs, Ukraine.

Brooks Tigner is a journalist on European Union and North Atlantic Treaty Organization issues for Defense News based in Brussels.

Denis Vaultier is a Brigadier General in the French Gendarmerie and a Senior Staff Officer in Gendarmerie headquarters in Paris.